Slaves, Slaveholders, and a Kentucky Community's Struggle toward Freedom

Slaves, Slaveholders, and a Kentucky Community's Struggle toward Freedom

Elizabeth D. Leonard

University Press of Kentucky

Scholarly publisher for the Commonwealth,
serving Bellarmine University, Berea College, Centre College of Kentucky, Eastern Kentucky University, The Filson Historical Society, Georgetown College, Kentucky Historical Society, Kentucky State University, Morehead State University, Murray State University, Northern Kentucky University, Transylvania University, University of Kentucky, University of Louisville, and Western Kentucky University.

Editorial and Sales Offices: The University Press of Kentucky
663 South Limestone Street, Lexington, Kentucky 40508–4008
www.kentuckypress.com

Library of Congress Cataloging-in-Publication Data

Names: Leonard, Elizabeth D., author.
Title: Slaves, slaveholders, and a Kentucky community's struggle toward freedom / Elizabeth D. Leonard.
Description: Lexington, Kentucky : The University Press of Kentucky, [2019] | Includes bibliographical references and index.
Identifiers: LCCN 2018047829| ISBN 9780813176666 (hardcover : alk. paper) | ISBN 9780813176680 (pdf) | ISBN 9780813176673 (epub)
Subjects: LCSH: Holt, Sandy, 1824?-1896. | African Americans—Kentucky—Biography. | African American soldiers—19th century—Biography. | Slaves—Kentucky—Biography. | Holt, Joseph, 1807-1894. | Slaveholders—Kentucky—Biography. | Judges—United States—Biography. | Kentucky—Race relations—History—19th century. | United States—Race relations—History—19th century. | African American soldiers—History—19th century. | Slaves—Emancipation—United States. | United States—Politics and government—1849-1877.
Classification: LCC E185.93.K3 L46 2019 | DDC 306.3/62092 [B] —dc23
LC record available at https://lccn.loc.gov/2018047829

This book is printed on acid-free paper meeting the requirements of the American National Standard for Permanence in Paper for Printed Library Materials.

Manufactured in the United States of America.

Member of the Association of University Presses

To my wonderful sons,
Anthony Bellavia and Joseph Bellavia,
and to all who continue the struggle
for social justice in grim, dispiriting times.

Contents

Preface

Some years ago, an African American student at the college in Maine where I teach undertook an independent study with me in which she strove to trace the details of her family's centuries-long history in America. Given that my Arkansas-born student's direct ancestors were enslaved people in the American South, we were curious to see how much specific and reliable information we could find. We used whatever archival and other primary sources we could get our hands on, which included many of the excellent databases of digitized material now available via the Internet. My student also talked extensively with living family members and traveled back to Arkansas for a week to conduct in-person research at various local historical societies. It was a hard slog. In the end, despite our shared determination and my professional training and experience, we found only a small portion of what we had hoped to uncover, especially once we tried to reach back beyond the 1870 federal census, the first to identify recently emancipated black Americans by name and the men, at least, as citizens.

In the course of our work together, my student and I periodically deviated from our central project to compare how easy it was for me to find abundant, detailed information about my always-free *white* family's history, particularly the history of the Leonard line (my father's), whose roots in America extend to the 1600s. (My maternal grandparents, who came here as impoverished immigrants from Italy and Hungary at the turn of the twentieth century, posed a much greater challenge.) There are many publicly available sources for learning about the Leonards, who, from generation to generation, continued to acquire wealth, security, and enhanced social status. They also carefully preserved and then privately handed down "stuff" that contains valuable data—not least a massive Bible from the late

1700s replete with notations pertaining to family births, deaths, marriages, and more. My student had no such "stuff" for reference: since before emancipation down to the present time, her family members have remained overwhelmingly poor and geographically scattered, moving frequently and accumulating little in the way of material goods they considered of historical or even sentimental significance. Doing this independent study together was fascinating and frustrating. It highlighted for us both that while scholarship in African American history has made great progress over the last fifty years, the obstacles to complete understanding remain enormous when compared to the history of always-free, literate, middle-class and elite white Americans, especially men.

Which brings me, in a roundabout way, to *Slaves, Slaveholders, and a Kentucky Community's Struggle toward Freedom,* for which the research experience has been, on a far grander scale, as fascinating and frustrating as it was for that independent study project. This is because of the magnitude of the enduring obstacles—first and foremost the gaps in the sources—that remain when trying to understand fully the stories of the African Americans who figure here, in contrast with the well-preserved, well-documented stories of the whites with whose lives the African American characters' lives were inextricably interwoven. The result is a story that is, ultimately, somewhat lopsided in the amount of detail it can present for some individual characters relative to others. Like my student's family history project, however, the story I have been able to craft from the available sources is illuminating nevertheless. I cheerfully encourage others to do what they can to take the story further, and deeper, than I have been able to do.

This book has two primary goals. First, it offers a close-up look at a few dozen slaves from Breckinridge County, Kentucky, who served in Company A of the 118th United States Colored Troops (USCT), mapping the courageous but also jagged and sometimes surprising journeys these men took from slavery through the Civil War and on into a postwar world where they hoped to capitalize on the promises of Union victory. A number of historians have studied the broad contours of black men's Civil War military service: classics by George Washington Williams (*A History of the Negro Troops in the War of the Rebellion*) and Dudley Taylor Cornish (*The Sable Arm*) come immediately to mind. Others have focused on particular facets of USCT soldiers' wartime and postwar experiences: their relations with their white officers, for example (Joseph T. Glatthaar, *Forged in Battle*), or their challenges as veterans (Donald R. Shaffer, *After the Glory*). Some have provided histories of single USCT regiments, including Edward A.

Miller (the 29th USCT) and James K. Bryant (the 36th). There are also a few precious, revealing memoirs by individuals associated with specific regiments, notably Susie King Taylor's *A Black Woman's Civil War Memoirs* and Thomas Wentworth Higginson's *Army Life in a Black Regiment.* Still other historians have considered the role black Kentuckians' USCT service played in the long process of emancipation in the state: I think here of Marion B. Lucas (*A History of Blacks in Kentucky: From Slavery to Segregation*) and Victor B. Howard (*Black Liberation in Kentucky*). Making the best possible use of the limited archival and other available materials, *Slaves, Slaveholders, and a Kentucky Community's Struggle toward Freedom* provides a narrative micro-history of a small number of black Kentuckians from one particular region of the state in order to show how, and how much, the war and its aftermath transformed their particular lives.

Second, this book depicts in specific detail the complicated tensions that characterized the intersecting communities—state, local, interpersonal—from which these black Kentuckians came and to which, in many cases, they returned after the war. Works such as Lowell H. Harrison's *The Civil War in Kentucky,* William C. Harris's *Lincoln and the Border States,* Aaron Astor's *Rebels on the Border,* and Anne E. Marshall's *Creating a Confederate Kentucky* offer rich insights into Kentucky's and Kentuckians' (including black Kentuckians') contributions to and experiences of the Civil War and Reconstruction. The current book, however, places a small slice of Kentucky and a small group of closely connected white and black Kentuckians under a microscope, not because doing so is easy but because it enables us to understand more viscerally what the war meant to actual human beings who inhabited interlocking worlds on the border between slavery and freedom. To do so, *Slaves, Slaveholders, and a Kentucky Community's Struggle toward Freedom* weaves together the stories of the men of the 118th USCT's Company A with the story of one prominent and distinctively relevant local, white slaveholding family. Why this family? Because until they escaped from slavery to join the Union army, several of the men who appear in this book were held in bondage by members of this extended family—the Holts of the region of Breckinridge County known, eponymously, as Holt's Bottom. Still others were owned by whites in the immediate vicinity. Additionally, as a family the Holts manifested in unusually striking and dramatic ways how—as Amy Murrell Taylor has shown in *The Divided Family in Civil War America*—bitter debates over slavery and then the Civil War itself could poison family relations and shred family ties, sometimes permanently. In this sense, given the vicious political divisions that are—as I write this preface—currently tearing American institutions, communities, and families apart, *Slaves, Slaveholders, and a Kentucky Community's Struggle toward Freedom* offers a welcome reminder that such brutal divisions are not new and that they can, in fact, be survived.

At the time the war began, almost all the Breckinridge County Holts (and their close kin the Stephenses), like most whites in the surrounding area, were actively and enthusiastically devoted to slavery, Southern nationalism, and the Confederacy. Most remained so long after the war ended and emancipation became law.[1] In contrast, the most professionally accomplished member of the extended family—the oldest surviving Holt son, Joseph, with whom the story begins—adamantly rejected the worldview that prevailed among his kin and community. Instead, he fervently embraced the cause of Union and, before long, emancipation, the USCT, and the hard work of establishing and permanently protecting black Americans' civil rights. Notably, Joseph Holt used his official roles within the federal government to accomplish these ends, first as President James Buchanan's secretary of war during the "secession winter" of 1860–1861 and subsequently as judge advocate general to Presidents Abraham Lincoln, Andrew Johnson, and Ulysses S. Grant. As readers who have found their worlds rent by harsh political conflicts will appreciate, Holt paid a high personal cost for his commitments, including painful emotional ruptures with family members and others back home that in many cases were, or at least seemed, beyond healing.

I have spent many years studying Joseph Holt, including trying to understand and explicate—in light of the world he came from—the evolution of his political views and choices with regard to slavery, emancipation, and black rights.[2] Rock-solid devotion to the Union as both a concept and a political reality represents the crucial starting point for this evolution: to Joseph Holt, *nothing*—including preservation of the system of human bondage from which he, his family, and millions of other white Americans had so long benefited—was more important than preserving the Union. Also of vital importance to his evolving consciousness, however, as the Civil War progressed and black enlistments became possible, was the impact of his observation of black soldiers' repeated demonstrations of stunning courage, and their willingness to sacrifice their own lives in order to save the nation that had so violently abused them and bring about emancipation and (they hoped) black citizenship. As black soldiers proved their devotion in the face of Confederate treachery—treachery in which so many of his own extended family members back in Kentucky were energetically complicit—Joseph Holt's commitment to black Americans' future welfare only deepened. At the same time, his ties with his own family unraveled. Years after Appomattox, some measure of reconciliation became possible, but only after his death did Joseph Holt return permanently, as it were, to the place where he was born.

Perhaps not surprisingly, it was my years of research into Joseph Holt and his political transformation that eventually led me to the fugitive slaves who comprised Company A of the 118th USCT. At some point it occurred to me that while many in Joseph Holt's extended family were engaged in supporting the Confederate rebellion (some doing so under arms), and while *he* was striving in the nation's capital to preserve the Union, defend President Lincoln's emancipation policies, and support the Federal troops, including the USCT, it would be interesting to know if any of the Holt family slaves had fled their bondage to enlist in the Union army. As it turns out, the answer was yes, and the unit they joined was the Kentucky-based 118th's Company A. Even more striking to me was to learn that among these fugitives was a middle-aged man whom Joseph Holt himself had purchased in Mississippi decades before the war, had brought to Kentucky, and then, when he moved to Washington in 1857 to join President Buchanan's administration, had transferred to the possession of his younger brother Thomas. As a slave this man was known only as Sandy; when he enlisted in the 118th USCT in August 1864 he did so as Sandy Holt.

Unfortunately, as was the case with my Arkansas student's independent study project, I have been able to uncover less specific detail about Sandy Holt's life than I had hoped, especially in contrast with what can be learned about Joseph Holt and his family. Still, by combining his story with the similarly incomplete stories of the other men in Company A, I have been able to produce a reasonably full collective biography. Ironically, it is unclear how much Joseph Holt himself knew about his former slave's military service or that of other fugitives from Holt's Bottom and the surrounding area. What Joseph Holt certainly *did* know—and helped to make possible—was that more than 20,000 black Kentuckians were among the 180,000 black soldiers of the USCT, and that their contributions to the Union's war effort, if different in kind, were at least as valuable to Union victory as his own. It took heroic efforts on many different fronts to bring about emancipation and Union victory in the Civil War. This knowledge inspired Joseph Holt, prodded him forward, and filled him with gratitude, even as the pro-slavery, pro-Confederate sentiments and actions of his kin—as well as what they cost the nation in blood, treasure, and cultural harmony—enraged and embittered him.

This book, then, is the story of a family and a community of black and white Kentuckians from Breckinridge County whose lives' sturdy threads were interwoven throughout the Civil War era. As was true elsewhere in Kentucky and across the border states, members of this particular family and this community understood and responded in disparate ways to the national debate over slavery, the collapse of the Union, the war, the Emancipation Proclamation, the Union's call for black men to enlist in the army, the immediate and long-term implications of Confederate defeat, the ratification of the Thirteenth Amendment to the US Constitution, and more. *Slaves, Slaveholders, and a Kentucky Community's Struggle toward Freedom* underscores the profoundly complex—but not unrecognizable—political and personal dynamics of the era for those who lived through it, particularly in regions on the border between slavery and freedom. It recounts a complicated story of interconnected lives, family and community rupture, institutions collapsing, self-determination, war, sacrifice, anger, cruelty, betrayal, and despair. It is also a story of individual transformation, courage, cross-racial alliances, and, to some extent, reconciliation. As such, not least in this time of renewed crisis for the nation, it is a story not entirely devoid of hope.

Map by Joseph Bellavia

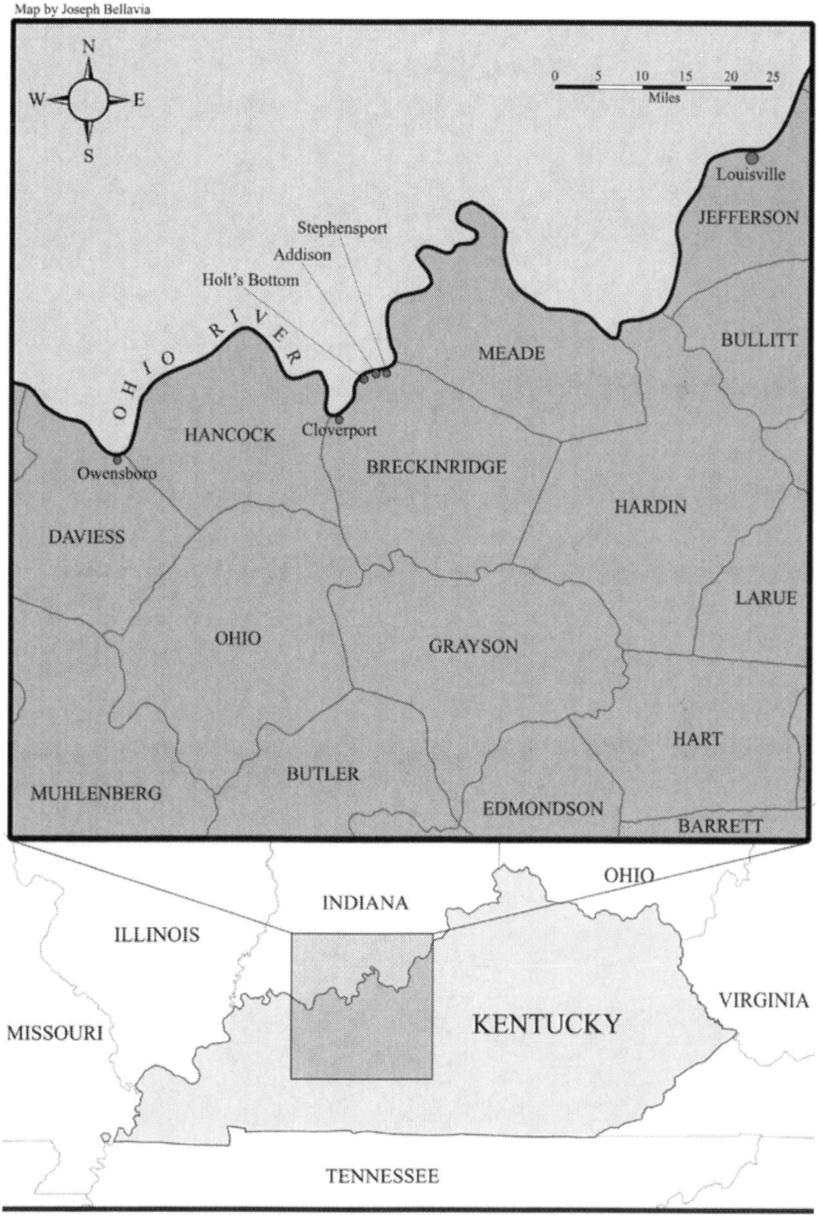

Approx. distance from Holt's Bottom to Washington, D.C.: 650 mi.
to Brazos Santiago, TX: 1200 mi.

Part One

Once a Slaveholder

The Journey of Joseph Holt

In the years before the American Civil War began, few could have predicted that Joseph Holt would become a key figure—judge advocate general—in President Abraham Lincoln's War Department as well as an enthusiastic supporter of emancipation, black men's military service to the Union, and black Americans' civil, political, and human rights more generally. Most whites in the region of Breckinridge County, Kentucky, where Holt was born and raised and where most of his extended family continued to live, were dyed-in-the-wool secessionists, fiercely dedicated to Southern nationalism, white supremacy, and the defense of slavery. In contrast, Joseph Holt became one of the most resolute and influential allies of Lincoln, the Union cause, the United States Colored Troops, and black freedom. His manifold contributions to all of these have long been underestimated. Fortunately for modern-day students of the Civil War era, however, thanks to his racial identity, his superior education, and his social and political prominence, Joseph Holt left a robust the paper trail for us. Indeed, as will be seen, even less intellectually advantaged members of his white family bequeathed to scholars sufficient documentary evidence to enable us to map their lives and thought processes with relative ease.

Pulling Up Roots

Born in 1807 in a corner of Breckinridge County known as Holt's Bottom, Joseph Holt grew up in a large and affluent slaveholding family, and by the time the war began he had been a slave owner, buyer, and seller in his own right for much of his life; he also married twice into substantial slaveholding families. Moreover, in 1861 Holt, already in his fifties, had always lived in places where slavery was woven tightly into the cultural fabric and most whites believed that human beings of African descent were destined to be their property to do with as they saw fit. Over the course of his antebellum professional life as an attorney and Democratic Party activist, Holt had also publicly defended the institution of slavery: during his legal training, in his practice, and in his political speeches. As a young man Holt had idolized Andrew Jackson, and he had come of age and to political prominence during the period when the Democratic Party was most closely identified with slavery's perpetuation and expansion. His speeches and much of his work before the Civil War reflected the party's values.[1]

It is also true, however, that since his youth Holt had occasionally displayed some ambivalence about slavery. While a student at Centre College in the mid-1820s, for example, Holt had encountered—probably for the first time—individuals like the Reverend Jeremiah Chamberlain, the school's president, who considered slavery a sin and believed Kentucky should commit to gradual emancipation. Perhaps under Chamberlain's influence, young Holt had given at least one speech at the college sharply critical of human bondage. Holt's private correspondence, too, offers evidence that as a young man he was not irrevocably committed to the perpetuation of slavery in the United States. Indeed, in a no longer extant fall 1845 letter to his maternal uncle, Robert Stephens, Holt gave the distinct impression that he considered slavery a "social political or moral evil," though he saw no obvious means at that time by which to safely abolish it. For his part, Uncle Robert vehemently challenged Holt's negative characterization of the institution, at the same time expressing his concern that his nephew might some day "settle in a free state." Should such a disaster take place, Uncle Robert wrote, he hoped that Holt would draw the line at becoming an abolitionist.[2]

Of course, any discomfort Joseph Holt felt about the institution of slavery in the prewar years must be measured against his overall acceptance. As late as July 1856, in a Frederick, Maryland, speech on behalf of Democrat James Buchanan's presidential candidacy, Holt vigorously defended the right of states to manage their own affairs and protect their "domestic institutions." He spoke at length about the threats to the Union that arose from growing sectional tensions over slavery and insisted, as Andrew Jackson had done before him, that the life of the Union *must* be preserved. It would be foolish beyond measure, Holt declared, to destroy the Union simply in order to destroy slavery. But for now he directed his anger at the abolitionists for stirring up trouble. For the last twenty years and more, he railed, they had consistently turned up the heat under Americans' discussions about slavery. And now, he went on, the "Black Republicans" seemed bent on transforming the abolitionists' rantings into law by means of the electoral process, perhaps demolishing the nation in the process.[3]

Holt's 1856 speech in Frederick echoed many of his era's most troubling ideas about slavery's "blessings" for white Southerners, even as it also conveyed some uncertainty about the institution's overall value. For Holt in 1856, slavery was "a problem" that had "long and painfully exercised the brightest intellects and the noblest hearts of the world" to no avail; an "excrescence" that had been "planted upon this continent, not by Americans, but by foreigners"; and a tumor that was "growing upon the body politic" and "twining [its] roots so closely above, beneath and around the very seat of life, that skillful surgeons when consulted, refuse to dissect them out, fearing lest death should ensue upon the operation." At this point in time, then, Holt did not so much endorse slavery as revile its activist opponents; he was not unshakably eager to preserve slavery per se, but he clearly feared that the "cure" the abolitionists and "Black Republicans" proposed for it would prove far worse than the disease itself: rebellion, race warfare, perhaps even the nation's collapse. With these perceived threats in mind, he strove to use his oratorical skills and fierce dedication to the party and the Union to promote cool-headed leadership as a corrective to hot-headed rabble-rousing of all sorts. At the same time, he worked to encourage patience and popular confidence in the virtues and ultimate justice of the electoral process. These things alone, Holt believed, would ensure national peace and the survival of America's republican experiment. Slavery's demise would have to wait.[4]

The year after he gave this speech, Holt and his second wife, Margaret Wickliffe Holt, left Kentucky for Washington, DC, when the newly elected Buchanan appointed him commissioner of patents. The move separated Holt by almost seven hundred miles from the family, community, and slave-based culture he had known for fifty years, and as he prepared for the move, the practical question of what to do about his and Margaret's several slaves inevitably arose. As historian Marion Lucas notes, "Though slaves sometimes viewed moving with [an] owner or his relatives . . . as a personal tragedy," there could be marginal benefits. Among other things, slaves who relocated with an owner could take some comfort that they were not being sold to someone else, "perhaps relieving anxiety regarding future treatment" and signaling "the possibility of continued contact with relatives and friends left behind." As he pondered what to do about the men, women, and children he and Margaret held in bondage, Holt weighed a wide range of factors. Among others, he wondered how particular individuals would adjust to the bustling, cosmopolitan capital city so far from the quieter landscape and cherished family members and friends of Kentucky. It bears noting that the move would also bring a distinct change in the racial dynamics and demographics with which the Holts and any slaves who accompanied them were familiar. There were virtually no free blacks in Breckinridge County in the late 1850s, and about 16 percent of the county's population was comprised of slaves. In contrast, both free and enslaved blacks had lived for a long time in the District of Columbia; by the late 1850s they made up approximately 30 percent of the District's overall population. In both places, of course, black Americans were central to the area's life, economic development, and prosperity.[5]

Also noteworthy is that Washington, DC, had a long history as a significant slave-trading center: "Slave dealers," writes historian Elizabeth Clark-Lewis, "not only made the District their headquarters but also 'used the federal jails freely to house their chattel in transit.'" But the proportion of the resident black population that was *enslaved* had dropped from about 50 percent in 1830 to roughly 22 percent by the time the Holts settled into their elegant home at 236 New Jersey Avenue SE, near Capitol Hill. Meanwhile, the overall number of black residents in the District continued to grow. That an increasing proportion of Washington's blacks were "free" clearly does not mean that they were free in the same way that whites were. Like their counterparts across the South, free blacks in DC were subject to a host of legal constraints and indignities, not least the requirement that they carry their "free papers" at all times on penalty of arrest, possible imprisonment, even sale. Despite these constraints, however, Washington's free black community had steadily established "many of the necessary social, educational, and religious institutions to sustain itself during the early decades of the nineteenth century." Some individuals and families were even able to enjoy a measure of affluence.[6]

For Joseph Holt and any slaves he and Margaret chose to bring with them, Washington in 1857 would be a new experience. It is impossible to know precisely to what extent practicality, household budget, demographic realities, and his individual feelings about slavery each factored into Holt's decision-making process with respect to how best to staff the new household. What is certain, however, is that the move became the occasion for him to transfer, either by sale or gift, all but one of the handful of people he still owned to the ownership of his younger brother Thomas in Holt's

Bottom. This decision pleased and benefited Thomas and his wife Rosina, whose commitment to slavery generally, and as a means for preserving the family's homestead and wealth at Holt's Bottom specifically, was unswerving.[7]

Joseph Holt showed little inclination to bring Margaret's remaining human property to Washington, either; he preferred to hire local servants instead, as other whites in the capital frequently did. Once again, although his views were surely shaped to some extent by raw household economics, Holt also considered the question of how his wife's bondsmen and bondswomen would adjust to the new environment, especially given the wrenching separations from family and friends they would have to endure. Regarding Margaret's dining room "servant," Holt wrote to his wife in April 1857, "I have had several chats with John." John "says he is willing to go to Washington to live with you for a while," but Holt added that "any attempt to retain him there, as a member of our household, would I am sure result in rendering him discontented & useless." In the end, Holt persuaded Margaret they should replace John with a hired man.[8]

In this same letter Holt also reminded Margaret that they had agreed to leave Annie and her son William with Margaret's family in Bardstown where William, he pointed out, would be more useful as a field hand than he could possibly be in urban Washington. Holt expressed particular concern about separating Margaret's personal maid, Jane, from *her* son. Jane, he observed, was "very far from being destitute of the maternal instincts." Alas, Margaret's desire to have Jane with her in DC outstripped her sympathy, and Jane was forced to come along. When the District's census taker came to the Holt house in 1860 he listed Jane Clark, age twenty-two, cook, as one of the household's two black residents, along with a thirty-five-year-old "hostler" (caretaker for horses) known as Alfred Semmes. Additional names appear in the historical record in connection with the Holts' Washington household: members of the hired black staff who helped Jane and Alfred—now Joseph Holt's sole remaining bondsman—keep the household running, tend the garden, and care for the Holts' carriage, horses, and dogs.[9]

Joseph Holt had already demonstrated some philosophical ambivalence about slavery as a youth; the 1857 move to Washington, DC, occasioned his first decisive, practical steps away from the institution. He took these steps, perhaps not surprisingly, even as the national debate over slavery was reaching a new level of intensity. In the fall of 1859, abolitionist John Brown's violent attack on Harpers Ferry pushed the question of slavery's future and the stability of the nation itself to the brink. A year later, just weeks after Margaret died following a long period of declining health, and as pro-slavery and Southern nationalist sentiment increasingly gripped the bulk of his family and community members back in Breckinridge County, Holt took another important step, emancipating Margaret's slave Jane. In his October 1860 statement manumitting the young woman Holt spoke with genuine warmth and appreciation of the "faithfulness and kindness" Jane had always shown to Margaret, and then declared her "henceforth free, manumitted, and discharged from all manner of servitude or service to me, my executors or administrators forever." Soon after, he received a letter from a friend, fellow Kentuckian and longtime slaveholder James Speed of Louisville, who later became President Lincoln's attorney general. Like Holt, Speed's views on slavery were changing. "The case of the girl you liberated is really touching," Speed wrote. "I am persuaded that this great evil, this terrible national sin, slavery, must die, but it will be in one of two ways: it will either go out in blood or perish because the master finds the slave has no value." Following her emancipation, Jane remained with Holt in Washington for many years as a highly valued and trusted employee whose affection and loyalty to him were steadfast.[10]

Choosing Union over Slavery

Joseph Holt's personal transformation from slave owner to committed emancipationist was well under way, then, by the fall of 1860. Still, for the time being his *primary* concern remained the preservation of the Union. Indeed, despite his recent emancipation of Jane, Holt's speeches and letters from this period—he was now Buchanan's postmaster general—ring with familiar criticism of the abolitionists who, he continued to insist, had been engaging in "incendiary agitation" for decades. They and the "Black Republicans" who supported them, Holt argued, posed the gravest danger to the Union. He urged white Southerners to remain calm in the face of such agitation because the Union still offered the best defense of all they held dear, including slavery.[11]

Holt pressed this case not only publicly but also in letters to his family, especially his brother Robert, to whom he was particularly close. Like most of Holt's family and community back in Breckinridge County, Robert—now a successful lawyer and planter in Mississippi and the owner of thirty-eight slaves—was a diehard pro-slavery Southern nationalist. Indeed, he viewed Abraham Lincoln's victory in the November 1860 presidential election as "a declaration by northern people individually & collectively through the ballot box of a purpose to emancipate the slaves of the South, and to involve Southern states in all the horrors which that event would plainly entail." In Robert's view, the time for secession—including the secession of Kentucky—had come, and he fervently hoped his oldest brother, whose ambivalence troubled him deeply, would remain true to his Southern roots and upbringing. "Your voice against us," he warned, "would strike your Southern friends like a cold dagger in their bosoms." As it happens, in the weeks following Lincoln's election Robert's doubts about Joseph Holt's ultimate fealty to the slave South and its culture were confirmed. As he watched slaveholders, including most of his own family members, increasingly prioritizing their commitment to slavery over their commitment to the US Constitution and the federal government, Joseph Holt's allegiance to his roots declined precipitously. "I feel a positive personal humiliation as a member of the human family in the events now preparing," Holt confessed to Pennsylvania Democrat and federal judge John Cadwalader in late November. "If the Republic is to be offered as a sacrifice upon the altar of American servitude, then the question of man's capacity for self-government is forever settled."[12]

On December 20, 1860, South Carolina declared its independence from the United States, and less than two weeks later, with his cabinet collapsing around him, President Buchanan named Joseph Holt secretary of war. As he strove without success to stem the nation's continuing dissolution, Holt's resentment of the institution that was driving the rebellion increased dramatically, and Robert's continued warnings about the potential hazards of betraying his Southern slaveholding roots only provoked him. "Providence," Robert wrote on February 11, "has united the destiny of ourselves & our slaves, of our and their posterity forever." For the first time in history, Robert continued, "the master holds in his hands the destiny of two races, the power of fixing for all time their relationship to each other, of framing the social and political institutions by which both are to be governed and beneath which each race is to work out its proper destiny." Indeed, if one sought to identify the moment when Joseph Holt finally abandoned all of his previous defenses of slavery and embraced, once and for all, his earlier doubts about its benefits, a likely contender would be the moment he read this letter, which could easily have served as a draft of the notorious "Cornerstone Speech" Alexander Stephens gave the following month. Unfortunately for historians, Holt's response to Robert, if any, is no longer extant.[13]

Thanks in good measure to Secretary of War Holt's efforts to ensure his safe, peaceful inauguration, Abraham Lincoln became president on March 4, 1861. Two days later, Simon Cameron took over the War Department and Holt stepped down, now turning his attention to Kentucky which, if his own family members' views were any guide, seemed at least as likely in spring 1861 to abandon the Union as it was to remain loyal. "During those critical days," recalled Kentuckian and future Supreme Court justice John Marshall Harlan's wife Malvina years later, Kentucky's Unionists "fairly haunted the lobbies of the State House, doing what they could to stiffen the backs of the men opposed to Secession. My husband and a few others of the younger men actually slept in the State House during several all-night sessions."[14]

Holt now focused much of his energy on doing what he could to keep Kentucky in the Union. Meanwhile, as the war got under way he could not fail to notice and be affected by the changes taking place around him, not least in terms of the attitudes of the District's black residents, several of whom he interacted with daily in their capacity as his paid employees, and two of whom also lived and worked in his household. As was true across America, black Washingtonians quickly recognized that the war might ultimately have consequences for slavery and blacks' civil, political, and human rights. Indeed, to this end, just over a week after Lincoln issued his April 15 call for militia to put down the rebellion, black Washingtonians eagerly expressed their willingness "to offer their lives in defense of the city and the Union." Soon, too, slaves in and around the city began to flee the sites of their bondage for places where they hoped the gathering Union forces would provide protection and perhaps also employment. Some found what they were looking for, but many did not. "In those first few weeks" of the war, Clark-Lewis writes, over seventy fugitive slaves were captured in the federal capital. Some were "detained and returned," while others, whose Confederate owners could not be identified, were kept behind bars. "In a short period of time," she continues, the District's jails "became overcrowded, making deplorable conditions even worse. Inmates were herded like cattle and forced to sleep on cold stone floors."[15]

Observing the momentous developments taking place wherever he turned his gaze, Joseph Holt became more certain than ever that slavery and slaveholders were to blame for the crisis and that slavery itself must be destroyed. In an open letter written in late May to Louisville's Joshua F. Speed—James Speed's brother and Lincoln's close friend—he argued against Kentucky's claim of "neutrality," no longer criticizing the abolitionists and "Black Republicans" as relentless provocateurs but instead excoriating white slaveholding firebrands whose Southern nationalist perspective, he knew, almost all of his family members shared. They and their elected representatives at every level, he now insisted, were in fact the ones responsible for the decades of rabid agitation on the slavery question that had preceded secession. It was *they* who had recklessly kept the issue of slavery alive, shamelessly rallying others around the myth of Northern oppression. Slaveholding zealots had initiated the "extraordinary and discreditable spectacle of a revolution . . . on the ground that guarantees for the safety of their institutions are denied them." Ironically, he pointed out, should these zealots ultimately succeed, they would lose the protections for slavery they so eagerly sought, while demonstrating to the world that the concept of representative government was a failure.[16]

By May 1861 Joseph Holt's revised analysis of the causes of secession separated him ideologically as far from his birth family and community back in Breckinridge County as he was separated geographically. So it is hardly surprising that when Holt followed his letter to Joshua Speed with a personal visit to Kentucky to speak on behalf of the Union and against "neutrality," he eschewed a visit to his family's Holt's Bottom homestead. Instead, he gave a series of speeches reiterating the letter's themes and boldly declaring himself "for this Union without conditions, one and indivisible, now and forever." Referring to the shock he and others had experienced upon realizing that Southern nationalists were prepared to destroy the Union regardless of the cost, Holt confessed, "We feel as one awakened from the suffocating tortures of a nightmare, and realize . . . [of] what a traitorous swindle we have been made the victims." In turn, he bitterly attacked those who criticized Southern-born Unionists like himself for rejecting slavery in favor of Lincoln, the federal government, and the Constitution. "We are told by the disunionists," he exclaimed—perhaps with many of his family members in mind—that in "supporting a Republican Administration in its endeavors to uphold the constitution and the laws, we are 'submissionists.'" But, he countered, "in this submission to the laws is found the chief distinction between good men and devils." Over the next few weeks Holt spoke similarly to the soldiers gathered across the river in Indiana at Camp Jo Holt, named in his honor, and to the members of the Chamber of Commerce at Irving Hall in New York City. By the end of September, Holt's efforts had contributed mightily to Kentucky's decision to abandon "neutrality" and affirm its loyalty to the federal government, though most white Kentuckians—even Unionists—remained deeply committed to slavery.[17]

During the months that Holt was campaigning for Kentucky's loyalty, his recently adopted hometown of Washington, DC, continued to experience firsthand the war's consequences for slavery more broadly. The capital, writes Clark-Lewis, had become "a magnet for contraband" and the influx of fugitives from places where slavery persisted dramatically altered the city's demographics. As the fugitives poured into and dispersed across the District, they established enclaves in various places, the most fortunate individuals clustering in a section of Georgetown where free black residents as far back as the 1830s "had established their own businesses, churches, and schools." In contrast, the poorest immigrants occupied hovels in what became the city's "new slums," whose names, writes historian James Whyte, "indicated their condition: Goose Level, Vinegar Hill, Foggy Bottom, Hell's Bottom, Bloodfield, Prather's Alley, and Nigger Hill," even "Murder Bay." At least one settlement, located at Duff Green's Row on East Capitol Street, was very near where Holt, Jane, and Alfred lived, ensuring direct and regular experience with the runaways' plight and no doubt bolstering Holt's disdain for slavery. At the same time, the massive and transformative influx of slavery's fugitives contributed significantly to Congress's decision in the spring of 1862 to abolish the institution in Washington. Unsuccessful efforts to accomplish this goal had begun back in the late 1820s. Now, almost three and a half decades later and still five months before he issued his preliminary Emancipation Proclamation, President Lincoln signed into law the District of Columbia Emancipation Act, "the only instance of compensated emancipation in U.S. history." This new law "allocated one million dollars to compensate slave owners" in the District for the approximately thirty-two hundred black men, women, and children they still held in bondage, at an average rate of not more than $300 per slave. The law also established a three-man commission to evaluate the claim of each individual slave owner applying for compensation.[18]

It is impossible to know why Holt had waited until now to set his one remaining slave, Alfred, free. But on May 24, 1862, he did so. In his petition to the emancipation commission Holt described Alfred as a "faithful and efficient" coachman, hostler, and gardener "of black complexion, standing about five feet eight or ten inches high, and being thirty-four years of age and of sound health and good habits." Holt requested between $900 and $1,000 in compensation for the hostler's labor; he received $569.40, most of which, one hopes, went to Alfred. As was true when he emancipated Jane, Holt's petition served as the basis upon which the commission could accurately prepare the official certificate of emancipation that Alfred, like Jane, would need to carry on his person in the future. "In the latter years of slavery," writes Clark-Lewis, slaves like Alfred came to be known as the "First Freed," who "embodied the hopes of the African Americans who remained enslaved. They were proof that legislated freedom, sustained by Congress, was possible." Clark-Lewis also notes that once emancipated, most of the District's former slaves "departed their masters' homes immediately and sought employment elsewhere." Like Jane, however, Alfred remained in Joseph Holt's employ for years following his emancipation and he and Jane eventually married. Some of the First Freed also volunteered or were drafted for military service; Alfred appears to have been among them. According to the Civil War draft registration records from 1863 to 1865, a thirty-four-year-old black man named Alfred, occupation "coachman," enlisted for "military duty in the fourth district of the District of Columbia"—Holt's district—sometime in June or July 1863. Unfortunately, in contrast with the abundance of historical evidence one can mine to tell the story of prominent, privileged whites like Joseph Holt, no other information is available about the nature or duration of the freed slave Alfred's military service.[19]

Less than two months after emancipating Alfred, Holt's deepening commitment to black freedom led him to file another petition with the emancipation commission, this one pitting him against some of his former in-laws. On this occasion Holt addressed the predicament of a Kentucky-born bondswoman known as Caroline Robinson, who may well have been Jane's mother and who belonged to William and Mary Wickliffe Merrick. Mary was Margaret Holt's sister, and the Merricks and Holts had once been close. But the Merricks' unwavering support for slavery had alienated Joseph Holt to an extent that even their shared grief over Margaret's death could not ameliorate. The Merricks lived in the District most of the time; William was a US circuit court judge. They also had a residence in his home state of Maryland, however, where slavery remained legal until 1864, and the Merricks' slaves, including Caroline, must have traveled back and forth between the two locations. Perhaps for this reason Mary and William felt justified ignoring the District's Emancipation Act. As a result Caroline, aware that Holt had emancipated both Jane and Alfred, turned to him for help. In his September 30, 1862, petition, Holt claimed that the Merricks had "neglected and still neglect to file with the clerk of the circuit court for the District of Columbia the schedule required to be filed by them by the ninth section of the Act," thereby preventing Caroline "from receiving the certificate of her release & discharge." Although the Merricks were surely displeased with Holt's interference, Caroline received her certificate and was finally free.[20]

By the spring of 1862 a new day had begun to dawn in Washington, DC, for Jane, Alfred, Caroline, and the thousands of other black Americans who resided there. This became even more apparent when, on May 21, Congress declared all black Washingtonians subject to (and therefore also beneficiaries of) "the same laws and ordinances as whites." Such sweeping legal changes further influenced Joseph Holt's thinking, not just about the wrongness of slavery but also about the need to guarantee the fundamental human, civil, and political rights of the hardworking, intelligent, and loyal black men and women he knew personally, as well as others with whom he interacted, or whom he simply observed, on a daily basis. Interestingly, despite his prominence, Holt's changing views were by no means always immediately obvious to outside observers. In October 1861, for example, although Holt had already spent weeks publicly excoriating white Kentuckians for putting slavery above the Union, the *Liberator* described him as someone who had been "brought up under the befogging and befooling influences of Slavery" in the Bluegrass State and could never be expected to overcome the prejudices associated with his upbringing. There was some indirect justification for this assumption, of course: other prominent Kentucky Unionists in the fall of 1861 remained deeply and vocally supportive of slavery and white supremacy, including Holt's own former father-in-law Charles A. Wickliffe, a former governor then serving as a member of Kentucky's delegation to the US House of Representatives. In his frequent speeches Congressman Wickliffe boldly denounced the principle that the federal government or its army could legitimately confiscate Southern property, especially human property, and declared angrily that the abolitionists were succeeding in their effort "to convert this war into . . . a John Brown raid upon a national scale."[21]

Lincoln's Judge Advocate General

Through the summer of 1862, in fact, the *Liberator* continued to lump Joseph Holt in with others who, the editors believed, would surely advise Lincoln against considering national emancipation, even as a war measure. But Lincoln himself knew better, and on September 3, 1862, he appointed Holt judge advocate general of the army under the auspices of Secretary Edwin M. Stanton's War Department. In his new role Holt set to work immediately as the nation's chief arbiter and enforcer of military law, providing opinions on the court-martial and military commission cases and procedures that relentlessly came before him for review, and offering interpretations of the law as it pertained to the Union army and its agenda. Even before the president suspended the writ of habeas corpus, Holt also began taking aim at civilian disloyalty.[22]

Then, less than three weeks after appointing Holt, Lincoln issued his preliminary Emancipation Proclamation. When he selected Holt for the job, and even more so after he issued the final Emancipation Proclamation on January 1, 1863, Lincoln surely expected his judge advocate general to use the considerable weight of his office to support black freedom. He was not disappointed: Holt was ready. Indeed, Holt's willingness to accept the post to which Lincoln had appointed him indicates just how far he had come in his thinking on slavery and black freedom. Still, although the rupture with most of his family members back home had disrupted their lines of communication, some old friends continued to plead with him to use his newfound influence and power to thwart Lincoln's policies rather than enforce them. "Stop him! Hold him!" implored one correspondent in late September. "Beg him . . . never to publish a proclamation," Hugh Campbell urged. "Suggest to him that a dignified retreat from his present position is the only road to a restoration of peace and quiet. . . . Can you not prevail on him to be entirely silent on 'negro-ology'?"[23]

Whether Holt responded directly to Campbell's plea is not known, but a month later he penned an open letter to Hiram Barney, collector of customs for the port of New York, in which he once again expressed publicly and unequivocally his feelings about the value of the Union relative to other "human institution[s]," specifically slavery. Holt's letter to Barney, which appeared in the *New York Times,* reiterated what he had been saying with increasing force since the winter of 1860–1861: that he simply would not endorse slavery at the expense of the Union. "No earthly interest," Holt wrote, "shall ever by me be weighed in the scales against the life of my country. Least of all . . . an institution, the fountain of whose being—the African slave-trade—the laws of my country have for more than forty years denounced as a crime worthy of death." On November 15, Hugh Campbell responded to Holt's letter to Barney, praising Holt for his eloquence and patriotism but sternly criticizing his point of view. "Of course you know," wrote Campbell, "that I do not agree with you in (even indirectly) acknowledging the right of the President to deprive any man, woman, or child of their property (negroes) any more than I admit his right to deprive them of their oxen or sheep."[24]

Holt was unmoved. Instead, he only dug more vigorously into the work Lincoln had committed to his trust. Observers who had failed to notice before now acknowledged the change, some with great joy. "As a Kentuckian," the black newspaper the *Christian Recorder* declared in early December 1862, "Mr. Holt naturally desired [at first] to save the Union without injury to slavery." Now, however, Holt could be counted on to uphold the Emancipation Proclamation openly and with courage. About two weeks later an article in the *Liberator* enthusiastically described Holt as an "abolitionist," the term his uncle Robert had feared, and trumpeted Holt's growing commitment to the principle that "the white man has no more moral right to enslave the black than the native African has to enslave the unfortunate mariner who finds himself cast upon a barbarous shore." The paper also thoughtfully (and accurately) acknowledged the personal and political price Holt was sure to pay among those whose worldview he had summarily rejected: secessionists, "rebel sympathizers," and "peace Democrats" in the North as well as pro-slavery Unionists in the border states.[25]

Indeed, hints of the price he would pay in the public domain for his "sable faith" were already apparent in an article in the Vincennes, Indiana, *Weekly Western Sun,* which now "consigned" Holt and others like him to "everlasting infamy" as traitors to Democratic Party principles. Still, Holt persisted in his efforts to support emancipation and undermine slavery, and not just in his official capacity. When he learned in October 1862 that his former in-laws, the Merricks, had failed to free another slave, just as they had "neglected" to file the proper paperwork on Caroline Robinson, he stepped in again to help. Like Caroline, twenty-four year-old Ellen Cox—probably Caroline's daughter and Jane's sister—reached out to Holt for assistance, and on October 13 he filed a petition on her behalf. The District's emancipation commission approved the petition, which was supported by Jane's testimony, and Ellen received her certificate of freedom. Subsequently, Ellen left the Merricks' household and she, too, went to work for Holt.[26]

Holt's correspondence with Unionist friends from Kentucky whose views on slavery were in flux did not weaken his resolve. "I don't know what is to become of our poor divided state," wrote his old friend Jesse W. Kincheloe from Hardinsburg in late November 1862. According to Kincheloe, a judge and slaveholder, Lincoln's preliminary Emancipation Proclamation had "greatly dispirited the Union men of the state" and "greatly emboldened the opposite party." Kincheloe himself increasingly doubted the value of slavery as an institution and claimed that he would happily surrender all of his slaves if doing so could bring forth what he termed "a satisfactory adjustment of our present difficulties." Other slaveholding Kentucky Unionists clearly felt differently, however, and even Kincheloe wondered if perhaps Lincoln had gone too far. "Is it not too much," he asked Holt, "for the government to ask of its friends, who have put in peril all, even life for its defense," to give up their property, too? A month later, Holt's friend E. T. Bainbridge of Louisville cautioned him against becoming too closely identified with what Bainbridge called the "higher law party," the Radical Republicans. Bainbridge reminded Holt that back in the summer of 1861 they had discussed the importance of fighting the war "on strictly constitutional principles," and that "every departure from the constitution and the laws"—not least the laws about slavery—"would necessarily produce or breed a necessity for a dozen more violations of the law." Bainbridge admitted that even then he had worried that Holt's "just and patriotic anger and disgust with the treason of Jeff Davis and his crew" would incline him to support emancipation. And so it had.[27]

Among several distinctions between September's preliminary Emancipation Proclamation and the proclamation Lincoln issued on January 1, 1863, was the latter document's explicit declaration, building on the Militia Act of July 1862, that former slaves in "suitable condition" in the states and portions of states still in rebellion against the federal government would now be "received into the armed service of the United States" as soldiers and sailors "to garrison forts, positions, stations, and other places, and to man vessels of all sorts in said service." Although the final proclamation exempted loyal Kentucky by definition, many Kentucky Unionists expressed revulsion nevertheless. Among their concerns was the possibility that white soldiers might soon find themselves under the authority of black ones. "I care not who commands these black volunteers," Charles Wickliffe declared at the end of January 1863, "General Sambo or General Hunter, or General anybody else. But I should like to know whether, if Colonel Sambo is in command on the field of battle of a regiment of these contrabands, whose commission is older than those of the white colonels in the same brigade, and the general of the brigade is slain, would not, in accordance with the rules and articles of war, this black Sambo colonel take command of the brigade without any possibility of preventing it?"[28]

In Wickliffe's view, enlisting blacks in the army would have the dreadful result of making them the equals—or worse, superiors—of the "gallant" white soldiers who had already been fighting the war for nearly two years. Wickliffe was also convinced that black men, especially those who had been slaves, would prove unfit for the pressures of battle. "They will not stand the firing of a gun," he declared. "They will fall upon the ground or run away." Furthermore, allowing slaves to enlist, he warned, would provoke a full-scale slave rebellion leading to "the destruction of women and citizens and property, and everything which can be destroyed."[29]

Regardless of their former relation as in-laws, and for the same reasons that he was willing to throw his support behind the emancipation of the Merricks' slaves, had Charles Wickliffe been an officer in the US army at this time, Joseph Holt would have sought ways to punish him for his anti-administration, anti-emancipation statements. Holt had already demonstrated his willingness to turn away from his own birth family and community when their views on the Union and slavery diverged from his, and the archival records of the judge advocate general's office confirm that he subsequently used his authority to take (or advise) action against others who took similar positions. On March 13, 1863, for example, Holt recommended to Secretary of War Stanton that surgeon Levi Oberholtzer of Pennsylvania be court-martialed or simply dismissed from the service for recent remarks criticizing the Emancipation Proclamation and seeking to "incite hostility to the administration, in the struggle which it is making to suppress the rebellion." Oberholtzer's status as a military surgeon, Holt pointed out, "necessarily gives to his pernicious and coarse denunciations great weight, and should not be submitted to by a Government by which he is fed and clothed and housed."[30]

Also in March, Holt referred Stanton to the case of the Reverend Peter H. Burghardt, chaplain of the 65th New York Infantry, who had recently given a speech attacking the government's policies, including the Emancipation Proclamation. "Such discourses," Holt wrote, "weaken the government . . . by chilling or estranging the sympathies of those upon whose courage and determination the administration must rely for its support." He recommended Burghardt's immediate dismissal. Similarly, Holt wrote angrily to Assistant Adjutant General E. D. Townsend about the anti-emancipation sentiments expressed by Colonel Isaac J. Wistar of the 71st Pennsylvania. "An officer capable of entertaining or uttering [such] sentiments," he wrote, "is no more fit to be in the military service of the United States, than if he held a commission from Davis himself." And in early April 1863 he informed Stanton of a letter one Captain J. M. Garland had written, in which he called the Emancipation Proclamation "as unconstitutional as it is unjust." "It is difficult to conceive of a position of deeper dishonor than that in which this officer has placed himself," Holt wrote. "No public interest can be safe in the hands of an officer so hostile to the administration charged with the conduct of the war, and so profoundly sympathizing with the rebels, as Captain Garland has confessed himself to be."[31]

In addition to pressing for the dismissal of individuals in the army who challenged Lincoln's emancipation policy, Holt devoted time and energy to undermining the obstructionism of the so-called Peace Democrats, whose anti-Lincoln, anti-emancipation, typically racist ranting often echoed the rhetoric of the most passionate Southern nationalists. In June 1863 Holt conferred with Stanton about a Copperhead newspaper in Ohio that he considered "dangerous and highly disloyal" for giving voice to both military men and civilians who denounced the government's war policies, particularly emancipation. To prove his point Holt selected a quote in the paper supposedly from a Union soldier who declared the war "a total failure" and who said, colorfully, that the Emancipation Proclamation had "proven a pill that has well nigh vomited all the patriotism and confidence out of this once noble army." "In a period of active hostilities, with either a foreign or domestic foe," Holt wrote, "no Govt. has ever tolerated open traitorous utterances or publications within its military lines; nor indeed can any Govt., however strong, do so without imminent hazard to its own honor and the lives of its own people."[32]

Joseph Holt's strong stand against the military and civilian enemies of emancipation paralleled his strong support for black men's military service. Black Union army regiments had begun to form officially in early 1863, though some had already come into existence *semi*-officially a few months earlier. Then, on May 22, 1863, the War Department issued General Orders No. 143, authorizing the establishment of the United States Colored Troops—the 1st District of Columbia Colored Volunteers became the 1st USCT regiment—and expediting the process of black recruitment in the rebel states. Just over two weeks later, three recently organized black regiments courageously engaged in the battle of Milliken's Bend in conjunction with General Ulysses S. Grant's Vicksburg campaign, a strong indication of what could be expected from the USCT troops going forward. According to Assistant Secretary of War Charles A. Dana, the battle at Milliken's Bend was extremely hard fought, involving a considerable amount of hand-to-hand combat, and the black soldiers' performance under fire had exceeded expectations. "It is impossible," one white officer exclaimed, "for men to show greater gallantry than the negro troops in this fight." In the weeks and months ahead, nothing contributed more forcefully to solidifying Holt's commitment to black freedom and uplift than the black soldiers' own steadfastness and the enormous sacrifices they proved willing to make for a restored Union where they and their loved ones could be free.[33]

Among other things, Holt quickly became aware that along with the usual grave risks associated with armed conflict, black soldiers faced lengthy (perhaps permanent) separations from their homes, and that their family members, if slaves, faced harsh punishment from their owners for the men's decision to enlist. Black soldiers also confronted frequent manifestations of their white comrades' enduring prejudice and disrespect as well as the possibility, upon capture, that they could be sold (or resold) into slavery or even murdered. Indeed, on May 1, 1863, the Confederate Congress passed legislation—the so-called Retaliatory Act—declaring that "all negroes and mulattoes who shall be engaged in war, or be taken in arms against the Confederate States, or shall give aid or comfort to the enemies of the Confederate States, shall, where captured in the Confederate States, be delivered to authorities of the State or States in which they shall be captured, to be dealt with according to such present or future laws of such State or States." The law promised that white Union officers, too, "who shall voluntarily use negroes or mulattoes in any military enterprise, attack or conflict, in such service, shall be deemed as inciting servile insurrection, and shall, if captured, be put to death, or be otherwise punished at the discretion of the court."[34]

In June 1863 Holt received a letter from his friend Francis Lieber, a German-born legal scholar and author of the April 24 General Orders No. 100, also known as the "Lieber Code," detailing proper conduct for soldiers in wartime. For Lieber, the Retaliatory Act's threat of shameless and unprovoked murder of black soldiers off the battlefield demonstrated that the Confederate leaders "dare to do things which no civilized people, even in periods of the highest passion, have had sufficiently depraved courage to do, for nearly two centuries." Lieber implored Holt to impress upon President Lincoln the need for a "severe proclamation" on the matter, but Holt needed no prodding. "We should either disband our colored troops," he replied, "or give them in all respects the same protection which is given to our white soldiers. . . . If we lead them into battle, & even place them in its path, & then permit them to be butchered when captured & held as prisoners, the world will justly denounce our conduct as both criminal & cowardly. Besides," Holt added, more practically than philosophically, "unless the negroes can be assured of protection they will fly from instead of to us, & this mighty resource which might become irresistible in the prosecution of the war if developed, will be lost."[35]

About a month later, Holt spoke even more forcefully about the importance of the USCT and the need to support its black enlistees. Responding to an open letter in the *New York Times* by US federal judge Hugh Lennox Bond of Maryland, Holt detailed the legal foundations of the government's policy, arguing that "the right of the government to employ for the suppression of the rebellion persons of African descent held to service or labor" was grounded in the fact that the slaves were, in the eyes of the law, both property and persons. As property, slaves could be confiscated and put to use just like any other enemy property. As persons (and, implicitly, as citizens), blacks bore the same obligation as all other persons to defend their government, and the government had the obligation to enable them to do so. Enlisting black men in the US army to defeat the Confederate rebellion served this purpose. But Holt did not rest here. Instead, he went on to emphasize the "tenacious and brilliant valor" black troops had already demonstrated and to praise their "loyalty" and "obstinate courage." These soldiers, he insisted, had proved themselves "a most powerful and reliable arm of the public defense." And, he added significantly, "when soldiers of this class lay down their arms at the close of the war," they should at once be able to "enter into the enjoyment of that freedom symbolized by the flag which they have followed and defended." In short, it was not enough to free black Americans from bondage for an uncertain fate. That freedom needed to mean something real, good, and enduring.[36]

In the grim shadow of the July 1863 New York City draft riots that left over a hundred innocent black civilians dead, and less than two weeks after the black 54th Massachusetts launched its heroic, unsuccessful, and extremely costly attempt to capture Fort Wagner in Charleston Harbor, President Lincoln responded officially to the Retaliatory Act. "It is the duty of every government," Lincoln declared, "to give protection to its citizens, of whatever class, color, or condition, and especially to those who are duly organized as soldiers in the public service. The law of nations and the usages and customs of war as carried on by civilized powers, permit no distinction as to color in the treatment of prisoners of war as public enemies. To sell or enslave any captured person, on account of his color, and for no offence against the laws of war, is a relapse into barbarism and a crime against the civilization of the age." Lincoln promised that the federal government would protect *all* of its soldiers and sailors equally, and that Confederate attempts to "sell or enslave anyone because of his color" would lead immediately to harsh punishment for Confederate prisoners of war. "For every soldier of the United States killed in violation of the laws of war," the president declared, "a rebel soldier shall be executed; and for every one enslaved by the enemy or sold into slavery, a rebel soldier shall be placed at hard labor on the public works and continued at such labor until the other shall be released and receive the treatment due a prisoner of war."[37]

Lincoln certainly did not need any prompting from Holt to encourage him to demand fair treatment of black Union soldiers who might be captured by the Confederates. Still, there is no doubt that Holt fully endorsed the president's response to the Retaliatory Act. Moreover, the paper trail Holt left behind is rich with evidence of his efforts as judge advocate general to influence the president whenever he sensed that black soldiers were being treated poorly, including by their own white officers and by the courts that examined their alleged offenses while in uniform. On July 13, 1863, for example, Holt presented Lincoln with his opinion in the case of Sergeant Robert Sutton, a black soldier in Company G of the 1st South Carolina, which later became the 33rd USCT. Sutton had recently been convicted of mutiny and sentenced to death, though the court then recommended mercy in light of Sutton's faithful service and value as a soldier. According to the record of the trial, a number of the black enlisted men in Sutton's regiment had refused, for reasons that are unclear, to go ashore during an expedition off the coast of Florida. In response, Captain William J. Randolph (white) ordered Sergeant Sutton to disarm one of the men "who appeared to be most active and persistent in his disobedience." When Sutton failed to obey, shots were fired, two of the enlisted men were killed, and two others were wounded. Holt's review of the trial record led him to conclude that Sutton had simply misunderstood Randolph's orders. He urged Lincoln to approve the court's recommendation for mercy.[38]

Holt's growing determination to use the power of his office to intervene on black Americans' behalf extended to civilians as well. Here again, one sees the distance he had traveled from his family, his roots, and his prewar worldview. In late January 1864, for example, Holt urged Lincoln to reject the findings of a military commission in the case of a white Tennessean, Robert Taylor, who had brutally killed a fugitive woman slave. After she escaped, Taylor had pursued her, and when he caught her, he beat her to death, but only after he tortured her first by partially hanging her. "Finding that the woman protected herself by taking hold of the rope," Holt wrote with disgusted detail in his review,

> it was slackened, and her hands tied, and again she was drawn up so that her toes barely touched the ground, and in this position

> she was held until her head fell on one side. The rope was then loosened, and an opportunity given her to revive. . . . Some of [Taylor's] neighbors standing by, who appear to have had a latent spark of humanity, advised him not to hang the woman, and he seems to have decided upon other means for accomplishing his end. He stripped off all her clothing, except her chemise, tied her hands and knees together, and with a leather thong whipped the lower part of her body and legs, at short intervals, for two hours and a half. She became exhausted and fell over on her side, and the bystanders advised him that he had "whipped her enough for that time." She was then untied, and, being unable to walk alone, was assisted towards the kitchen, on the threshold of which she fell into the presence of [Taylor]'s wife, and a few moments thereafter expired.

"It is impossible to conjecture," Holt raged, "by what principle of law, what conception of justice, or sense of duty, the Court were guided in their decision and judgment." He urged Lincoln to overturn Taylor's sentence of only five years in a New York state prison in favor of something harsher, and to punish the members of the military commission for their poor judgment.[39]

It is important to note that Holt's deepening commitment to black Americans' freedom and welfare did not blind him to some blacks' capacity to perpetrate crimes as heinous as those of whites. In March 1864, for example, he urged Lincoln to confirm the conviction and death sentence of a black civilian whom a military commission had found guilty of attempting to rape an eleven-year-old white girl. Following the attack, Holt explained, "an examination of her clothes and her person, made by women and by a physician, disclosed all the confirmatory evidence of attempted ravishment, for which the law looks; and an examination of the negro's parts, by the doctor, corroborated the other proof." Holt called the crime "hellish" and recommended that Lincoln approve both the verdict and the sentence.[40]

In a related vein, Holt was persuaded that black soldiers should not receive inordinately sympathetic treatment simply on account of their race. In March 1864 Privates Sterling Bradley and Charles Davis of the 63rd USCT were convicted of mutiny and sentenced to death. Two months earlier a vigorous disagreement had arisen among several of the enlisted men in the 63rd's camp in Tennessee. When Lieutenant William Striblen tried to subdue the men, Bradley attacked and wounded him with his bayonet, sending Striblen to the hospital. Davis apparently fired his weapon, though he does not appear to have hit Striblen with a bullet. Defense witnesses testified that before the altercation erupted, Bradley and Davis were distressed over news they had received that day that their family members, many of whom had set up camp nearby, were to be dispersed. In addition, Striblen and another officer that morning had, in the enlisted men's presence, severely wounded a black civilian for no apparent reason, and he was heard to boast that he had "nearly killed one damned nigger" that morning, and "expected to kill another before night." On this occasion Holt agreed with the court that the alleged extenuating circumstances did not justify Davis's and Bradley's violent behavior. "It is vitally important to the success of the great and promising experiment of employing negroes as soldiers," he declared, "that, while no unjust distinctions should be made between them and other troops, neither benevolence nor sympathy should deter us from the enforcement of a rigorous discipline, alike adapted to their training and to the necessities of the service." Holt recommended that the sentences of Bradley and Davis be sustained.[41]

Defending Blacks' Rights

Shortly before he wrote this particular opinion, Holt attended a speech given to the House of Representatives by the British abolitionist George Thompson, an outing that would have been unthinkable for him a few years earlier, when he still considered abolitionists the leading threat to the republic's future. An April 15, 1864, article in the *Liberator*—which had once deemed Holt a hopeless Kentucky apologist for slavery—noted his presence at Thompson's speech and described him as "one of the purest and most conscientious statesmen of our country" in light of his now widely recognized pro-emancipation views and efforts. Then, in mid-July, Holt faced what must have been, at some level, a particularly challenging personal test: Secretary of War Stanton sent him to Kentucky. Holt's official task was to meet with Governor Thomas Bramlette and Major General Stephen G. Burbridge to discuss the military situation there. Apart from the hazards of traveling outside the well-guarded federal capital, emotionally the visit cannot have been easy. Leaving his assistant, Judge Advocate Addison A. Hosmer of Massachusetts, to tend to business in DC, Holt spent about a week in his deeply divided home state, primarily in Louisville, where he had lived for many years before the war. Once again he did not travel to Breckinridge County, where he would have had to confront his family and community members' abhorrent politics directly. He might also have faced real physical danger, possibly even from his own kin.[42]

Indeed, among those from the Holt's Bottom area whose animosity toward Holt was particularly bitter was his brother Thomas's older son John R. Holt. Back in April 1861, Holt's maiden aunt Mary Ann Stephens—the only other Unionist in the family and to a great extent a laughingstock to the rest—had described the twenty-one-year-old John as a red-hot secessionist "determined to 'sett them all against the government.'" Moreover, she noted, John had expressed a willingness once the war began to kill his turncoat uncle Joseph if their paths ever crossed. Personally, Mary Ann found John's passionate denunciations of Lincoln, his uncle Joseph, and the federal government positively silly. "I never heard such babblin in all my life," she confided in one of the many lengthy letters she wrote to her nephew in Washington throughout the war. But she observed that John's parents, Thomas and Rosina, "thought he was brilliant."[43]

Two months after the war began—while his uncle was giving pro-Union speeches in Kentucky and elsewhere—John R. Holt enlisted in Company G of the 1st Kentucky Infantry (Confederate), also known as the Dixie Guards. Seven weeks later he was discharged due to a severe but unidentified illness that was declared, at the time, "absolutely incurable." This grim diagnosis clearly overstated his incapacity, however, for as soon as he was able, John reenlisted, now joining the 2nd Kentucky Cavalry's Company C. While serving with this regiment he was captured at Salineville, Ohio, following a July 26, 1863, battle that resulted in the destruction of John Hunt Morgan's forces and Morgan's own arrest and imprisonment. Sent initially to Ohio's Camp Chase, John was later transferred to Camp Douglas outside Chicago. Fearing that John would be executed for his actions, Aunt Mary Ann had begged Joseph Holt to use his influence as judge advocate general to save the young hothead, but there is no evidence and little likelihood that he did so. John remained at Camp Douglas—sometimes called "the North's Andersonville"—until he was transferred to Point Lookout in Maryland near the end of the war. Meanwhile, back in Holt's Bottom, his father Thomas was arrested at least once for being involved in local anti-government guerrilla activities. Joseph Holt's family members were fervent secessionists, and the dangers he would have faced visiting Holt's Bottom in 1864 were real.[44]

And so on this visit he remained in Louisville, meeting with General Burbridge, Governor Bramlette, and other civil and military leaders, probably including his longtime Louisville friend and fellow Unionist Dr. T. S. Bell. From there Holt also corresponded with Jane back at his Washington home, one of the people closest to him among his small circle of trusted intimates. Apologizing repeatedly for her spelling—Holt himself may have taught her to read and write—Jane reassured him that "every thing is getting on as usual." She encouraged him to "write soon," noting fondly that she had had several anxious dreams about him since his departure. Jane reported that the garden was doing well, producing "a mess of corn" and delicious beets, and that Alfred was "very slowful" in returning from somewhere. "I shant look for him," she concluded, "unlest I hear that he is coming."[45]

By August 5, Holt was safely back in his War Department office, where he set about composing a detailed report for Secretary of War Stanton of what he had learned during his trip west. In this report, Holt focused considerable criticism on an anti-government, anti-emancipation booklet military authorities had seized from the office of Daniel W. Voorhees, a Democratic member of Congress from Indiana and a staunch Copperhead. "In the divine economy," Holt recited from the pamphlet, "no individual of the human race must be permitted to encumber the earth, to mar its aspects of transcendent beauty, nor to impede the progress of the physical or intellectual man." Human beings who were *incapable* on their own of either "virtuous action" or "progress onward and upward"—human beings, presumably, like the black men, women, and children white Americans had enslaved since the seventeenth century—deserved to be "subjected to a just and humane servitude and tutelage to the superior race"—whites—"until they shall be able to appreciate the benefits and advantages of civilization."[46]

Words like these, Holt wrote in his fall 1864 report, encapsulated "the whole theory of human bondage": whites' presumption that "because they are strong" they had the right "to despoil and enslave the weak, because they are weak!" It was a perverse theory, he observed, and one that now served as the "corner stone for the government of [the] rebellion, every fiber of whose body and every throb of whose soul is born of the traitorous ambition and slave pen inspirations of the South." Holt described the grisly purposes of groups like the Organization of American Knights (OAK), which included "the cold blooded assassination of Union citizens and soldiers," especially black soldiers. He noted that members of the OAK's Louisville branch had conspired some weeks earlier to derail a train full of black troops, with the sole purpose of "seizing the opportunity to take the lives of as many as possible." Here he seems to have been referring to an incident involving the 13th USCT, a Tennessee regiment, whose men were performing railroad guard duty on the Nashville & Northwestern Railroad that summer. According to the *Nashville Daily Union* of June 26, 1864, a number of the 13th's enlisted men were wounded around that time in a mysterious derailing "accident."[47]

On the positive side, Holt was pleased to report that black recruitment into the Union army had been going well in Kentucky despite many obstacles. As Captain and Provost Marshal John R. Grissom later reported to Provost Marshal General James B. Fry, the organization of black regiments at Owensboro—the closest Federal recruiting station to Holt's Bottom—was challenging but had been successful on the whole. "It was extremely difficult," Grissom recalled, "to obtain services of suitable persons to act as enrolling officers, and in many cases after commencing the work they gave it up on account of personal abuse, insults, and threats of personal violence made by citizens and owners." Nevertheless, at Owensboro alone about sixteen hundred former slaves had signed up. "A great degree of enthusiasm was manifested by the Negroes on the subject of volunteering," Grissom observed, and "when they felt sure of protection they presented themselves in such numbers that it was difficult to make suitable provision for them."[48]

For Joseph Holt, and for the Union generally, this was good news. The more black men the Union army could recruit in Kentucky the better: their familiarity with the state's contested terrain offered the federal government a distinct advantage in the conflict. In an earlier endorsement of General Stephen Burbridge's request "to mount two colored regiments" in the state—"the horses to be seized from citizens of known disloyalty"—Holt had commented, "These regiments, composed of men almost raised, as it were, on horseback, of uncompromising loyalty, and having an intimate knowledge of the topography of the country, would prove a powerful instrumentality in ridding the State of those guerrilla bands of robbers and murderers which now infest, and oppress almost every part of it," including, he might have added, Breckinridge County. As a result, the 5th and 6th US Colored Cavalry regiments were organized. In October 1864 the 5th was engaged at Saltville, Virginia, about sixty miles east of the Kentucky border. In a gruesome but familiar pattern, following the Confederate victory there an unknown number of the wounded Union soldiers who remained on the battlefield or had been moved to field hospitals—especially blacks—were mercilessly killed by armed Confederates.[49]

As the war moved into its final months, Holt brought to his War Department work a heightened awareness of the manifold cruel and murderous injustices black Americans—including black Kentuckians—continued to experience, whether they were in slavery or in Federal uniform. Now serving as judge advocate general *and* head of the War Department's Bureau of Military Justice, Holt continued to review the courts-martial, courts of inquiry, and military commissions involving black Americans, but with a sharpened focus on their particular struggles. It is impossible to know how much regret over his own previous active participation in the South's "peculiar institution" factored into his opinions and decisions now. One suspects that it was considerable.[50]

Many of the cases Holt examined during the war's final months involved enlisted men. In one, a white officer, Lieutenant Edwin R. Fox of Company C, 2nd US Colored Cavalry, had been acquitted of murdering one of his black troopers. Lieutenant Fox, it appears, had ordered a series of punishments (including tying him up) for Private Henry Edwards for allegedly feigning illness. When Edwards resisted punishment, Fox simply shot him in the head. The court acquitted Lieutenant Fox on the grounds that he had acted according to what he understood to be his duty and his conviction that it was "a mistake to treat his men with kindness and punish them lightly." But they simultaneously determined that Fox's readiness to kill Edwards for a relatively minor infraction rendered him unfit for duty with a black regiment. In his review of the case, Holt argued that Fox had clearly gone "far beyond the necessity of the case in his attempt to enforce discipline" and he strongly recommended Fox's dismissal. In early 1865 Holt also reviewed the case of Private James Castle of the 11th US Colored Heavy Artillery's Company D. A former cook from Rochester, New York, Castle was convicted of "leaving his guard and getting drunk," "shooting with intent to kill a man who had offered him no provocation," and "alarming the camp by the discharge of firearms." He received a sentence of ten years in prison at hard labor "wearing a ball and chain." Holt did not dispute the verdict and sentence in the case. But he insisted that the white officers in the 11th USCHA should not benefit from Castle's lapses while Castle's family suffered. Holt therefore endorsed the convicted soldier's request that the officers, to whom he had entrusted almost $400 "for safe keeping," be compelled to surrender the funds to Castle's family, which was "in a state of extreme destitution."[51]

On numerous occasions Holt still sought to mitigate punishments to black soldiers that he considered much too harsh. For example, Sergeant Major Adam Laws of the Maryland-based 19th USCT was charged with having cursed violently at the unit's white commander, Colonel Henry

Thomas, on one occasion saying, "God damn you, don't lay your hands on me, if you do it will be the last man you will ever put your hands on." The court sentenced him to six months' imprisonment at hard labor, but Holt encouraged leniency, drawing attention to the fact that Laws, who had requested a pardon, was previously known to have been a good, respectful, "dutiful and obedient soldier," perhaps even "the best soldier in the regiment." Holt also continued to review the work of military commissions involving civilians whose actions hindered the army's ability to achieve its goals. Of particular interest was the case of William Burns, a white Kentuckian charged with "impeding and preventing the enlistment of negroes into the armies of the United States." According to the trial record, Burns and another man had taken extreme measures toward this end, including cutting off the left ears of two black recruits before beating them and imprisoning them for a night for maximum intimidation. Holt vigorously affirmed the military commission's decision to sentence Burns to ten years' imprisonment at hard labor, noting that such a sentence would also "be of salutary influence upon [other] disloyal and traitorous citizens of the Southern states," notably Kentucky, in connection with their routine violence against innocent blacks.[52]

In the case of nineteen-year-old Clarence Joyce, also of Kentucky, Holt expressed even more forcefully his determination to protect black soldiers from whites' shameless cruelty. An avowed secessionist, Joyce was charged with trying to kill Private Robert Richardson of the 61st USCT's Company H. Witnesses, including a number of other black soldiers, testified that the white man was intoxicated when he came upon two black enlisted men on the streets of Louisville, called upon them to stop, then cursed them as "God damned nigger sons of bitches" when they ignored him. A few yards away, Private Richardson—a former clerk from Michigan who was "so nearly white that his negro origin was barely perceptible"—overheard the altercation and crossed the street in order to avoid getting tangled up in it. Joyce then trained his attention on Richardson, demanding to know whether he was a black man or not and eventually stabbing him "with an open penknife in the abdomen," exclaiming, "I am a God-damned rebel, and I don't care who knows it, and I'll kill all the damned soldiers I meet."[53]

One defense witness at Joyce's trial insisted that it was Private Richardson who provoked the attack by bumping up against Joyce in the street and then "put[ting] his hand to his breast as if to draw a weapon." Holt found this testimony completely implausible. The witness admitted, after all, that he had been drinking alcohol on the evening in question and probably did not really know for certain what had happened. Holt went on to disagree with the sentence the commission had imposed on Joyce: a single year at hard labor in the state penitentiary at Frankfort. He was disgusted, too, with the pardon that some of Joyce's white friends requested. Holt observed that the officer who arrested Joyce had heard Joyce saying that he attacked Richardson because "he did not allow any damned negro to give him any impudence." Holt further declared that Joyce possessed a "ferocious and wicked spirit" manifest in his assumption of the right to attack "any man whom he considers as holding, by the accident of color, a lower position in the scale of humanity than himself," and noted that Joyce had shown absolutely no remorse. "On the contrary," Holt emphasized, "there is an air of exultation in his demeanor, as if he were rejoiced that he had wiped away in blood the imaginary stain which a lack of humility in one whom he regards as belonging to an inferior race, had left upon his manhood." It was "only proper," Holt concluded, that the convicted man's imprisonment should be "disagreeable and painful" given the crime that he had committed against another human being—even worse, a Federal soldier—simply on account of the man's race. Thanks to Holt's intervention, Joyce's sentence was upheld and Private Richardson received a promotion to sergeant.[54]

In numerous reviews from the final months of the war Holt provided observations like the one he offered in the case of James T. Andrew (white), convicted of murdering a free black man named Thomas Waller. Holt described the killing as "a ruthless, brutal murder" that "evidently belongs to a numerous and revolting class of crimes . . . being perpetrated upon the . . . colored population of the South by their late traitorous and exasperated masters." Indeed, he emphasized, "this long down-trodden, but now emancipated, race have the strongest claims upon the national gratitude, growing out of their loyalty in the midst of the traitorous white population by which they were surrounded, and out of the courage and faithfulness with which they have laid down their lives on so many battlefields in defense of the Union." For Holt, the decisive contributions and sacrifices black soldiers continued to make to the Union cause on a daily basis reinforced the fundamental legitimacy of black Americans' claims to citizenship and federal protection.[55]

At least one case suggests that Holt had a special concern for the welfare and safety of black women, whom he considered slavery's greatest victims. For several months in 1864, Chaplain William H. Corkhill had allegedly been well known around the contraband refugee camp at

Benton Barracks, Missouri, where he served as superintendent, for treating the women there as his own personal prostitutes. Evidence indicated that Corkhill had habitually visited the female refugees "in their rooms at late hours of the night, locked their doors, extinguished the lights they may have had burning, got into their beds, felt of their persons in the most indecent manner, made advances to them in disgusting language, and in every way shown himself to be abandoned to his passions, and to have renounced all regard for the respect of those under his especial charge." In exchange for the women's involuntary "favors," Corkhill had distributed "clothing and other comforts" among them, saving the best-quality materials for those who proved the least resistant to his sexual advances. "If the evidence in this case is to be believed," Holt wrote to President Lincoln, Corkhill

> is guilty not only of immoralities, but of practicing those immoralities with so much indecent lewdness as to show a most depraved and abandoned nature, and a total forgetfulness of his duty not only as a Christian minister, bound by the sacred office he fills to set an example of purity and elevation of character, but also as a guardian of the morals of a degraded and ignorant class of beings just redeemed from the dangers of involuntary servitude, and toward whom a sense of honor should induce any man, capable of appreciating the responsibilities resting upon him in such a position, to act with especial care and fidelity in the inculcation of modesty and chastity.[56]

Strains of paternalism are certainly evident in Holt's attitude toward the contraband women in this case, but his fundamental concern for their well-being is undeniable. This attitude surely arose at least in part from, and was reinforced by, his ongoing relationship of mutual interest and fondness with Jane and her sister Ellen who, along with Alfred, still worked as his household employees. Like the mounting evidence of black soldiers' dedication to the Union cause and their brave sacrifices for their freedom, Holt's warm and enduring relationship with Jane, Ellen, and Alfred underscored for him the depth and persistence of black Americans' oppression. Indeed, some months earlier Holt's close friendship with a white woman named Mary Cash had gone completely to pieces when the emotionally insecure Cash had wildly accused Jane and Ellen of trying to poison him against her. Rather than taking Mary's side in the dispute, Holt stood firmly by Jane and Ellen, earning Mary's resounding approbation. "Your faith in the African race is complete," Cash wrote when she realized that her plan to alienate Holt from his black employees had backfired. "I think it will bring you but little happiness in this world." Joseph Holt had come a long way indeed from his slaveholding Kentucky roots and past.[57]

Part Two

Once a Slave

The Journey of Sandy Holt

Part One of this volume traced the remarkable evolution of Abraham Lincoln's judge advocate general, Joseph Holt, from longtime Kentucky slaveholder and Southern Democrat to staunch defender of emancipation, the United States Colored Troops, and, more generally, black Americans' civil, political, and human rights. The historical record for understanding Holt's evolution is robust, as is true for so many privileged and prominent white Americans in the nation's past. What follows in Part Two is a parallel study of the context and journey of a very different figure from the Civil War era: a man who was born into slavery, spent virtually his entire life as a poor laborer, never had the opportunity to learn to read and write, and came to be recognized by the US government as a whole and free human being—and a citizen—only when he was in his forties. Like Joseph Holt, this man had deep roots in Breckinridge County, Kentucky; indeed, from the time he was a youth he, too, considered Holt's Bottom his home. Like Joseph Holt, this man, too, committed himself during the Civil War to the cause of black freedom, and he sacrificed mightily, in the ways that were available to him, to make that freedom a reality. Unlike Joseph Holt, however, the historical record for this man is predictably and sometimes excruciatingly thin, and the historian must gather, scrutinize, and piece together a host of less traditional (and less readily accessible) sources in order to tell his story. It is, nevertheless, well worth telling, not least because of the intriguing ways his story is intertwined with Joseph Holt's.

Slavery in Kentucky

In May 1861, when Union general Benjamin F. Butler refused to return to their "masters" the first three fugitive slaves who sought his protection at

Fortress Monroe, Virginia, he surely did not imagine that by the time the war was over, as many as 180,000 black men would serve in uniform as Federal soldiers. Approximately two-thirds of these men had previously been slaves, and nearly 40,000 of them died in the service. The black men who enlisted in the Federal army joined more than 170 regiments of the United States Colored Troops and were engaged across both the eastern and western theaters of the war. Especially significant here is that more than 20,000 of them, about 13 percent, came from Kentucky, which held over 225,000 black men, women, and children in bondage at the time the war began.[1]

Slavery was firmly embedded in Kentucky's economy and culture in 1861. In the years following the American Revolution, Kentucky took shape across forty thousand square miles of land that had previously belonged to Virginia, joining the Union as a new state in 1792. "Blacks and whites entered Kentucky together," historian Marion B. Lucas has written, with blacks typically representing between 10 and 20 percent of the pioneer population. While blacks "undertook the drudgery of carving [farms] from the Kentucky wilderness," white men drew up the state's first constitution, taking as their model the guidelines and language set down in the constitution of Virginia. In essence, Virginia's laws pertaining to slavery became Kentucky's, applicable to the more than 12,400 bondspeople who were living there when the state was created.[2]

In 1798, the Kentucky legislature expanded the state's original laws regarding slavery into a forty-three-article slave code, which then persisted, with few changes, throughout the slavery era. Predictably, the 1798 code consigned black Kentuckians "to an inferior position in every aspect of life," prescribing specific, harsh punishments for all offenses against its directives. In addition to defining slaves as real estate that "shall descend to the heirs and widows of persons departing this life, as lands are directed to descend," the code deprived bondsmen and bondswomen of such fundamental rights as the right to serve on a jury or as a witness in any court action involving whites as well as the rights to assemble freely, engage in trade, or own weapons. The code also constrained slaves' mobility, stipulating that any unfree person who left the property of his or her owner for more than four hours must carry a pass, which could be issued only by a member of the owner's family, an overseer, or an employer (presumably white) to whom the slave was hired out.[3]

Kentucky's slaves still managed to move about with some impunity as the laws designed to inhibit their physical freedom were often, writes Lucas, "loosely applied and unevenly enforced." Kentucky's rural character and limited transportation network, too, made effective implementation of the laws extremely difficult. Nevertheless, slave patrols operated everywhere and state law insisted on "special vigilance" by whites living in counties that bordered the Ohio River, across which freedom (of a sort) lay in the territories that became Ohio (1803), Indiana (1816), and Illinois (1818). Unsurprisingly, regulations pertaining to *fugitive* slaves were also central to Kentucky's 1798 code. "Any person who [even] suspected a Negro of being a runaway slave," Ivan McDougle explained a century ago, "could simply take him before a justice of the peace, and swear to his belief in the guilt of the accused." Once the local justice of the peace provided the accuser with a certificate detailing the location of the capture, the accuser could return the accused to his or her purported owner for a reward. In cases where an owner could not be determined immediately, the suspected fugitive was jailed while county officials tried to track the owner down. After a year or so, if an owner did not appear, the sheriff could put the accused up for sale, retaining any proceeds to cover the expenses incurred.[4]

Kentucky's slave code afforded whites strong, even violent, control over their human property. Slaves in Kentucky "were not regarded as persons," wrote one agent for the Federal Writers' Project in the 1930s, following a series of interviews with former bondspeople. They "had no civil rights and were owned just as any other chattel property, were bought and sold just like horses and cattle, and knew no law but the will of their white masters." In theory, the code also offered terms whereby an owner might emancipate a slave. However, an owner's individual power to free a slave remained "subject to the rights of [his or her] creditors" and heirs. In addition, owners were required to guarantee that any slaves they emancipated did not become "an economic burden to the community or state." In the end, few of Kentucky's slaveholders freed their slaves during their own lifetimes. More often, they bequeathed their slaves to their heirs or ordered that, like other property, the human property "be sold to pay debts and support family members." Kentucky's slave code further established "an essentially intermediate status between slavery and freedom for free people of color" (all blacks in the state were presumed to be slaves unless they could prove otherwise whenever a white person demanded). In addition, in 1808 the state legislature determined that free blacks elsewhere could not legally immigrate to Kentucky, and that any free black attempting to do so must leave the state within twenty days on penalty of being sold into perpetual bondage.[5]

Unlike slave codes elsewhere in the South, the Kentucky code did not officially forbid masters to educate their human property. However, former slaves from Kentucky routinely recalled being denied the opportunity to learn to read or write. As one former slave from Boyd County explained, "Before freedom, the negroes in [my] neighborhood were allowed no books, [and] if found looking at a book a slave was whipped unmercifully." The state's slave code further required that owners treat their slaves "with humanity," provide them with sufficient clothing and food, and "abstain from all injuries to them extending to life or limb." The extent to which individual owners observed these protections, however, varied widely. "I remember one slave named Adams," recalled George Henderson of Woodford County, "who ran away and when he came back my old master picked up a log from the fire and hit him over the head." "I once saw a light colored gal tied to the rafters of a barn," remembered former slave Edd Shirley of Tompkinsville, "and her master whipped her until blood ran down her back and made a large pool on the ground." A former slave from Clay County described two women killing themselves because their master was so cruel. "You would ask if I had been whipped," Robert Anderson of Green County commented in his memoir, *From Slavery to Affluence.* "Indeed I have. My entire body is covered with scars from punishments, so that when I am undressed my body looks like a board that is full of knots." According to the Kentucky slave code, when owners mistreated their bonded laborers the state could intervene. But state intervention did not mean the victim went free. Rather, when the state stepped in it typically did so to sell the abused slave to another, presumably more benevolent, master.[6]

Kentucky's climate and agricultural conditions led the state to be dominated by small farms rather than massive plantations, and nearly 90 percent of Kentucky slaveholders in the antebellum period had fewer than twenty slaves; the average was closer to five. There were 182,258 slaves in Kentucky in 1840 and 210,981 ten years later. By far the majority of these men, women, and children were field laborers who performed the "hardest, dirtiest, most laborious agricultural tasks a working farm required," jobs that at the same time were, "for the most part, routine and could be learned easily and checked without difficulty." Field slaves, writes Lucas, "arose early and fed the horses, mules and oxen. They tended the chickens and slopped the hogs. Slaves hauled salt blocks to the fields, counted the farm animals, and drove cattle and sheep from one pasture to another. Bonds[people] plowed the fields and raised corn, sweet potatoes, and wheat for the farm, as well as the cash crops of tobacco, hemp, and flax. They weeded and harvested garden vegetables and trucked produce and staples to market . . .

broke horses and mules, chopped out briar patches, cleared additional pasture or cropland, and shelled corn."[7]

Other slaves were, relatively speaking, more fortunate: selected for domestic labor in their owners' homes, their responsibilities might be somewhat less physically taxing. Nevertheless, house slaves in Kentucky, as elsewhere, lived and worked under the constant glare of whites, whose control over them was absolute, at least in theory. Perhaps even more so than those who worked in the fields, house slaves were "always subject to their owners' whims and wills" and faced the constant threat of physical and sexual abuse and of being sent out to the fields should they fail to meet their owners' performance standards or demonstrate sufficient "devotion." Indeed, many house slaves routinely spent time laboring in the fields anyway, especially during the harvest season. Both house slaves and field slaves were also susceptible to sale at any time should they prove "troublesome." "Negroes who were unruly," wrote a Federal Writers' Project agent for Kentucky, "or were caught attempting to escape, were usually sold to planters in the far south where they could not hope to escape, and were forced to end their days in unremitting toil in the cotton and cane fields."[8]

Together these enslaved black men, women, boys, and girls provided much of the backbreaking labor that produced Kentucky's antebellum prosperity. They also formed families and communities, despite the overall disdain with which whites' laws—and many slave owners individually—treated their personal commitments. "As a rule," recalled a former slave named John from Boyd County, "negro men were not allowed to marry at all," and "any attempt to mate with the negro woman brought swift, sure, horrible punishment." On many farms the slave population was "propagated by selected male negroes, who were kept for that purpose." According to another former slave, John Sturgill of Floyd County, "Slave traders came into the county to buy up slaves for the Southern plantations, and cotton or sugar fields," and "slave families were very frequently separated." "De white folks jes made niggers carry on like brutes," a white interviewer—clearly struck by her subject's speech patterns—quoted Annie Boyd of Christian County as saying. "One white man uster say ter nuther white man, 'My nigger man Sam wanter marry yer nigger gal Lucy what does yer say' en if he said hit war all right why dat couple war supposed to be married." "Only the strong healthy slave women were allowed to have children," wrote another Federal Writers' Project agent, "and [they] often were not allowed to mate with their own husbands but were bred like livestock to some male negro who was kept for that purpose because of his strong physique." In addition, as was true across the slave South, "often the father of a comely black woman's child would be the master himself, who would heartlessly sell his own offspring to some other master, without regard for his welfare." Like slaves everywhere, Kentucky's bondspeople did what they could, both implicitly and explicitly, to challenge the dehumanizing features of the institution, but the obstacles were enormous.[9]

Although some Kentuckians, particularly members of the Presbyterian and Baptist Churches, had begun calling for the institution's demise almost as soon as it came into existence, most whites in the state considered slavery "almost sacred." Contemporary observers as well as historians later—and even former slaves themselves—sometimes cast slavery in Kentucky in a favorable light as a "benign form of bondsmanship," especially compared to the institution's manifestations elsewhere in the South. In reality, however, race-based human bondage could be as harsh in Kentucky as anywhere else. "I will never forget how mean old Master Nolan Barr was to us," recalled Joana Owens, who spent years in slavery in Hawesville. Barr "had a big farm," Joana continued, "and owned lots of slaves, and when the old master got mad at his slaves for not working hard enough he would tie them up by their thumbs and whip the male slaves till they begged for mercy. He sure was a mean old man. I will never forget him as long as I live." Former slave Susan Dale Sanders, who grew up in Spencer County, remembered that some of the owners she knew "wo'ked the women and men both in the field and the children too," and when they "thought they was'n't do'n''nuf wo'k," they would take the men and "strip off their shirts, and lash them with cow-hid[e] whips until you could see the blood run down them poor niggers' backs." To suggest that slavery in Kentucky was less brutal than it was elsewhere in the Deep South, warns historian Lucas, only understates "the evil of both systems."[10]

The USCT Comes to the Bluegrass State

It comes as no surprise, therefore, that like the fugitives who found their way to Fortress Monroe in May 1861, slaves in Kentucky began to flee their owners as soon as Federal troops arrived on state soil that September. "The appearance of soldiers in 1861," writes historian Victor B. Howard, persuaded many of Kentucky's bondspeople that "the day of jubilee had arrived." For their part, slave owners around the state were irate about this development, especially in light of the state's official decision to remain in the Union. If the state remained loyal to the Union, should not their slaves remain loyal to them as well? Not all Union commanders welcomed the fugitives, either, despite their awareness that Confederate forces had also begun impressing Kentucky's male slaves for their labor. In mid-October 1861 General William T. Sherman, then in overall command of Union forces in Kentucky and stationed at Louisville, wrote to the 19th Illinois's Colonel John B. Turchin to convey rumors that "some negro slaves" had "taken refuge" in the 19th's Louisville camp. "The laws of the United States and of Kentucky," Sherman reminded Turchin sternly, "compel us to surrender a runaway negro on application of the negro's owner or agent. . . . My orders are that all negroes shall be delivered up." How Turchin responded to Sherman is unknown.[11]

Because slaves running to Union lines in loyal Kentucky strained the patience of Unionist slave owners, wrote General Alexander M. McCook to Sherman in early November, efforts to stem the tide were considered "of vital importance." The continued fidelity of Kentucky whites to the Union depended in large part on their faith that the federal government and the army would defend their right to own human property. "Ten [slaves] have come into my camp within as many hours," General McCook informed Sherman, and he expected "a general stampede" before long. McCook added that he had put the fugitives to work—"They will be handy," he remarked, "and generally useful"—but in the long run he was concerned that harboring fugitive slaves would prove counterproductive. "I would respectfully suggest," he wrote, "that if they be allowed to remain here our cause in Kentucky may be injured." Sherman agreed.[12]

Nevertheless, as 1861 gave way to 1862, fugitive slaves in Kentucky continued to seek protection from the Federals. Although government and army policy maintained that they must be returned to their owners, some officials were increasingly reluctant to comply. "I learn from Colonel [Nicholas] Perczel," General Ulysses S. Grant wrote in January 1862 to General Eleazer A. Paine at Fort Jefferson, in the southwestern corner of the state, "that there are many now in camp who have flocked there through fear. Some discretion will have to be used in forcing these people out of camp now that they are in." Still other commanders proudly announced their commitment to protecting the fugitives. "The charges against me of 'nigger-catching' and of returning slaves to their owners, or agents," declared General Quincy A. Gilmore to General Gordon Granger from near Lexington, "have not the slightest foundation." In fact, Gilmore added heatedly, "I have never, that I know of . . . hindered any slave of his liberty in any way, shape, or form."[13]

At the same time, pro-slavery Kentuckians continued to warn of the potentially dire consequences for white loyalty of Federal officers harboring the fugitives. "The conduct of a few of the officers of the Army in forcibly detaining the slaves of the Union Kentuckians," wrote one white Lexingtonian to President Lincoln, "may provoke a conflict between citizens and soldiers. To prevent such a catastrophe we desire you to say . . . that military force will not be permitted for the detention . . . of such property . . . especially in resistance and contempt of the legal process of a civil tribunal." In November 1862, Brigadier General Jeremiah T. Boyle, district commander for Kentucky, went so far as to threaten to expel permanently all fugitive slaves who were found within US army lines. Boyle's threat elicited a sharp response from Washington. In a letter to Secretary of War Stanton, recently appointed Judge Advocate General Joseph Holt himself highlighted the negative implications, questionable legality, and immorality of Boyle's proposal. Holt argued that while commanding generals might have the right to issue orders of this sort, they should only do so in cases where they were certain that "the presence of slaves within their camps" would prove "injurious or dangerous" to the white soldiers and the army's work. Should a commander issue an order such as the one Boyle proposed simply for the purpose of placing the fugitives back "within the reach of those claiming to be their owners," Holt added, the order would violate section 10, chapter 195 of the Second Confiscation Act of July 1862 by driving runaway slaves "from our military camps into the meshes of men who thrust them into prison as fugitives, with the intention of having them afterwards sold into servitude."[14]

Not infrequently, white civilians and local officials also actively interfered with the army's efforts to protect fugitive slaves and employ them to the Union's advantage. In the summer of 1862, two men escaped from their masters in eastern Tennessee and sought refuge with Major General James S. Negley's command. Negley decided to employ the fugitives as "servants" in various capacities, including tending to the animals that made up part of the command's wagon train. Subsequently, when the command was in Kentucky en route to Louisville, the two men were "seized as fugitive slaves by the civil authorities," thrown in jail, and quickly advertised to the public as slaves for sale. Once again, Judge Advocate General Holt responded, condemning the actions the local authorities had taken against the two fugitives. At the time they were captured, he wrote, the two black men were "virtually in the military service of the United States" and were also protected, at least in theory, by the fact that they had previously been "the property of a man known to be in open rebellion" against the federal government. "It is understood," Holt thundered, "that the disgraceful practice of kidnapping negroes declared to be 'captives of war and free' under the act of Congress, with a view to their sale into slavery under local laws, extensively prevails, and it should be repressed with a vigorous and decided hand. The supreme law, and the right it gives to the military custody and control of the victims of these shameless oppressions, should be enforced with the whole power of the government if necessary."[15]

Determined to continue holding Kentucky in the Union, President Lincoln was reluctant even to appear to be encouraging the state's slaves to run away: when he signed the Militia Act on July 17, 1862, initially authorizing the enlistment of blacks into the Union army as laborers, the president had exempted Kentucky from the law's authority. Lincoln was also well aware of the resolutions Kentucky's representatives had been introducing in Congress for months, which condemned the enlistment of black men in the army as "uncivilized, unchristian, and infamous, and an admission that the white men of the country were not equal to the task of subduing the rebellion." Deeply concerned lest Kentucky renege on its support for the Union, Lincoln moved cautiously.[16]

As it turns out, however, the exemption of Kentucky from the Militia Act meant only that the state's fugitive slaves found ways to join the army by crossing into neighboring free states where black enlistment was possible, such as Indiana and Union-occupied portions of Tennessee. "A Hopkinsville correspondent for the *Louisville Journal*," writes historian Victor Howard, "reported that hundreds of slaves were leaving Christian and Todd counties every night for Clarksville" in Tennessee, and "many blacks were sent back to recruit others." According to the Militia Act, black enlistees received $10 a month: $7 pay plus $3 for clothing, a total of $6 *less* per month than the $13 pay plus $3 for clothing that white enlisted men received. Their diminished military pay undoubtedly struck black soldiers from Kentucky, as elsewhere, as an insult. At the same time, the promise of freedom and the opportunity to fight for the permanent destruction of slavery offered considerable compensation.[17]

Progress toward the active enrollment of black soldiers in Kentucky accelerated in early 1863 after Lincoln issued the Emancipation Proclamation. Although the proclamation, like the 1862 Militia Act, technically did not apply to slaves in Kentucky, Lincoln allowed authorities to undertake a census of black males in the state who were between the ages of eighteen and forty-five. The census results indicated that over forty thousand black men were available to help fill Kentucky's quota of "volunteers." Still, as Marion Lucas notes, well into 1863, "Lincoln continued to promise Governor Thomas E. Bramlette . . . that no Commonwealth slaves would be recruited." Again, however, this did not stop black Kentuckians from joining the army. In February 1864 Adjutant General Lorenzo Thomas, on a tour of Missouri and Kentucky, informed Secretary of War Stanton from Louisville that Kentucky's slaves—especially from those counties like Breckinridge that bordered free or occupied territory—were now "constantly crossing the lines and quite a number of them enlisting," some enrolling in regiments based in states as far away as Massachusetts. For his part, Thomas recommended that in exchange for white Kentuckians' loyalty, the federal government allow this arrangement to persist, at least for the time being, rather than enlisting black Kentuckians directly.[18]

The situation, though, was untenable. As the war dragged into its fourth year, the relentless demand for able-bodied soldiers to put down the Confederate rebellion convinced Lincoln to order an "aggressive" recruitment program in Kentucky, including offering locally determined bounties as an incentive. On March 7, 1864, Provost Marshal General James B. Fry issued orders that called for enrolling free blacks and slaves across the state. Subsequently, General Orders No. 34 from the Headquarters of the District of Kentucky—dated April 18, just days after the appalling massacre of perhaps as many as two hundred black soldiers at Fort Pillow in neighboring Tennessee—gave the following instructions:

> The Assistant to the Provost Marshal General of the State, the Provost Marshals of Districts, and the Deputy Provost Marshals in each county are directed to receive and regularly enlist as soldiers in the service of the United States all able-bodied negro slaves and free colored persons of lawful age who may apply to them to be enlisted. . . . As soon as enlisted, the recruits will be at once forwarded to the Provost Marshal of the District for muster into the service of the United States; and as soon as mustered, and squads of such recruits are collected, they will be at once forwarded to the general rendezvous at Louisville, thence forwarded by the commandant . . . to the nearest rendezvous or camp of instruction . . . for the purpose of being equipped.[19]

Across the Bluegrass State, the presence of the army recruiters, who typically included representatives of the United States Colored Troops from regiments that had been created earlier, served as a powerful draw to local male slaves. "Nothing impressed fellow blacks," historian Joseph Glatthaar has written, "like the sight of handsomely uniformed and fully armed black soldiers." Male slaves flowed toward recruiting stations from across Kentucky, most of them "slip[p]ing quietly away from their cabins as opportunities arose." Marion Lucas describes one former slave who recalled as a child "being awakened late at night by his mother, who whispered for him to tell his uncles 'good-bye.' The startled child opened his eyes to see four of his uncles leaving to join the army, 'the light of adventure shining' on their faces."[20]

Conscious of the need to preserve Kentucky slaveholders' already shaky loyalty despite now directly enrolling their human property in the army, Federal agents initially strove to provide owners with certificates "guaranteeing compensation of up to three hundred dollars a recruit," along with other types of "assurances." President Lincoln hoped such safeguards would minimize the slaveholders' resistance to what many considered the federal government's unjustified impressment of their property. Instead, however, white slaveholders and nonslaveholders alike, including numerous pro-Confederate guerrillas who were active in the state, made the work of the recruiters as difficult and dangerous as possible. On March 14, 1864, Major W. H. Sidell wrote to Provost Marshal General Fry that some districts in Kentucky were so "overrun with guerrillas" who were determined to halt the recruiting effort that the work ahead seemed almost impossible. "All of the [local] provost marshals speak of the necessity for military force" to protect the recruiting stations, Sidell observed, and he noted that General Burbridge had "accordingly placed one company of mounted infantry at [the] headquarters of each." Three weeks later, Burbridge conceded that white Kentuckians' "deep-rooted prejudice against the abolition of slavery" made it essential "to deal with negro enlistments in this state with great caution."[21]

Some slave owners, especially those who foresaw the end of slavery as a consequence of the war, came to embrace the enlistment of Kentucky's blacks as a welcome opportunity to avoid military service themselves while minimizing the financial losses they would incur if their slaves ran off to enlist. They also welcomed the enlistees' bounty money when they could pocket it. "Applications have been made to me by the owners of slaves to enlist them into the military service of the US," wrote Captain and Provost Marshal John R. Grissom on March 16, 1864. "If I am authorized to enlist I think that quite a number of recruits can be obtained. What bounty or compensation would I be authorized to offer?" In July the federal government belatedly decided that slaves who enrolled in the USCT were entitled to keep whatever bounties they received. Predictably, this decision only exacerbated white Kentuckians' frustrations with the whole recruiting process and contributed to a surge in their resistance. One officer in a Kentucky cavalry unit (Union), Colonel Frank L. Wolford, expressed his anti-black recruitment sentiments so stridently that he was dishonorably discharged.[22]

Despite the threat of arrest, many individual slave owners and their allies stepped up their attempts to undermine the enlistment process, including through violent guerrilla activity. "Efforts have been made in several of my subdistricts," wrote one recruiter in the state's fourth congressional district in late May 1864, "to suppress enlistments by intimidating Negroes. In several counties colored men desiring to enlist have been severely handled. Two were lately caught in Marion County, and their left ears cut off." Some slaveholders traveled directly to recruiting offices and camps and tried to use force, persuasion, or blackmail to get their slaves back. Others, writes Lucas, "attempted to entice recruits into returning home by taking their wives or girl friends to Federal camps, alternately promising the enlistees a better life if they returned home or threatening retribution against loved ones if they refused." Recruiting officers diverged on how to respond. Those who were themselves ambivalent or unsure of the government's policies sometimes handed the fugitives over, but many courageously refused, at great peril to their own safety.[23]

Meanwhile, the federal government doubled down, "enrolling all available, able-bodied slaves, 'regardless of the wishes of their owners,'" which, "in theory, excluded only the severely infirm and the physically handicapped." Kentucky slaveholders were furious, but the slaves themselves continued to respond with enthusiasm. By enlisting in the army, Kentucky's slaves—like their counterparts across the South—expressed first and foremost their desire for freedom. They sought as well to declare their humanity and their manhood, and they hoped that military service would provide them with a sure pathway to citizenship. More practically, fugitive slaves who enlisted in the US army sought the wages associated with military service, which in June 1864 were raised for black soldiers to equal those of whites. In addition, black recruits hoped the enlistment bounties would increase their "potential for land ownership, independence, and a better life after the war," whether they returned to Kentucky or moved somewhere else. In the end, more than 56 percent of the black men in Kentucky who were eligible became USCT soldiers, serving in twenty-two different regiments: two of cavalry (the 5th and 6th US Colored Cavalry), three of artillery (the 8th, 12th, and 13th US Colored Heavy Artillery), and seventeen of infantry (the 72nd, 107th, 109th, and 114th through 125th US Colored Infantry). As Joseph Holt observed during his visit to the state in late July 1864, black recruitment in Kentucky was "a decided success" that was "full of encouragement for the future." Holt went on to express his respect and deep admiration for the black enrollees from his home state, observing, "When we consider the perils and menaces which these downtrodden men have to brave in making their way to the recruiting stations, we cannot but regard the example of their courage and loyalty and zeal as among the noblest and most cheering signs of the times."[24]

Sandy Holt

As USCT recruiting in Kentucky proceeded in the summer of 1864, agents set up a station in the town of Owensboro, located on the Ohio River in Daviess County, about forty-five miles west and slightly south of Joseph Holt's family homestead at Holt's Bottom in Breckinridge County. As the regiments became organized, Owensboro also served as a departure point for the troops to other locations. "A few nights since," the Owensboro *Monitor* reported in late June, "80 negroes enlisted at this place [and] were shipped by one of the steamers up the river" to Louisville for transfer to the front. Black soldiers' leave-taking from Owensboro was not always smooth or pleasant. "On Monday," the *Monitor* continued, "160 more departed on the 'Star Grey Eagle'—making 240 sent from this point. The captain of the Eagle received his ebony freight in a somewhat ungracious manner, swearing to the soldier who bore the order to convey to them that 'they should stand, lay, eat and sleep with a lot of mules on board.'"[25]

The area around Owensboro and extending east toward Holt's Bottom had suffered steadily from guerrilla violence since earlier in the war, and the turmoil only increased after the USCT began recruiting there. "On Tuesday about 4 o'clock in the afternoon," the Maysville, Kentucky, *Weekly Bulletin* reported in late June, "some 250 guerrillas" had "left Cloverport, where they had been committing their outrages" after an earlier visit to nearby Stephensport, where they "robbed the stores and citizens, and carried off a number of horses." Joseph Holt's family homestead lay directly on the path between these two towns, and members of his family—and their human property—experienced the mayhem. Indeed, as his summer 1863 arrest suggests, Holt's brother Thomas—whose son John was then stewing in a Federal prisoner of war camp—probably even contributed to it. The guerrillas, the *Weekly Bulletin* continued, "entered the town of Cloverport . . . broke open the stores and helped themselves to what they wanted, stole a number of horses . . . and then left for Hawesville, to which place a portion of the gang had previously been sent. The guerrillas had things all their own way in Hawesville, and robbed and rioted indiscriminately. . . . In the evening they left Hawesville, as they stated, and as is believed, for Owensboro, which town they declared they intended to attack and capture and burn." Any attempt to destroy Owensboro, or halt black recruitment there, would be a failure, the article cautioned, "as there is a sufficient Federal force stationed there for its defense." Even so, one can imagine the raw terror such guerrilla violence provoked among those who became its victims, not least the black men from the area who took huge risks just to join the Federal army. And yet the determined fugitives kept coming.[26]

Among those who came to Owensboro that summer was a former bondsman named Sandy, a native of Virginia's Culpeper County, where more than half the residents at the time he was born—in about 1824—were enslaved persons of African descent. The identities of Sandy's parents are unknown and precisely how long he remained in Virginia is uncertain. By the time Sandy was in his early twenties, however—he first appears by name in the historical record in 1846—he was living in Kentucky and had been sold at least twice. Five feet seven inches tall when he was full grown, with dark skin, black eyes, and black hair, as a youth Sandy must have shown great promise as a hearty laborer. His first sale resulted in removal from his Virginia home, probably as a very young child and perhaps immediately to Mississippi, where he could provide muscle for the new state's cotton boom. A subsequent purchase sometime between 1837 and 1840 brought the Virginia-born bondsman to the Holt family homestead in Holt's Bottom. It was none other than Joseph Holt, who spent several years living and working as a lawyer and Democratic Party activist in Mississippi, who acquired Sandy. At the time, neither he nor Sandy could have possibly imagined the distinct but intertwined roles they would eventually play in saving the Union and bringing about slavery's demise.[27]

When Joseph Holt purchased Sandy he purchased several other slaves as well, principally for the use of his brother Thomas and Thomas's wife

Rosina, who had gradually taken over the management of the family property and slaves in the face of Joseph and Thomas's father's increasing infirmity (John Washington Holt died in 1838). "I have determined to ask a favor of you," Thomas wrote to Joseph in July 1837. "It is that you purchase for me 2 Negro men or a man and Boy 15 or 16 years of age." Thomas found it "almost impossible," he wrote, to handle the farm labor with the slaves he already had, and he had heard that bondspeople were selling inexpensively in Mississippi. Instead of the two new slaves Thomas requested, however, Joseph—still decades away from rejecting the central "domestic institution" of the world where he grew up—bought thirteen. Sandy, then in his early to mid-teens, was probably meant to be the "Boy" Thomas had requested. According to Joseph and Thomas's brother Robert, who escorted Sandy and the other recently purchased slaves to Holt's Bottom, the new arrivals settled in quickly and seemed to be "contented and cheerful." Thomas, Robert informed Joseph, planned to find "profitable employment" for them "in the cultivation of Tobacco, cutting wood, &c."[28]

Young Sandy had been in bondage to white people his entire life when he arrived in Kentucky; surely he found few if any of the slave institution's broad local contours surprising. The types of labor that the Holts expected Sandy to perform in the decades before the war—the prime years of Sandy's life and strength—were familiar, whether he was working at the family homestead tending the crops (including tobacco, wheat, and oats) and the animals (especially pigs), or on the numerous occasions, beginning in 1842 or 1843, when he and other family slaves were sent to Louisville to perform domestic chores and look after the ample gardens and grounds surrounding the elegant residence Joseph Holt and his first wife, Mary, acquired there. New to Sandy when he arrived in Kentucky, of course, were the individuals who comprised the particular community of whites and blacks he joined: Breckinridge County had a total population of 8,979 in 1840, of whom 1,722, or about 16 percent, were slaves. The Holts and their closest kin, the Stephenses, were among the area's major slave owners.[29]

Probably the most important member of the local slave community Sandy joined in the years before the Civil War was Matilda, the cook of Joseph Holt's cousin, James G. Stephens and his wife, who lived only about a mile away from the Holt homestead. Over time, Sandy and Matilda grew very close, and in 1853 they "jumped the broom" at the Stephenses' home. Needless to say, Sandy and Matilda's marriage did not alter their legal status or their living arrangements. After their wedding they continued to live with their respective owners, and although they enjoyed regular opportunities to visit, there is no evidence in the historical record that they had any children.[30]

During his years at Holt's Bottom, Sandy worked with many other black men and women, some of whom came and went very quickly, like Betsey, who drowned—perhaps by her own design—in a well at Holt's Bottom soon after she and the others arrived from Mississippi. Others, like Sandy, remained in place for decades and became particularly close friends. This was true for Dick who, like Sandy, spent most of his time at Holt's Bottom but also sometimes provided labor at Joseph and Mary Holt's Louisville home. Indeed, Dick occasionally served as a courier between the two places, particularly when Joseph Holt, who all his life dearly loved flora of all sorts, sent carefully selected items from his own grounds or a nearby nursery back to the family homestead for the garden there. At some point Dick also married. The details of Dick's marriage are unclear, but we do know that when Holt and his second wife, Margaret, moved to Washington in 1857, one of the arrangements he made with his brother Thomas was to trade Dick for the unmarried Alfred (who later married Jane) so that Dick could remain at Holt's Bottom with his wife.[31]

Two other close friends in Sandy's slave community were Wesley, who belonged to Joseph Holt's "maiden" aunt Mary Ann Stephens, and Wesley's wife Joanna, who belonged to Thomas. Indeed, in summer 1848 when Wesley and Joanna jumped the broom at the Holt family homestead, Sandy was in attendance. Joanna went on to bear eight children, but only two survived to adulthood: a girl named Elizabeth, born in about 1857, and a boy, born in 1862, whom she and Wesley named after Sandy. Also among the extended Holt-Stephens family slaves whom Sandy got to know well in these years was John, born in the late 1830s, owned (like Sandy's wife Matilda) by James G. Stephens and married to Thomas and Rosina's slave Sarah. Years later Sarah recalled that for the first few years they were married, she and John—like Sandy and Matilda—continued to live with their respective owners, but that John "came on foot each Saturday night to stay with me until the following Monday morning." Sandy and Matilda sustained their relationship in a similar way.[32]

Somewhat ironically, almost a decade before the Civil War began and when he was still living in Louisville, Joseph Holt took out a rather unusual and expensive short-term slave insurance policy on Sandy. This is the only slave policy Holt is known to have ever purchased, and it was designed primarily to cover Sandy's fall 1853 trip by steamer to Louisville from Holt's

Bottom, where he had been laboring during the harvest. Thomas Holt had convinced his brother to buy the insurance, apparently concerned that the strong and valuable Sandy, by then in his late twenties, might try to escape or perhaps drown or be injured during the roughly ninety-mile journey on the Ohio River. On this occasion Sandy would be traveling alone, unsupervised by any white family member, though he would apparently be working as a "fireman and deck hand" on board under some white man's watchful eye. Still, "it is common now," Thomas wrote to Joseph, "to have Negroes insured when they run on a steamboat and I think it would be a very good plan with Sandy."[33]

The six-month policy Holt purchased in the fall of 1853 cost $29.75, roughly equivalent to $800 today. It guaranteed a substantial benefit of $700 (now almost $20,000), though the exemptions were so numerous as to make the expense seem hardly worthwhile. Moreover, as it turns out, the Holt brothers need not have worried about Sandy striking out for freedom at this time. To the contrary: Sandy, who had recently married Matilda, arrived safely in Louisville, and in the years ahead, in accordance with the brothers' apportionment of his labor, he went on to make the journey between Louisville and Holt's Bottom several more times without incident. Indeed, long after the war, whites in Breckinridge County who had known Sandy since his youth described him as thoroughly reliable, "honest," "industrious," and completely lacking in any "vicious habits," presumably including the tendency to run away.[34]

The 118th USCT Goes to War

In the summer of 1864, however, Sandy *did* run away, to Owensboro, to join the 118th United States Colored Infantry regiment. "All of us slaves were made to enlist under our owners' names," recalled Henry Barrett, who enlisted with Sandy in Company A, "they saying they could keep up with us much better that way." As required, therefore, Sandy enlisted as "Sandy Holt," identifying Thomas Holt of Stephensport (the closest "town" to Holt's Bottom) as his owner (it will be recalled that Joseph Holt gave or sold Sandy and all but one of his other slaves to Thomas in 1857 when he and Margaret moved to Washington). More than a dozen other slaves from the area around Holt's Bottom also enlisted with Sandy in Company A on August 10, 1864, including his friend John, whose enlistment papers erroneously identified him as "John Steves" instead of "John Stephens." Still more fugitives from the area followed in the days and weeks ahead. In the end, twenty-nine, or almost a third of Company A's enlistees, came from the part of Breckinridge County that surrounded Holt's Bottom, and others from the area enlisted in the regiment's Company H. All together these men represented approximately half of the male slaves living in and around Holt's Bottom who were between the ages of seventeen and forty-five in the summer of 1864 and therefore eligible for military service in the US army. In September, Sandy's close friend Wesley enlisted for three years in Company I of the 107th US Colored Infantry, enrolling as Wesley Stephens.[35]

In the enrollment papers he prepared for the overwhelmingly illiterate new recruits at Owensboro, the provost marshal and recruiting agent for Kentucky's second congressional district, Captain John R. Grissom, identified Sandy Holt and most of his comrades simply as "laborers." A former tailor, Grissom was intimately familiar with the institution of slavery: his father Alfred Grissom was a slave owner, although Captain Grissom himself owned none. Grissom also recorded each new recruit's approximate age. At forty, Sandy Holt was one of the oldest soldiers in Company A, but his age did not pose an obstacle to service. Notes historian Victor Howard, "The regulations governing the age and fitness of conscripts were applied very loosely. It was assumed that the young slaves did not know exactly how old they were, and it was generally suggested in Kentucky that no one be taken who looked younger than sixteen." At the same time, "If an older man seemed to be in good health, the upper age limit was not strictly observed." "I went in [to the army] on my birthday when I was 14 years old," recalled Company A's Owen G. K. Barrett, who came from Owensboro, "but of course I put up my age to get in." Besides Sandy, only five enlistees out of the hundred who eventually made up Company A were identified as forty or older. Service records indicate that most of the other enrollees were between seventeen and twenty-two.[36]

Indeed, even Sandy's commanding officers were younger than he: Company A's captain, John Lapham Bullis of Macedon, New York, who joined the regiment in Owensboro on August 18, was only twenty-three, and the 118th's lieutenant colonel at the time, John C. Moon of Wilmington, Ohio, was in his early thirties. Given his age and the generally diminished life spans for American slaves (life expectancy for male slaves was around thirty-six years in 1850), it is hardly surprising that Sandy was already a widower when he enlisted: Matilda had died the previous year. With Matilda gone and having no living children, Sandy did not have to worry—in the way that some of his comrades surely did—about his former owner punishing his immediate family members in response to his escape and enlistment. Indeed, it is likely that when the recruiters came to Owensboro, the middle-aged and recently widowed Sandy saw no reason *not* to risk his life for the Union, and especially for emancipation.[37]

As he filled out the recruits' enlistment papers, Captain Grissom recorded each man's height as well as the color of his hair, eyes, and complexion (for example, "black," like Sandy Holt, or "copper," like some of the fairer-skinned men). Each enlistee then signed his enrollment papers with an X: having been deprived of an education, Sandy and virtually all of his former slave comrades in Company A were unable to read or write. Once their enrollment papers were complete, Sandy and the others underwent physical examinations meant to identify recruits whose severely debilitated physical condition might bar them from service. "There were 5 or 6 [men] there when I was examined," recalled enlisted man Alexander Robinson many years later when he applied for a pension. "I don't know how many of them were doctors. We were stripped naked and taken into the room one at a time and they said they wished they had a Reg[imen]t as sound as I seemed to be." Robinson's description notwithstanding, the physical examinations were generally cursory and superficial. Still, they could be illuminating to the doctors who performed them, a number of whom, Joseph Glatthaar notes, reported experiencing considerable shock when they encountered abundant incontrovertible evidence of the physical abuse the men had routinely endured in slavery.[38]

Even when they identified recruits whose physical disabilities were likely to prevent them from serving effectively, examining doctors were often reluctant to reject the men outright. Isaac Bugg was mustered into Sandy Holt's company despite having an "unreducable" dislocation of the right shoulder, the muscles of his arm and shoulder never having developed properly after he was supposedly bucked off a horse as a child. Doctors may have allowed some men with relatively serious disabilities, like Bugg, to enlist as a way to fill the regiments. But they also knew that most fugitive slaves whom they turned down for Federal service would have no place to go but back to their masters, who were likely to punish them harshly for having absconded in the first place. Indeed, "in view of the cruelties practiced in the State of Kentucky by owners of slaves towards recruits rejected by recruiting officers for physical disability," in June 1864 Adjutant General Lorenzo Thomas recommended that recruiters proceed to enlist even those fugitives who seemed physically unqualified for anything more than the minimal exertions associated with duty in the quartermaster's or the commissary department.[39]

The physician whose name appears on Sandy Holt's enrollment documents and those of most of the other men who enlisted with him in Company A was Dr. John W. Compton of Owensboro. Like Captain Grissom, Dr. Compton does not seem to have owned any slaves himself, and he may well experienced some of the shock Glatthaar describes as he examined the fugitives who came before him that summer. Upon examining Sandy, however, Dr. Compton declared him "free from all bodily defects and mental infirmity" that might "disqualify him from performing the duties of a soldier." Sandy Holt and the others who were found fit for duty then took the oath to "bear true faith and allegiance to the United States of America," to "serve them honestly and faithfully against all their enemies or opposers whomsoever," and to "observe and obey the orders of the President of the United States and the orders of the officers appointed" to command them, "according to the Rules and Articles of War." One can only imagine what it must have felt like for a man like Sandy Holt, who had been in bondage to whites his entire life, to take this oath, with its explicit promise of impending danger and its implicit promise of freedom and citizenship should the Federals' cause prevail.[40]

Danger presented itself immediately to the men of the 118th USCT, beginning with the energetic efforts many of their owners undertook to recapture their valuable human property. Somewhat surprisingly, there is no extant evidence that Thomas Holt or anyone from the family came after Sandy; although he may well have been past the prime of his physical strength and health, he still represented a precious capital investment. Other slave owners, however, deployed professional slave catchers and even specially trained "negro dogs" to recapture the black laborers they had lost to the US army. Historian Victor Howard notes that on at least one occasion during the recruitment of Sandy Holt's regiment, Lieutenant Colonel Moon arrested three whites in Owensboro for disrupting the process, and then sent a group of soldiers into the surrounding countryside to arrest others who were harassing the enlistees.[41]

Angry resistance to the enrollment of black men as US soldiers persisted among whites living in the area surrounding Owensboro. It persisted, too, at the highest levels of the state government. "In common with the loyal masses of Kentucky," wrote Governor Bramlette to Abraham Lincoln in early September 1864, "my unionism is unconditional." But, the governor added pointedly, "we are for preserving the rights and liberties of our own race, and upholding the character and dignity of our position. We are not willing to sacrifice a single life or imperil the smallest right of free white men for the sake of the negro." Even as he launched his scorched-earth campaign through Georgia that fall, General Sherman, too, continued to express opposition, to no avail. "I know," wrote Adjutant General Thomas to Secretary of War Stanton, "that Genl. Sherman has been and is opposed to the organization of Colored troops, but he ought to bear in mind that they guard a long line of his communication, and that on the Mississippi they are greatly relied on, for holding the important points. Not a commander on the river but has to confess that they are perfectly reliable." In Kentucky, General Thomas added, "we are getting the very best class of men."[42]

Meanwhile, many white Federal enlisted men contributed to black soldiers' unease by openly expressing their disgust with having to serve together. Marion Lucas describes the experience of Kentucky's 5th and 6th US Colored Cavalry regiments in late September 1864 as they marched away from Camp Nelson, about eighty-five miles southeast of Louisville. "The insults, taunts, and ridicule from their fellow white soldiers began almost immediately. Along the march black soldiers quietly endured the humiliation of having their hats knocked off, their horses stolen, and verbal charges that they were cowards who would run away at the first sound of enemy fire." More than a hundred of these black cavalrymen died in the battle that followed at Saltville in southwestern Virginia, and the morning after the battle Confederate soldiers murdered dozens more who had been wounded.[43]

Black volunteers in Kentucky often experienced their first actual violence as soldiers from the white civilians who bitterly resented their efforts to serve the Union. Lucas describes a group of recruits from Boyle County who were "'pretty severely injured' by a mob of angry whites" on their way to the front; others who were waylaid in their progress toward the front long enough for local whites to subject each recruit to a hundred lashes; and eight other enlistees who were murdered. Sandy Holt and his Company A comrades personally experienced a gruesome example of guerrilla violence when, on October 5, 1864, Union forces discovered the lifeless body of eighteen-year-old Robert Eaves near the Henderson-area farm of a white man named John J. Towles. An investigation proved that Eaves, who had enlisted in the company about a week before Sandy, was the victim of a lynching: local pro-Confederate guerrillas had forcibly removed the young recruit from a private residence near where company soldiers had been engaged in some skirmishing in late September, and they hanged him.[44]

Two weeks before Eaves's murder, Lieutenant Colonel Moon had warned Acting Assistant Adjutant General E. B. Harlan that Owensboro had recently been "visited" by "a band of guerrillas, who murdered 3 U.S. soldiers after they had surrendered, and 1 citizen who had once been an officer in the Federal army." Moon was probably referring to the attack on the town by a guerrilla named Jack Bennett who, according to the Washington, DC, *Daily National Republican* had, "at the head of seventeen men, dashed into Owensboro" at the beginning of September and, "as they rode down the street, fired in a reckless manner at every person that exposed himself to view." The "scoundrels," the article continued, "exhibited a heartlessness and depravity of feeling worthy of devils and fiends," including killing a Captain Walters of the 3rd Kentucky Cavalry.[45]

By way of explanation, the newspaper pointed out that "for some time Owensboro was garrisoned by a battalion of negro troops," but "they were withdrawn from the post, ten being left to guard the wharf-boat against guerrilla attacks." Bennett then proceeded to attack the boat and demand the black soldiers' surrender. The soldiers were appropriately "frightened by the imposing front presented by the thieving band, and at once laid down their arms," at which point "an indiscriminate slaughter" began. Bennett and his men killed seven of the black men immediately; three others escaped into the boat's hold. "The boat was then plundered of light artilleries of value and set on fire, the dead bodies of the murdered negroes still stretched upon the blood-stained deck." To their credit, once the guerrillas had left town, local citizens put out the fire and rescued the three black men they found "crouched in the darkest corner" of the ship's hold, sending them "across the river to Indiana for safety." Robert Eaves's subsequent lynching demonstrated that the guerrillas' appetite had not been satisfied. Fear of suffering a similar violent fate even before he had the chance to reach the front may well have factored into enlistee David Heston's decision to desert within a week of his enrollment. He was the only member of the 118th's Company A to do so.[46]

In addition to the dangers posed by angry former owners and their guerrilla allies, Sandy Holt and his comrades confronted numerous biological threats in the form of the powerful, silent, and invisible pathogens their sudden gathering unleashed. As historian Jim Downs has written, "Union camps at first represented a safe haven" to fugitive slaves, but as they soon discovered, "life behind Union lines proved to be toxic." Among the most profoundly toxic pathogens the men encountered immediately was the smallpox virus, which had been spreading across the North American continent in epidemic proportions since the winter of 1862, in complete disregard for the sectional political divide. "Military authorities," Downs explains, "often responded to the outbreak of smallpox in their camps by placing afflicted soldiers in pest houses to isolate the virus, or by vaccinating and sometimes revaccinating vulnerable troops." However, Downs notes, "due to the unsanitary conditions of the camps and the constant movement of soldiers," the "military's efforts at preventing the virus from spreading often failed." Former slaves like Sandy Holt and his comrades who came from rural areas were particularly vulnerable and were "disproportionately infected."[47]

To compound the problem, vulnerable black soldiers faced considerable discrimination when it came to their access to medical care, and as a result, Glatthaar writes, "illness took a much heavier proportionate toll on the USCT than it did on white volunteer units." In the 5th US Colored Infantry Regiment, organized in the summer of 1863 primarily among free blacks from Ohio, even before a surgeon was assigned to the unit, fifteen of the new recruits died of a variety of illnesses including pneumonia and smallpox and thirty more fell gravely ill. The consequence of "such woeful and discriminatory medical care," Glatthaar observes, was that black soldiers died from disease at a rate more than twice as high as that of white soldiers; more than twenty-nine thousand of them—five thousand more than the total number of black soldiers who enlisted from Kentucky—succumbed during the war to illnesses like smallpox, pneumonia, dysentery, typhoid fever, and malaria.[48]

Sandy Holt's regiment was fortunate in having a surgeon in place even before most of the regiment's recruits had begun to arrive in Owensboro. Twenty-three-year-old Russell D. Adams of Onondaga, New York, a graduate of Long Island College of Medicine, was appointed surgeon for the 118th in late July, and two assistant surgeons came on board in October. For his part, Sandy Holt was fortunate to avoid a debilitating encounter with the smallpox virus. But a number of his comrades in Company A became seriously ill soon after they enlisted, either from smallpox or some other disease, their suffering made visible to us by medical records literate whites devised and included in the men's military service records. For the first three months of his military service, Ellis Ayer was hospitalized; he did not become available for active duty until November. Robert Dent suffered even longer, spending most of his first seven months in Company A in a pest house and becoming fit for duty only in the spring of 1865. John Christian developed a fever in early September that was followed soon after by a long period of alternating constipation and diarrhea.[49]

Indeed, some of Sandy's comrades who got sick right away never made it out of the hospital, including Dick Rapier, who died of smallpox just a month after he enlisted and before the 118th ever left Kentucky. Jack Younger died of chronic diarrhea in October after being transferred to the Corps d'Afrique General Hospital at New Albany, Indiana. Jefferson Gibson was sent to the aptly named General Eruptive Hospital in Louisville soon after he signed up, and in the weeks before he died his misery was profound: Gibson's graphic hospital record indicates that he was covered in pustules, delirious with fever, and had a "pneumonic" cough and great difficulty breathing. Finally, on October 30, he died of a combination of "variola"—smallpox—"and supervening pneumonic typhoides." Preceding Gibson to the grave was newly enlisted Henry Houston, who died on October 19 of "malignant variola" at the same Louisville hospital after receiving treatments of magnesia sulphurica, whiskey, beef tea, carbonate of ammonia, and "simple syrup."[50]

As Sandy Holt's former owner Joseph Holt and others in distant Washington enthusiastically endorsed black men's continued enlistment in the Union army, enraged former owners, slave catchers and "negro dogs," guerrillas, and disease threatened their ability to be successful. And these were by no means the only hazards Sandy Holt and his comrades encountered even before they made it to the battlefield. The service records reveal numerous examples of insufficient training by their white officers: Company A's James Bell bled to death less than two months into his enlistment after being accidentally shot through the knee by another inexperienced recruit, Jacob Grundy. Despite these and other dangers, however, through September and early October 1864 the recruiters continued to gather earnest enlistees into the 118th from within a roughly fifty-mile radius of Owensboro on the Kentucky side of the Ohio River. And although white opponents of black enlistment in Kentucky remained fierce, the behavior of the recruits gradually garnered some positive attention. On September 15 the Maysville, Kentucky, *Weekly Bulletin* observed that the men's "deportment at all places where they have been stationed, has been spoken of much to their credit as quiet and peaceful, showing a fine state of subordination and discipline." Of the enlisted men in one USCT regiment then stationed near Maysville, the *Weekly Bulletin* commented that they were "so perfectly quiet and well behaved" that "during their whole stay we never heard a single complaint against them. They were polite and respectful at all times to the citizens." "Negroes," the paper concluded, "have been accustomed all their lives to obedience, and hence they carry into the army their habits of subordination."[51]

As soon as Sandy Holt's 118th USCT reached "minimum organizational strength" in early October, its skeleton staff and the nearly nine hundred enlisted men who were not too sick to travel embarked on a journey of more than seven hundred miles from Owensboro to Baltimore, Maryland. According to historian Dudley Cornish, "Once a regiment was raised," the Bureau for Colored Troops "ordered it to report to the commanding general of the department to which it was assigned, and it then passed from bureau control to the direct control of the army in the field." On October 8, Adjutant General Lorenzo Thomas informed Secretary of War Stanton that he had "designated six Regiments"—totaling about five thousand soldiers—to proceed to City Point, Virginia, via Baltimore, including the 118th. "The movement," Thomas elaborated, "will commence the tenth instant, and five Regiments will start as fast as transportation can be provided." Thomas added that he planned to "send a staff officer with the first Regiment to see that the troops are properly supplied at Baltimore with what is necessary for the field."[52]

Nine days later, General Thomas wrote a similar letter from Baltimore to General Benjamin F. Butler, commanding the Army of the James at City Point. Thomas announced that he had begun dispatching the Kentucky USCT troops to Virginia. "One Regiment left here yesterday; two others are here, and will leave tomorrow. The fourth should be here tomorrow; the fifth the next day and the sixth maybe a week later. All will receive their additional equipments here." According to Thomas, the regiments from Kentucky represented, physically, "the best I have organized," though he regretted that they had "not had more time for drill." Still, he added, "I am satisfied they will do the work assigned them." In Baltimore the 118th left behind the remains of yet another Company A comrade who never made it to the battlefield: George Martin, who had died of dysentery on October 20. Then, en route to the "Monumental City" some of the men endured a vicious bout of the measles. Nevertheless, when they reached Baltimore they were mustered in to the United States army, receiving their uniforms, blankets, shoes and socks, haversacks, knapsacks, canteens, guns, and ammunition. Soon after, they traveled 170 miles south to City Point, about 100 miles from Sandy's birthplace in Culpeper County.[53]

In Virginia the regiment's lack of training and overall unpreparedness for combat became unmistakably clear, though the 118th was hardly unique on this score. On October 24 a noticeably unenthusiastic Colonel Arnold A. Rand of the 4th Massachusetts Cavalry offered his impressions to Assistant Adjutant General Captain Israel R. Sealy. "I have the honor to report the arrival at this post," wrote Rand, "of the One hundred and eighteenth Regiment U.S. Colored Infantry" with its 871 enlisted men, of whom now 76 were absent due to illness. Noted Rand, "The lieutenant-colonel"—Moon—"was left in Baltimore, it seems, and the major commanding is unable to give me any roster." What was clear was that in addition to being thoroughly "green," the regiment as a whole still lacked the requisite number of commissioned officers—typically about thirty-five—and Rand recommended that unless more could be appointed quickly, "competent non-commissioned officers or men be detailed from white regiments to instruct squads in the school of the soldier."[54]

Still, the day after Rand expressed his concerns about the regiment's condition, Sandy Holt and his comrades in the 118th were formally assigned to the 3rd Brigade of the XVIII Corps's 3rd Division. About a week later, the regiment was reassigned to the 1st Brigade, still in the XVIII Corps's 3rd Division, along with the 22nd, 36th, and 38th US Colored Infantry regiments, whose enlisted men came mainly from parts of Virginia and North Carolina. Despite their official status, however, until the Kentuckians could be "thoroughly drilled and disciplined" and fully prepared for active duty, the 118th was ordered to "retire from the line and encamp" along with the 117th USCT, an eastern Kentucky regiment that had been organized in July. Meanwhile, illness continued to stalk the soldiers: shortly after their arrival in Virginia, Company A's Henry Moorman died of measles at a pest house near Jones Landing, and around the same time, George Sawyer died of unknown causes at the XVIII Corps's general field hospital near Aikens Landing. Both men came from the area around Holt's Bottom and had almost certainly known Sandy before the war. So too had Henry Robinson, who contracted the measles during this period and possibly the mumps as well. Robinson recovered.[55]

Lieutenant Colonel Moon soon rejoined the regiment, and in the weeks ahead his dedication to preparing his men for active service elicited great appreciation from the regiment's other officers and, no doubt, from the men themselves. On November 3 fifteen of the regiment's white commissioned officers—including the commander of Sandy's company, Captain John L. Bullis—recommended Moon's promotion to the rank of colonel in recognition of the fact that "almost without assistance" he had not only "recruited in Owensboro, Ky, every man in the Regiment, under the most trying circumstances," but since then had also been "making the greatest exertions to fit it for the field." Moon's bravery, declared his subordinate officers, was beyond doubt. Moreover, "his character is exemplary, his fitness for the position is beyond question, he enjoys the full and entire confidence of every officer and every man in his command, [and] his military life also, which has been varied and extensive, is without reproach." The 118th's officers urged Moon's promotion as "a man most eminently fitted for, and well worthy [of] the position we ask for him." Later that month, General Butler appointed Moon the 118th's colonel.[56]

Their deployment to Virginia in October meant that, like so many other black regiments, Sandy Holt and his comrades in the 118th participated in General Grant's protracted Richmond-Petersburg campaign. Indeed, General Butler's Army of the James "contained the largest percentage" of USCT regiments "of any Civil War command," with black soldiers representing "as much as 40 percent of its maximum strength of 40,000 officers and men." The campaign to capture the Confederate capital followed a series of failed assaults on the lines protecting Petersburg and included the disastrous battle of the Crater on July 30, about two weeks before Sandy Holt enlisted. Several USCT regiments that had been active in the area during the late spring and summer departed at the end of 1864. Others, like the 118th, arrived in the late summer and fall after the Federal army had already settled in for the siege. In the end, almost three dozen USCT regiments, including eight that were organized in Kentucky, joined the prolonged effort to drive the Confederates out of Richmond. "Nearly one in every eight soldiers in the siege of Petersburg," writes Glatthaar, "was black."[57]

Initially, the 118th was stationed near Chaffin's Farm on the heights north of the James River. There, black and white Union troops together had recently fought a hard battle in which the armies on both sides had suffered significant casualties. At Chaffin's Farm, writes Glatthaar, "black units had to charge over difficult terrain against strong Confederate works. After working their way through a maze of felled trees, troops from the 4th and 6th U.S. Colored Infantry had to wade a swamp as they approached the Confederate fortifications. Officers had instructed troops to fix bayonets and not to fire, but as their advance slowed to a crawl in the swampy area and Confederates began to shoot down the attackers, the black troops could not resist firing back. When they stopped to reload, Confederates cut them down in huge numbers." By the end of the battle, black units had endured more than 40 percent of the Union army's casualties. Not surprisingly, it was at Chaffin's Farm that a Marylander—Sergeant Major Christian Fleetwood of the 4th USCT—earned black Civil War soldiers' first Congressional Medal of Honor.[58]

In contrast with the soldiers who fought at Chaffin's Farm, army returns indicate that Sandy Holt and the men of the 118th saw little action against General Robert E. Lee's forces during their early days on active duty. The regiment's inexperience combined with the Federals' turn toward trench warfare on the Richmond-Petersburg front meant that the men initially focused on training, preparation, and labor. The increasingly unfavorable weather also obstructed opportunities for the Federal forces as a whole to advance. As James M. McPherson has written, "The onset of Virginia's coldest winter of the war" soon necessarily "curtailed operations." "Cold November rains poured down on the Petersburg front," concurs A. Wilson Greene, "and the dirt roads upon which the armies depended turned to mud, the weakening November sun taking longer to dry them between storms."[59]

Consequently, Sandy and his comrades spent their early weeks in Virginia drilling in field maneuvers and the use of their weapons as well as performing essential if unglamorous guard and fatigue duty. The latter included arduous tasks like maintaining their camp's sanitary facilities, such as they were, chopping down trees and gathering wood for fires, and constructing roads and defensive works, especially trenches, which the soldiers then manned. Although some whites ungenerously expected the black Kentuckians to display "habits of indolence and carelessness" as a result of their previous lives in slavery, in fact, they displayed great diligence. "The new line of works . . . progressed rapidly during the week," wrote the acting chief engineer for the Department of Virginia and North Carolina, Lieutenant Peter S. Michie, at the end of October. "Abatis is being laid in front of the whole line as fast as it possibly can be done. . . . Woods . . . have been slashed for a distance of 250 yards from them and will be continued to beyond the rifle range." Writes A. Wilson Greene, "Both armies embraced the spade as warmly as the sword."[60]

In his history of the Ohio-based 5th USCT, which participated in the Richmond-Petersburg campaign from May 1864 through the battle of Chaffin's Farm, Versalle F. Washington emphasizes the grave hazards of fatigue duty. This sort of duty, Washington writes, "could be tedious, but it also could be deadly." In particular, the duty in the trenches on which the ultimate success of the campaign depended was brutal. Trenches were both disease-ridden and subject to relentless harassment by enemy fire, and service there could sharply increase a regiment's casualty rate. "The constant sniping from the Confederate lines wounded and killed soldiers," Washington explains, "but the natural conditions were the real killers. The trenches did not have overhead cover, so the soldiers were constantly exposed to the sun or to the rain." In a three-month period from May through July 1864, roughly 10 percent of the 5th USCT's soldiers were hospitalized with injuries, typhoid fever, or sunstroke as a result of their work in the trenches. The extreme cold of that Virginia winter contributed, too, to many soldiers falling ill. Indeed, Sandy Holt's dear friend from Holt's Bottom, Wesley Stephens of the 107th USCT, died of chronic diarrhea three months after his regiment's November arrival in the area. According to his own service record, Sandy himself was hospitalized twice while the 118th was in Virginia, first for four days in late November and early December 1864 for "parotitis," an inflammation of his salivary glands (probably mumps), and again several weeks later for diarrhea, for which he was prescribed quinine powder. Company A's Ambrose Cooper, too, battled mumps during the 118th's early weeks in Virginia, and although he was eventually able to return to active duty, the disease caused lasting damage to his testicles, rectum, and eyes.[61]

The enlisted men in Company A struggled to remain healthy under the harsh conditions in Virginia, and sometimes they failed. Among those who succumbed during this period was George Wilson, who died unexpectedly on October 31, apparently of heart disease. As was true of so many of his USCT comrades who died in the service, Wilson's personal effects were scant: he left behind only a few items of military gear including his knapsack and straps, two haversacks, and two canteens. Company A's John Peyton also died in Virginia, of liver disease. Thornton Stout died of chronic diarrhea and was buried at nearby Hampton, Virginia, where he had been serving on detached duty at Fortress Monroe. Sandy Moorman died of typhoid fever, as did Charley Turner. Joseph Roberts, Charles H. Tickenor, and George Steves died of pneumonia. These losses were followed by the death of Edward Boyd, who was later remembered by his company for his regular efforts to send a portion of his meager earnings home to his mother back in Kentucky. Roland Dent and Samuel Scott testified that Boyd had "perform[ed] faithful service in his company" right up until the time he contracted pneumonia, which was "induced by cold exposure and fatigue incidental to the duties of a soldier, and . . . not caused or aggravated by any personal habits."[62]

Company A's Sidney Smith also suffered from pneumonia while the regiment was stationed in Virginia, but he survived. Not so the initially "stout and vigorous" George Rowan, who died of heart disease and the effects of smallpox after spending several weeks at the General Eruptive Hospital in Louisville, where his comrades Jefferson Gibson and Henry Houston had died in October. At first George Rowan had seemed likely to recover. In the end, however, the treatments he received of "tonics, stimulants, & nourishment" as well as "quinine and milk punch," "egg nog," warm water sprayed into his ears, and a "warm embrocation [lotion] of olive oil and . . . camphor to the face" were insufficient to save him. Some of Company A's soldiers' long-standing physical ailments became exacerbated during this period, leading to discharge rather than death. This was true for Benjamin F. Baker, who was eventually released from the service on account of having been unfit for duty basically since his enlistment "because of want of physical development," which suggests that Baker had in fact never been a viable soldier. Around the same time Isaac Bugg, too, was discharged due to his irreducible shoulder dislocation. At the time of his release, Bugg was also suffering the effects of a protracted struggle with smallpox, for which he had been hospitalized in October and which produced pronounced long-term weakness and pain in his back.[63]

Company A's Richard Thompson was discharged in Virginia, too, after having proved, like Benjamin Baker, "unfit for duty" for an extended period. In Thompson's case the presenting problems included evidence of smallpox, pneumonia, and a "hard cough." Thompson's discharge papers also noted that he suffered from "scrofula" (tuberculosis), which had already been evident at the time he joined the regiment. For his part, Company A's Jacob Miles had in fact never even managed to join his regiment in Virginia, instead spending most of his time in the service in a military hospital in Indiana. Miles's discharge papers indicate that he was "incapable of performing the duties of a soldier because of Rheumatism and general debility," and that he had been "unsound upon enlistment." One recalls that recruiters of fugitive slaves in Kentucky were under instruction to enlist men even when their physical condition was marginal, simply to protect them from the wrath of their owners should they be rejected at the time of enlistment and returned.[64]

Given how many of Sandy Holt's Company A comrades fell gravely ill, died, or were discharged in the first few months of their military service, it is easy to forget that the "effectives"—among whom Sandy himself numbered most of the time—remained actively on duty, contributing their valuable strength to the Union effort through drilling, performing guard and fatigue duty, and sometimes undertaking special tasks or assignments in support of the company, the regiment, and the siege. Service records indicate that Elijah Bates and Caleb Nelson, for example, both spent time serving as company cooks, while Jack Griffith and Walter Whitinghill were assigned to oversee the company's rations. Jim Johnson and Sam Webb guarded the brigade commissary and subsequently Johnson was posted as an orderly to a white officer. Joshua Howard, Alfred Stiles, and Rolly Reed all served as company musicians, Robert White was Company A's designated bugler, and Lewis Beverly, Jerry Moorman, and—when he was not sick with pneumonia—Sidney Smith had assignments with the ambulance corps.[65]

In late 1864 and early 1865, as their health and strength permitted, Sandy Holt and many of his Company A comrades also performed hard and perilous physical labor in support of General Butler's Dutch Gap Canal project, which Butler hoped would provide Union gunboats with a shorter, safer passage up the James River toward Richmond. Back on August 9, just as the 118th was beginning to organize in Owensboro, Captain Melancton Smith had described the plan to Acting Rear-Admiral Samuel Phillips Lee. "General Butler," Smith wrote, "has decided to cut a canal across Dutch Gap," a 174-yard-long piece of land also known as "Farrar's Island," he explained, "created by a sharp bend in the River." Butler planned to break ground on August 10th—the very day that Sandy Holt and most of Company A enlisted—and to that end, Smith explained, "about 1,500 laborers were sent over . . . with a large picket force," numerous "implements for excavating," and a host of horses, carts, and wheelbarrows.[66]

"Simple in design," writes one historian, the Dutch Gap Canal plan was "brutal to execute." Butler had assured General Grant that only fifty-five thousand cubic yards of soil would need to be removed, which he estimated would take between ten days and three weeks using the labor of about a thousand men. As it turns out, however, "despite the aid of heavy equipment including a steam-powered dredge," the job required more than four months of steady hard digging and soil removal by thousands of overwhelmingly black soldiers, usually in detachments of between 100 and 150 at a time. They worked in shifts throughout the day and night in exposed conditions and under constant attack from enemy artillery. To protect themselves the soldiers frequently dug small "burrows" into the banks of the river and devised other sorts of bomb proofs into which they dove, if time permitted, when they heard enemy shells coming. According to Secretary of War Stanton's annual report for 1865, "There were thrown in the vicinity of the working parties" at Dutch Gap "over twenty thousand shells during the whole period of the work." And according to the *Army and Navy Journal,* as many as thirty-five men were injured or killed just on the day the digging began.[67]

"The canal was a horror," recalled one eyewitness in 1870, "the dread of all troops liable for detail." In his pension application decades after the war, Sandy Holt's Company A comrade Alexander Robinson described his own experience: "I was 17 years of age when I went into the army," Robinson recalled. "I was perfectly free from disease or injury of any kind when I enlisted." Sometime in November or December 1864, however, while engaged in dredging a portion of the canal, Robinson was hit in the leg by a shell fired by Confederates who were determined to obstruct the project. As Robinson remembered it, "I was standing on the bank" of the river when "a piece of the shell struck the beam of the dredge & the piece of shell glanced off of the beam which was covered with straps of iron, and struck me on the left leg some four or five inches above the ankle on the front or shin part." Robinson recalled being in so much pain from the shell's impact, which tore the skin and muscle from bone, that "it knocked me down." He received some initial treatment from the regimental surgeon later that day, and then spent about a month recuperating and doing light duty. Robinson's wound never healed properly, and it caused him considerable pain for the rest of his life. Many other USCT soldiers who worked at the Gap were even less fortunate.[68]

"The soil," noted Lieutenant Michie, "consists of a layer from twelve to sixteen feet thick in the average, of an indurated clay and sand, not easily moved by the pick, underneath which is a layer of heavy gravel and sand, the gravel the size of ordinary paving stones." In *A Regiment of Slaves,* Edward G. Longacre describes the contributions of Medal of Honor winner Christian Fleetwood's 4th USCT to the project. "In detachments working simultaneously from different points, the 4th dug at the hard earth with shovels and picks, and loaded the soil on horse-drawn wagons that carted it away. As the men worked, the greenish waters of the James were held in check by earthen bulkheads fifteen feet thick. The final job would be to remove those barriers with an explosive charge." Over time the work's difficulty increased, while the laborers grew even more susceptible to disease. "The sun shone fixedly, the yellow earth radiated the blaze of heat, and set free the malaria of newly turned earth and sedgy shores," recalled one eyewitness. "Fever and ague, and bilious fevers, attacked the working party; and these diseases were aggravated by the cellar-like holes in which the constant fire of the enemy forced the troops to live. The sick-list speedily enlarged, and the death-rate increased." Soldiers working the Gap also experienced constant shelling from Confederate mortars, at a rate, according to one source, of one every five minutes. "The artillery and picket firing in the region of the Dutch Gap Canal has been quite heavy for the last fortnight," announced the *Army and Navy Journal* on December 10, "the enemy having shelled the small squad of negroes there employed with great persistency." At one point, General Butler briefly assigned Confederate prisoners of war to work on the dig for punishment, after discovering that captured black soldiers had been put to labor on the Confederate fortifications around Richmond. Learning of Butler's action, and aware of the terrible conditions at the Gap, the Confederate leadership backed down.[69]

In recognition of the particular sacrifices they were making on behalf of the Union's war effort, the first men who pulled extra duty on the Dutch Gap project were entitled to extra pay: 8 cents additional per hour for a seven and a half hour day, plus a gill (about half a cup) of whiskey or its equivalent. By the time Sandy Holt and his Company A comrades were engaged there, however, the offer of extra duty pay seems to have been withdrawn. But the work continued. In addition to Sandy Holt and Alexander Robinson, the men from Company A who labored on the project included Frank Bell, David Howard, George Brashears, Walter Whitinghill, and Edward Boyd, who later died of pneumonia. George Brashears, too, fell ill as a result of his work at Dutch Gap and was treated at the hospital for constipation, pneumonia, rheumatism, and pleurisy. Walter Whitinghill, who developed hemorrhoids, later recalled that at the time he received orders to join the dig he was already "in a condition with the camp diarrhea [such] that the work was more than my physical condition could stand." Also engaged for a period of time at Dutch Gap was Lucius Bates, who suffered rheumatism and permanent injuries to his chest and back. As for Sandy, his assignment at the Gap involved throwing up breastworks to help protect the other laborers digging the canal from enemy attack, and in the course of these efforts he permanently injured his left wrist. As is true of so much of the piecemeal evidence that is available for studying these men's wartime experiences, a dominant theme of the service records is the relentless physical suffering they endured.[70]

On December 3, while the Dutch Gap project was still under way,

General Orders No. 297 reorganized along racial lines the two corps—the X and the XVIII—that had previously made up Benjamin Butler's Army of the James. Now the white regiments became the XXIV Corps and the black regiments, including the 118th, became the XXV Corps. Although General Godfrey Weitzel had previously opposed enlisting any blacks in the US army, he now energetically assumed command of the all-black corps, declaring the square the corps's official emblem "in view of the circumstances under which this Corps was raised and filled; the peculiar claims of its individual members upon the justice and fair dealing of the prejudiced; and the regularity of the conduct of the troops which *deserve* those *equal rights* that [they] have hitherto [been] denied." Weitzel urged the black men under his command to display uncompromising commitment to the Union cause. "Let History record," he proclaimed, "that on the banks of the James, thirty thousand freemen not only gained their own liberty, but shattered the prejudice of the world and gave to the land of their birth Peace, Union, and Glory." By now, of course, black men by the thousands had already been displaying—and sacrificing abundantly in connection with—their "uncompromising commitment," while banking on the promise that Union victory would lead to freedom.[71]

As 1864 gave way to 1865, preparation began for the removal of the bulkheads that had been holding back the James River since August while the soldier-laborers extended Butler's Dutch Gap Canal to impressive dimensions. By the end of 1864, reported the *Army and Navy Journal,* the canal was "522 feet long, about 120 feet wide at the top and 40 feet wide at the bottom, and about 70 feet deep." At least one of Sandy Holt's Company A comrades, William Williams, was among those who were "detailed to work the mine" that would presumably open the canal to traffic. Then, on January 1, 1865, Captain William A. Parker confirmed that "the ends of the canal at Dutch Gap were blown up with 12,000 pounds of gunpowder." Unfortunately, the results of the massive blast were less than satisfactory. "We heard no report of the explosion," Parker wrote, "and there was no perceptible commotion of the water at our anchorage. The earth was thrown up into the air about 40 or 50 feet and immediately after fell back into its original place." In sum, the blast was a failure and, for the time being, the canal remained closed. When it was finally opened in April, the war was almost over and the canal's utility was moot.[72]

Despite the project's failure, however, the grueling and courageous contributions of the USCT to the effort did not go unnoticed, and some black soldiers' participation drew particular attention. "The progress of the work has not been wholly unmarked by instances of rare bravery," noted the *New York Herald* on January 5, 1865. "In this respect it may be said that Sergeant William Robinson, of the Twenty-second United States Colored Troops, chief director of the carts and wagons, has constantly stood in the middle of the pit to place his vehicles in their proper positions. He has done his duty manfully." Added the *Herald,* "The same may be said of all the colored troops who, by reason of their color and the fact that their capacity for courage and endurance under a galling fire has been hitherto in a measure considered an experiment, are deserving of especial mention." Consumed with his own work in Washington on behalf of Union victory, black freedom, and justice and opportunity for the black soldiers, Judge Advocate General Joseph Holt could not have agreed more.[73]

As it turns out, however, the troubled Dutch Canal project further undermined President Lincoln's already tenuous faith in General Butler's abilities as a military leader, and on January 7, Lincoln replaced him with Major General E. O. C. Ord, bringing Butler's army career to an end. Soldiers in the USCT were deeply displeased by the news. "The colored portion" of the army, wrote one USCT sergeant to the black newspaper the *Christian Recorder* at the end of January, "lament his loss more than the losing of a right arm or even life itself." Butler, he wrote, was a "genuine friend of the colored people." In his farewell message on January 8, Butler displayed precisely the attitude this black sergeant valued so much, generously praising and giving credit to all the black soldiers under his command. "The best officers of the Union," he told the men of the XXV Corps bracingly, "seek to command you. Your bravery has won the admiration even of those who would be your masters. Your patriotism, fidelity, and courage have illustrated the best qualities of manhood. . . . You have unlocked the iron-barred gates of prejudice, opening new fields of freedom, liberty, and equality, of right to yourselves and your race forever." Butler's words were appreciative, encouraging, and optimistic. Sadly, they did not offer an accurate picture of what lay ahead in the black veterans' future.[74]

Last Days in Virginia

The Dutch Gap fiasco behind them, at the end of January 1865, Sandy Holt and the men of the 118th were involved peripherally in what came to be known as the battle of Fort Brady (or Trent's Reach), one of the last naval battles of the war, which Brevet Brigadier General and engineer Henry L. Abbot called "the most important event during the month on these lines." On January 23, a group of Confederate warships attempted to evade a series of obstructions on the James that were impeding rebel efforts to reach and attack the Federals' supply base at City Point. At about eight o'clock that evening, Captain Henry H. Pierce of the 1st Connecticut Artillery, commanding Fort Brady, informed Lieutenant C. A. Truesdell that a sentinel at the fort had observed the Confederate ships making their quiet approach. Pierce then ordered the soldiers defending the fort, including "colored supports," to fire at the enemy ships. The Confederates responded, inflicting damage of their own on the fort, the personnel assigned to garrison duty there, and the obstructions they had confronted before continuing down the river. Within two days, however, they were forced to return, and when they passed by for the second time on the 25th, the Union soldiers fired again. "Consider the rebel boats to have been much crippled in their passage down and up," wrote Pierce. "But three men—two engineers and one colored support—were killed inside the work." Some forty other soldiers were injured, though none seriously. In the weeks that followed, black soldiers assisted in the work of repairing the fort and strengthening the protective works surrounding it. In the end, the Confederate move against Fort Brady was unsuccessful.[75]

As winter gave way to spring, Sandy Holt and his Company A comrades continued performing an abundance of picket, guard, and fatigue duty, in the course of which a number of them earned promotions above the rank of private. Although virtually all of the commissioned officers in the USCT regiments were white, regiments also required a certain number of noncommissioned officers—typically five sergeants and eight corporals per company—to help maintain order, provide leadership, and assist with training and drill. Finding qualified men from among those who had entered the service directly out of slavery could be difficult, not because of their lack of innate ability but because most, like Sandy, had received no formal education, were illiterate, and had never been granted opportunities for leadership. "It is very seldom that negroes can be found in the southern states whose education is sufficient to fit them for positions on the non-commissioned staff of a regiment or for those of 1st sergeants of companies," wrote Inspector General R. B. Marcy to Adjutant General Lorenzo Thomas in November 1864.[76]

Still, some enlisted men in Company A proved themselves entirely competent. His service record indicates that middle-aged Sandy Holt remained a private throughout his time in the army, but others in his company achieved and even mustered out at noncommissioned officer rank, including Corporals Anderson Green, Samuel Scott, David Howard, Walter Whitinghill, and George McClarty, and Sergeants George Brashears, Owen Barrett, Jack Griffith, and Robert White. Men who reached noncommissioned officer status were returned to the ranks without hesitation, of course, if they proved unsuccessful in their new roles or committed any of a multitude of possible offenses or infractions. Company A's Alexander Ayer, John Smith, Henry McClarty, and Horace Morton all achieved the rank of corporal but could not sustain it: each was reduced to the ranks, sometimes quite quickly. Henry Barrett, Frank Bell, Sylvester Morton, Albert Delanor, and Silas Letcher made it all the way up to sergeant before being busted permanently back to private, Letcher for "incompetency," and the others for unknown reasons.[77]

Some enlisted men rose, fell, and rose again. Company A's James Atchison became a corporal in September 1864, was sent back to the ranks two months later, and was then promoted again to corporal and finally sergeant, the rank he held at the end of his service. John Craig eventually found his niche as a corporal. Promoted to sergeant shortly after his enlistment, Craig was reduced to corporal two months later, promoted again to sergeant in March 1865, and ultimately mustered out at the lower rank. Interestingly, of the eighteen men in Company A who at one time or another became noncommissioned officers, eleven (61 percent) were described in their enlistment papers as having "copper" or "mulatto" complexions. This is more than twice the proportion of men in the company as a whole whose papers identified them as having fairer skin. One has to wonder how much a "copper" complexion factored in to a former slave's likelihood for promotion, by his white superior officers, to a position of leadership and advanced skill. Having fairer skin, of course, may well have also played a role in the sorts of skills that individual slaves had been permitted to acquire while in bondage, skills that could in turn have privileged them in their regiments. Sandy Holt, it will be recalled, appears in his service record as "black."[78]

For their part, the 118th's white commissioned officer staff, led by the well-respected John C. Moon of Ohio, was of mixed quality and level of commitment to the black men under their command, over whose lives and service during the war they had significant influence. Far less impressive than Moon was Albert Royall, a native of Poland who became lieutenant colonel in early December 1864. Royall did not last long with the 118th: on March 24, 1865, Royall tendered his resignation, claiming that he was "not able to provide for my family," having not received any pay since the previous June. Even more significant, perhaps, was Royall's assertion that he had "never been able to please my superior officers, and the treatment that I have to undergo is of such nature, that I feel myself not able to perform the duties as faithfully as I wish." In accepting his resignation, General Weitzel noted that Royall, "through his ignorance of our language alone, is incompetent for his position." Eventually Isaac D. Davis of Elkton, Maryland, replaced Royall as the 118th's lieutenant colonel.[79]

Also among the 118th's commissioned officers was Major Edmund DeBuck, a Philadelphia merchant, and Lieutenant Martin V. B. Wagoner of Albany, New York, the regiment's adjutant and a former brick maker. Like Royall, but unsuccessfully, Wagoner attempted to resign from the post, claiming that he was "the only support of an aged, invalid mother in addition to my wife and two small children," and that "the pay I receive from the Government as a compensation for my services is entirely inadequate to meet contingencies." Moon rejected his resignation. The 118th's regimental quartermasters were Willard M. Farr of Ohio and George H. Willis of Massachusetts, and its physicians were surgeon Russell D. Adams of New York, assistant surgeon Joel T. Tevis of Indiana, who had a serious drinking problem that ultimately led to his dismissal, and assistant surgeon Alexander M. Winn of Maine. And then there was Asa E. Everest of New York, appointed chaplain of the regiment in March 1865. Forty-four years old and a graduate of Middlebury College (class of 1847) and Union Theological Seminary (class of 1850), Everest failed to establish a positive relationship with the regiment's leadership and, one suspects, with the men as well. Letters in Everest's service record from Colonel Moon and others depict the chaplain as "unworthy the position he holds" and "a useless encumbrance to this regiment." Everest was discharged five months after mustering in.[80]

At the company level, Sandy Holt and his comrades were fortunate to enjoy the steady leadership of John Lapham Bullis, who came to the 118th after two years' service in Company H of the 126th New York, which was engaged at Harpers Ferry in September 1862 and at the battle of Gettysburg, where Bullis was wounded and captured in July 1863. Bullis spent about three months in Richmond's Libby Prison before being exchanged, after which he returned to the 126th before mustering out in order to accept the appointment as captain of the 118th's Company A. Bullis served out the war with Company A, and although, sadly, there are no written records that directly present the enlisted men's views, an undated testimonial from one of his superior officers describes Bullis as "a most diligent and attentive officer, a strict disciplinarian, and a man of the best moral character I ever saw in the Army." In contrast, Bullis's first lieutenant, Robert Newlin Verplanck of New York, a graduate of Harvard College, hated his post, once telling Colonel Moon "that he did not like to remain in a Colored regiment as he did not like to associate with all the officers who received appointments in the Colored regiments." By June 1865, Verplanck was clamoring for a discharge, and soon his request was approved. Joseph A. Robinson, a native of Pennsylvania, served as Company A's second lieutenant and at least one of his superior officers considered Robinson at best a mediocre leader: "This officer has acted up to the requirements . . . as far as he is capable of doing," the man wrote. "He is by no means a competent officer but has tried to the best of his ability to perform his duties," but his "services can very well be spared." Ten months into his assignment with the 118th, Robinson, too, was released from duty.[81]

The commissioned officers of the 118th were thus of mixed quality, but the black soldiers' labor on behalf of the Union cause—fortifying rifle pits, bomb proofs, and other defensive works, digging and draining trenches, constructing corduroy roads, building the Dutch Gap Canal—was unremitting, wearying, and debilitating. Through it all, even as Joseph Holt and other prominent and powerful white allies in Washington as well as white regiments across the theater of war pressed forward toward the same goals, Sandy Holt and his comrades in the 118th joined all USCT soldiers in clinging to the promise of future freedom. In March 1865 the US Congress bolstered black soldiers' optimism about the future by passing legislation to ensure that should the Union cause prevail, not just the soldiers but also their wives and children would be forever free. "This act of justice to the soldiers," advised General John M. Palmer, who took command of the Union's forces in Kentucky on March 12, 1865, "claims from them renewed efforts, by courage, fortitude, and discipline, to win a good name, to be shared by a free wife and free children." The claims were not made in vain.[82]

Part Three

War's End and Returning to Kentucky

Part One presented the richly documented story of the white, educated Kentucky Unionist Joseph Holt's transformation from slaveholder to dedicated advocate of black Americans' freedom and rights, beginning in his youth and accelerating significantly as the nation descended into civil war. Firmly made, this commitment was one Joseph Holt's position as Abraham Lincoln's judge advocate general both required and strengthened. Using different types of sources and the methods of collective biography, Part Two pieced together the much more fragmented historical record of the education-deprived slave Sandy Holt's journey out of bondage and into Federal army service. Once counted as Joseph Holt's human "property"—and an eminently reliable, docile representative of the "peculiar institution's" benefits for privileged white Southerners *and* for slaves themselves—Sandy Holt at middle age absconded and became a fugitive. Soon after, along with dozens of other black men from the area surrounding the Holt family's Breckinridge County homestead, he became a soldier in the United States Colored Troops. In that capacity, like his highly advantaged white former owner now stationed in the War Department in Washington, DC, Sandy Holt flung himself wholeheartedly into the work of achieving the Union's wartime goals on the battlefield. Both men fought for the defeat of the Confederate rebellion, the nation's survival, and black freedom. Both strove and sacrificed toward these ends in the distinctive ways that were available to them in light of their disparate social positions. Part Three continues their stories through and beyond Reconstruction, weaving those stories together with the larger tale of the Kentucky and Breckinridge County communities they left behind and to which both men, eventually, returned, communities that were themselves transformed appreciably by the war.

War's Aftermath in Kentucky

In March 1864, a free black man and waiter from Philadelphia named Henry Hoyle enlisted as a private in Company F of the 43rd USCT. Initially assigned to guard the Army of the Potomac's supply trains during General Grant's Overland campaign that spring and summer, the 43rd then moved to the Petersburg front, was engaged at the battle of the Crater, and for the next eight months participated, like Sandy Holt's 118th USCT, in the Richmond-Petersburg siege. After Richmond fell in early April 1865, the 43rd joined the pursuit of Robert E. Lee and his collapsing Army of Northern Virginia to Appomattox Court House, where Hoyle and his comrades were present for the surrender. Subsequently, the 43rd spent several weeks at Petersburg and City Point before heading to Texas. From there in the fall of 1865, Hoyle wrote a letter to the editor of the *Christian Recorder*, a black newspaper published in Philadelphia. "Thank God!" he wrote, as if emancipation and Union victory had liberated free blacks like him, too. "We are now free! No more will the torturing whip be inflicted on gray-headed fathers and mothers. No more will families be torn asunder and sold as cattle. Those dark days are past, and bright laurels attend us. May God grant us a safe return and bring us up out of Texas, for we have great trials and tribulations to go through. May we soon return to our quiet homes, and enjoy the sweet comforts of life. God has brought us safely through the hottest of the raging battle." Alas, for USCT veterans like Sandy Holt who would return to Kentucky in the months ahead, Hoyle's optimism was premature.[1]

In the spring of 1865, Kentucky was in turmoil. Beginning in March, the commander of US forces in the state, General John Palmer of Illinois, struggled to enforce the implications of impending Union victory there in the face of widespread resentment among Kentucky's whites about emancipation and the January 1865 passage of the Thirteenth Amendment, which they refused to ratify. Kentucky at the end of the Civil War, writes historian Anne E. Marshall, was "a place where slavery was neither dead nor alive," and for a long time to come, black Kentuckians "found themselves in a unique and bewildering situation with respect to their status." The end of the war did not come easily or quickly to the state or its residents, black or white, who navigated as best they could the rocky terrain of reunion and emancipation in their families and communities.[2]

Despite the fact that Georgia's December 6, 1865, ratification secured the Thirteenth Amendment's authority regardless of local preferences, black Kentuckians received much "contradictory advice" from a range of sources about their current status—slave or free?—and about the best and safest path forward from bondage to whatever lay ahead. Federal officials proclaimed that Kentucky's former slaves were now free, while many erstwhile slaveholders sought to hold them in bondage as long as possible and otherwise hinder their progress toward freedom. "After the war had closed," recalled Will Oats, a freedman from Wayne County who was about ten years old in 1865, his family members were "all very happy" until they found themselves "wondering what they were going to do without a home, work, or money." Lacking obvious, unequivocally superior (and safer) options, many freedpeople continued to live with and work for their former owners, sometimes for life. Wes Woods, a freedman from Garrard County, remembered, "We were glad when the news came that we were free, but none of us left" the master's farm "for a long time." Ann Gudgel of Anderson County told an interviewer many years later, "We went on and libbed with Master Ball till us chilluns was bout growed up." "I remember the slaves on my grandfather's farm," recalled Ruby Garten, a white Kentuckian from Union County. "After they were freed they asked him to keep them because they didn't want to leave. He told them they could stay." According to Mary Wooldridge of Washington County, "Wen my Missis . . . told us we was free I was as happy as a skinned frog but you seed I didn't have any sense."[3]

Many emancipated black Kentuckians stayed put, but others responded to the overall state of confusion and the ambiguity in their status by packing up their few belongings and leaving Kentucky altogether, overwhelmingly heading north. Indeed, just a month after Appomattox, General Palmer issued an order permitting Louisville's blacks "the right to move freely within the Commonwealth" and, if they preferred, to cross the Ohio River to states where their freedom was not in question. Two months later Palmer extended these rights to all black Kentuckians, and by November 1865 more than ten thousand of them had taken Palmer at his word, initiating a decades long "trend of out-migration" from the state. By 1900, blacks represented only 13.3 percent of Kentucky's overall population versus the 20.4 percent they had constituted in 1860.[4]

Complicating the postwar situation in Kentucky was the question of the Freedmen's Bureau's jurisdiction over matters pertaining to the state and especially its black population. Predictably, the same spirit that caused them to reject the Thirteenth Amendment drove many white Kentuckians, including former Unionists, to resist the establishment of a branch of the bureau there. Like President Andrew Johnson, they considered the bureau's involvement in Kentucky affairs yet another effort on the part of the federal government to exert control over the state despite its official wartime loyalty. Nevertheless, in June 1865, Freedmen's Bureau Commissioner Oliver Otis Howard ordered Major General Clinton B. Fisk, then the bureau's assistant commissioner for Tennessee, to "begin extending his influence, if not authority" to Kentucky. Howard's reasoning centered on white Kentuckians' clearly demonstrated opposition to emancipation.[5]

During its short life, the Freedmen's Bureau's primary mission was to assist the former slaves in making the transition to freedom and economic self-sufficiency, not least by ensuring that labor contracts between landowners and the former slaves were fair. On June 24, 1865, General Fisk issued a circular informing his subordinates that Kentucky's freed slaves must not be compelled to work for any particular employer (or at all) unless they were paid, and that their wages must be "based on supply and demand rather than a fixed rate." Bureau agents were charged with investigating and prosecuting any violations of these regulations by either employers or employees. In addition, as if this job was not big enough, Freedmen's Bureau agents in Kentucky and across the South also "issued rations and clothing, operated hospitals and refugee camps . . . assisted benevolent societies in the establishment of schools, helped freed[people] in legalizing marriages entered into during slavery, and provided transportation to [those] who were attempting to reunite with their family or relocate to other parts of the country." To the Freedman's Bureau fell the responsibility, too, of assisting black veterans and their heirs and dependents in collecting any outstanding pay or bounty money associated with their military service. The bureau operated in Kentucky until the spring of 1872, although its functions were greatly diminished everywhere beginning in August 1870, and its funding and enforcement mechanisms were never sufficient for the massive work it was assigned to perform.[6]

Long after the shooting war ended, white Kentuckians displayed fierce and persistent resistance to emancipation, the introduction of the Freedmen's Bureau, and other manifestations of federal intrusion into state affairs. On September 30, 1865, the *Army and Navy Journal* reported an angry claim by the *Louisville Union Press* that the federal government was "interfering with the slave laws of Kentucky." For its part, the *Journal* opined that postwar Kentucky was proving even more recalcitrant and determined to return to the antebellum status quo than South Carolina. A week later the paper reported in greater detail on the conflict between the federal government and Kentucky's pro-slavery forces, which included the governor, still Thomas E. Bramlette. According to the *Journal,* Governor Bramlette continued to insist that Kentucky's decision not to secede in 1861 meant that slavery remained legal in the state in 1865; that General Palmer was treating the state's blacks far too leniently; and that black Kentuckians were becoming an increasingly heavy "burden on white people." General Palmer countered that "slavery is dead in Kentucky as elsewhere"; that white "malcontents" were "absurdly devoted to a defunct institution"; and that his governing practices and his efforts to protect the freedpeople were entirely appropriate as well as lawful.[7]

A month later the town of Lexington, where a young Joseph Holt had once studied law, seemed on the verge of a crisis. Precipitating the trouble was Mayor Joseph Wingate's declaration that "the congregation of colored persons in this city, claimed to be slaves by the neighboring farmers and others, has become an evil of such magnitude as to require correction." Wingate further announced that those to whom the blacks "belonged" must come and fetch them by November 25 or be prepared to face legal sanctions. General Palmer angrily characterized the mayor's threat as clear evidence "of the existence of a purpose on the part of many persons to avail themselves of the earliest opportunity of disregarding the rights of those inhabitants of the state who were once slaves, and again reducing them to the condition from which they have just escaped." Whites, in short, were simply refusing to accept the consequences of Union victory. Palmer ordered General James Brisbin, headquartered in Lexington, to inform the mayor that the federal government intended to use whatever tools necessary to safeguard the town's (and the state's) blacks from violence. He further ordered that those claiming to be the freedpeople's owners be prohibited from taking them anywhere involuntarily. "All the people of the State," Palmer reiterated—black *and* white—were now "presumed to be free." On this occasion Palmer noted that he considered any discharged men of Kentucky's USCT regiments and their families particularly vulnerable and therefore under the military's "special protection." At the same time, he reassured black Kentuckians generally that the state was still subject to martial law.[8]

Shortly after the Thirteenth Amendment went into effect in December 1865 and about six weeks before Sandy Holt and his comrades in the 118th began their journey home, General Palmer issued a formal proclamation declaring slavery in Kentucky dead, and the Freedmen's Bureau's General Fisk announced that henceforth the bureau would not just "influence" but would in fact "exercise supervision over Kentucky's former slaves."

The following month black Kentuckians met in Louisville, Frankfort, and Lexington to celebrate the third anniversary of the Emancipation Proclamation, and in March blacks met again in Lexington for a statewide convention to discuss the future. Participants at both gatherings adopted resolutions demanding black equality, which they presented to the state legislature for consideration. Their efforts faced strong headwinds: for some time to come local whites' lingering fury over emancipation—and the service of black Kentuckians in the USCT—only intensified. In his postwar report on the history and operations of the Owensboro recruiting office, where Sandy Holt and his comrades had enlisted, John R. Grissom wrote that many of Kentucky's former slaveholders who had once made "loud professions of loyalty and Unionism" had demonstrated clearly that they "could not stand the test when they were personally affected by the loss of Negroes," especially their slaves' "loss" to the Federal army. Former slave owners whose sentiments had favored the Confederacy from the beginning were even more bitter. As Kentucky's provost marshal General W. H. Sidell himself noted, the enrollment of local blacks in the US army had so enraged the state's slave owners that they had actively welcomed the "bands of armed partisans and guerrillas" who crisscrossed Kentucky "acting in the interests of the enemy." War's end brought no end to the violence.[9]

To the contrary, white Kentuckians across the state who had opposed both emancipation and black enlistment and who now opposed postwar federal intervention in Kentucky's affairs, with its implications for radical social transformation, seethed for years after Appomattox. In fact, they did more than just seethe. As Anne Marshall has written, for about two decades following the end of the Civil War, Kentucky represented "one of the most lawless states in America," the violence growing more fervent with the return of tens of thousands of local whites who, like Joseph Holt's nephew John R. Holt, had left the state to serve in the Confederate army. In this context, writes Marion Lucas, black soldiers and their families "were particular objects of hatred and suffered horribly." As General Palmer observed in early 1866, whereas veterans of the Confederate forces were typically "welcomed back to their former homes, in many cases by communities that regard them as patriots and heroes," Unionists and Union army veterans—especially if they were black—commonly found themselves to be "objects of prejudice, dislike," and "persecution." Moreover, because state and local courts did not allow blacks to testify against whites until 1872, and did not allow them to sit on juries for another decade, whites expected the courts to serve as "instruments of vengeance" under their exclusive control. Indeed, the federal government's supporters and its military representatives, black and white, feared quite appropriately for the security of their lives, property, "and all their dearest interests." In February 1866, General Palmer observed that despite the many "outrages" that the more than two hundred thousand former slaves who remained within the state's borders had endured in the months since Appomattox, not once had the civil authorities brought the (white) perpetrators to justice. Since locals seemed unwilling to do it, he concluded, the federal government must fulfill its solemn responsibility to protect all Kentuckians, *especially* those who had fought to defend it.[10]

According to Victor Howard, the gravest problem for Kentucky in terms of its transition out of slavery was "the existence of bands of white men, often disguised, who preyed upon the blacks in the rural areas"—places like Holt's Bottom and the surrounding region—"and drove them from their agrarian pursuits." For years these bands, some associated with the Ku Klux Klan, used violence and intimidation to achieve their goals, "persuading" white landowners not to extend fair labor practices to the freedpeople, especially USCT veterans, or even hire them at all, and pressuring lawmakers to reject attempts to enhance blacks' civil and political rights through the law. Looking back from the vantage point of old age, Mary Wright of Hopkinsville recalled, "De Klu Klux uster stick de niggers head on er stake . . . en dar de buzzards would eat them till nuthin' was left but de bones. Dar war a sign on dis stake dat said 'Look out Nigger You are next.'" A group of blacks in Frankfort eventually forwarded a document to Congress in which they described the horrors the KKK and other white supremacist organizations had been perpetrating in Kentucky since war's end. "We would respectfully state," they wrote, "that life, liberty, and property are unprotected among the colored race of this State. Organized bands of desperate and lawless men, mainly composed of soldiers of the late rebel armies, armed, disciplined, and disguised, and bound by oath and secret obligations, have, by force, terror, and violence, subverted all civil society among colored people; thus utterly rendering insecure the safety of persons and property, over-throwing all those rights which are the primary basis and objects of the Government, which are expressly guaranteed to us by the Constitution of the United States as amended." The signers of this memorial described instances of "the Ku-Klux Klans riding nightly over the country . . . spreading terror wherever they go by robbing, whipping, ravishing, and killing our people without provocation." They noted the Kentucky legislature's repeated refusal to pass any laws to confront the violence, which left the terrorists to assume that they were "licensed to continue their dark and bloody deeds under cover of the dark night." They appealed to Congress to assert federal power for their own and their families' protection, in order to enable them to properly "exercise the rights of citizens."[11]

General Palmer, General Fisk, and the Freedmen's Bureau agents who served in Kentucky fought an uphill battle to improve the lot of the state's emancipated blacks, including Kentucky's USCT veterans after they returned home. In early 1866 General Palmer optimistically proclaimed to several thousand blacks in Louisville that "hereafter, before the law, there shall be no other difference between the colored race and others than that of color," though he confessed his belief that "in the nature of things, for years to come, the colored people of this country must be laborers." Still, Palmer hoped that before long, in Kentucky and across the nation, "the question to be asked would be, not 'who is the whitest,' but 'who is the most honest, intelligent, and industrious.'" Soon after Palmer gave this speech, Kentucky's legislature declared the Civil War over and Palmer stepped down. Subsequently, although the state legislature that winter enshrined the legality of slave marriages if the marriages were "solemnized" by a "proper" authority, and "legitimized" the children those marriages had produced, lawmakers also signaled their intention to keep Kentucky blacks utterly subordinate to whites by leaving most of the rest of the old state slave code untouched. For good measure, the legislature also adopted a series of resolutions "requesting the removal of the [Federal] troops from the state, condemning the Freedmen's Bureau, requesting restoration of the writ of habeas corpus, and yet again rejecting" the Thirteenth Amendment in principle. Had they met a couple of months later, Kentucky's legislature surely would have joined Andrew Johnson in denouncing the federal Civil Rights Act of 1866, which Congress passed on April 9 over the president's veto.[12]

In the two months between the terrible race riots in Memphis in May 1866 and in New Orleans that July, the Freedmen's Bureau began full operations in Kentucky with Brevet Brigadier General John Ely, stationed in Louisville, serving as chief superintendent. Bureau agents strove vigorously and at great personal peril to combat white Kentuckians' rage toward the newly emancipated blacks. Notably, writes Marshall, "Bureau agents in Kentucky, unlike in other southern and border states, were not under the protection of Federal troops or a sympathetic state government": as a state that had not left the Union, Kentucky was technically not subject to postwar military occupation. This significantly added to the hazards the agents faced and led many other organizations that were dedicated to helping the freed slaves to stay away. Nevertheless, over the period of time it operated in Kentucky, the bureau rightly claimed some important achievements, not least in terms of the number of schools for black children it helped to found. "Kentucky," writes Victor Howard, "like all other Southern states, moved slowly to take responsibility for Negro education, and the Freedmen's Bureau acted to fill the vacuum." By March 1867, Kentucky was home to more than 50 Freedmen's Bureau schools, which collectively enrolled over three thousand students. Eighteen months later there were 135 schools, educating more than six thousand students. "The response of the colored children in the matter of education," reported one bureau agent in fall 1866, "is almost fabulous and gratifying to me." "The great interest the colored people of Kentucky take in the establishment of common schools," wrote another the following spring, "and the energy displayed not only by their youth, but also by them of middle ages, for acquiring the rudiments of knowledge is giving practical evidence" of the freedpeople's desire to be "*responsible free* citizens of the great and powerful United States."[13]

Predictably, most white Kentuckians maintained that "the educated freedman would be worthless as a laborer," and many continued to do whatever they could to thwart blacks' educational and other progress. As Howard observes, "Mass education implied a revolutionary transformation of blacks' traditional role" by preparing them "to function as enlightened citizens," and as a result, black schoolhouses became frequent targets of white violence. "I have the honor to enclose the written statement of Edmund Claybrook, a colored school teacher," wrote an agent stationed at Henderson, about sixty miles directly west of Holt's Bottom, two years after the bureau began its work in Kentucky. Claybrook reported that the Freedmen's Bureau's Henderson school had recently been burned to the ground; the agent was sure the KKK was responsible and he promised to "try and arrest the parties" involved. Around this same time, another Freedmen's Bureau school was burned down not too far from Holt's Bottom. Despite these grim developments, however, the Henderson agent reassured his correspondent that on the whole, "the schools are in a flourishing condition, and never at any time since the Bureau was established has there been so deep an interest by the freedmen in education." "Schools," he wrote optimistically, "are springing up as if by magic; and we think that if ample protection is afforded them they will soon be able to manage themselves."[14]

The 118th USCT in Texas

On April 2, 1865, the Confederate leadership evacuated Richmond and the final phase of the shooting war began. For Sandy Holt and the surviving members of the 118th USCT's Company A, however, almost a year would pass before their military service ended and they returned to face the turmoil of Reconstruction-era Kentucky described above. Plenty of arduous work remained to bring the war to a close and secure the Union victory upon which the future of black freedom, citizenship, and rights fundamentally depended. For starters, in the immediate wake of Richmond's fall, the 118th joined other USCT regiments as some of the first Federals to enter and occupy the devastated city, a stunning—if temporary—demonstration and experience of the "bottom rail on top." Indeed, it is difficult to imagine the pride and satisfaction that must have filled the hearts of these slaves-turned-soldiers when President Lincoln himself arrived on April 4 to tour the vanquished Confederate capital. Following Lincoln's visit, Sandy Holt and his comrades remained in Richmond until a few days after General Grant chased General Lee to Appomattox, "performing in and around the city the usual guard duties" and trying to maintain order. Subsequently, they received orders to travel with the rest of the XXV Corps's 1st Division to guard the railroad lines about three miles from Petersburg.[15]

It was there they mourned President Lincoln's April 14 assassination, and when Assistant Adjutant General T. S. Bowers requested that General Weitzel select "one of the best regiments of colored troops you have" to represent the USCT at Lincoln's funeral in the capital, the men from Kentucky surely would have liked to be chosen. Bowers stipulated, however, that the regiment must be one "that has seen service," meaning significant battlefield fighting, and like many other USCT regiments stationed in Virginia at the end of the war, the men of the 118th had more commonly poured out their energy and blood in other kinds of labor for the Union than combat. Consequently, the honor of marching in the funeral procession went to the 22nd USCT, a predominantly free black regiment from New Jersey whose soldiers had been involved in the late-September 1864 struggle for Chaffin's Farm. Meanwhile, the 118th remained on guard duty in and around the Petersburg area, where Company A lost yet another soldier, Jerry Moorman, who succumbed to an accidental shooting.[16]

Because their enlistments had begun later, USCT regiments were not demobilized as quickly as white volunteer regiments once the shooting war was over. Instead, beginning in late May, the 118th joined the bulk of the all-black XXV Corps as it began the long and complicated process of transferring by sea to Texas, "probably the worst location for occupation service," writes Glatthaar. "The Texas Expedition," which combined occupation duty with the US government's response to the ongoing French invasion of Mexico, "seems to have got off without any public excitement," reported the *Army and Navy Journal* on June 10. "It has been fitting out for the past fortnight, in Hampton Roads, and at Fortress Monroe and City Point. . . . The sailing orders prescribe a general rendezvous in Mobile Bay, where the steamers will be coaled and cleaned for the voyage further South." The paper predicted that good weather would "soon carry the whole fleet to its destination," adding that the men of the XXV Corps—including Sandy Holt's 118th—were "in good spirits and condition." Six days after this optimistic report, service records nevertheless indicate that Sandy's Company A comrade Jacob Green died of pneumonia while onboard the US steamer *Empire City*.[17]

A total of about thirty-two thousand men from the XXV Corps spent almost three weeks in spring 1865 traveling from City Point, Virginia, to Texas. "We are preparing to move and will probably soon be on the salt water southward bound," Company A's Captain John Bullis wrote home. On May 25, "the corps embarked in ocean transports" just "as rapidly as transports could be furnished," and five days later the men of the 118th were on their way. The transports carried the soldiers, officers, equipment, and supplies over two thousand miles down the Atlantic coast, around the state of Florida, and through the Gulf of Mexico, stopping for recoaling and resupply in Mobile Bay. Their destination was Brazos Santiago and the area surrounding it on the southern tip of the Lone Star State where the Rio Grande River flows into the Gulf of Mexico.[18]

At least some of the men in the XXV Corps found the prospect of duty in Texas unsavory. On June 17 the *Army and Navy Journal* reported that a group of black cavalry troopers anticipating deployment to Texas had mutinied in advance of their departure from Virginia, "owing, doubtless," the *Journal* hypothesized, "to the association in their minds of Texas with slavery." Union victory and the ratification of the Thirteenth Amendment ensured the ultimate death of the slave institution even in remote Texas, of course, but the black troopers may well have been concerned about how long and how vigorously local resistance to emancipation would endure in a frontier state so far removed from the nation's capital. Most likely the mutineers' calculations were influenced, too, by the threats posed by the various diseases and other unhealthful conditions to which they expected to be exposed, perhaps even en route. On July 8, the *Army and Navy Journal* cheerfully reported that the troops who had already made the journey "did not suffer much from the effects of the long voyage" to Texas, "and there were but few deaths from ship fever." According to historian Joseph Glatthaar, however, the soldiers of the XXV Corps "suffered so badly from fever, poor sanitation, and spoiled or insufficient food" on their way to Texas "that men in one regiment . . . died at a rate of twelve per day." The regiment to which Glatthaar referred was the 115th US Colored Infantry, a Kentucky-based regiment like the 118th, whose men also suffered. It has already been noted that Company A's Jacob Green died of pneumonia on the trip to Texas. In mid-June, shortly after the transports began landing at Brazos Santiago, Sandy Holt's comrade Edmund Reese died of the same disease.[19]

"Great trouble was experienced in the landing of the troops," wrote General Philip H. Sheridan in his official report of the operations in Texas, for which he served as commanding officer. According to Sheridan, this trouble resulted from a combination of "bad harbors," "the great draft of the vessels employed as transports," and "the absence of suitable lighters"—flat-bottomed barges used for transporting men and supplies in shallow waters—"to convey the troops across the bars." Moreover, Sheridan noted, at Brazos Santiago "the wharf had been destroyed" and a new one had to be built before the men could disembark. When they did, their first impressions of their new location were overwhelmingly negative. One black soldier described Brazos Santiago itself as "extremely hot . . . barren and desolated," with "scarcely a tree or shrub of any kind visible to the eye, nor even a blade of grass." The *Army and Navy Journal* called Brazos Santiago "a wild, inhospitable island . . . guiltless of spring or shade-trees." Compounding their discomfort and what must have seemed to most like isolation from all things familiar was the soldiers' discovery that "no one had made any preparations for them." Instead, both officers and men were compelled to set up their own tents in the blistering heat, bearing "the scorching summer sun as best they could" while also dealing with a severe shortage of fresh water.[20]

Sandy Holt and his comrades in the 118th did not remain long in Brazos Santiago. Soon they headed to Brownsville, about thirty miles west, directly across the border from Matamoros, Mexico, and home to several thousand freshly paroled Confederates and about half as many white Federal occupation troops awaiting the XXV Corps's arrival. The march there was grueling and slow and the men enjoyed little help from Mother Nature: as it often did in the spring, the Rio Grande had recently overflowed its banks and on at least one day the soldiers marched ten miles through mud and water that reached the tops of their trousers. "All of us had to wade the bayous," recalled Company A's Sergeant Owen Barrett. Finally, on June 30 they made it to the town's outskirts, an uninviting spot "infested" with "tarantulas, rattlesnakes, and mosquitoes."[21]

In the days ahead, those not completely debilitated by the long, unhealthy trip from Virginia or the exhausting march from Brazos Santiago focused on setting up camp and engaging in steady drill practice. The 118th's larger purpose in the region was to help establish a strong federal presence to counter any attempts by former Confederates or Mexican imperialist supporters of the French puppet emperor Maximilian to assert themselves militarily against the Mexican republican (or Liberal) government of Benito Juárez, the United States, or both. As General Sheridan wrote in his memoirs, it was General Grant's conviction "that the French invasion of Mexico was linked with the rebellion" from the start, and the XXV Corps was deployed to Texas to squelch any trouble. As commander of all US forces west of the Mississippi and south of the Arkansas River since May 17, Sheridan had orders calling on him to "concentrate at available points in the State an army strong enough to move against the [French] invaders of Mexico" and their former Confederate allies "if occasion demanded."[22]

The potentially profound international dimensions of the 118th's latest army duty was something Sandy Holt and his comrades in Company A could not possibly have anticipated when they first became fugitives from slavery a year earlier; their owners, too, would have scoffed at the idea. According to General Sheridan, however, in the summer of 1865, "the appearance of our troops and the knowledge that friends were on the border went like electricity to the homes and hearts of the Mexican people," which in turn must have bolstered the pride of the men in Federal uniform whom the law had so recently deemed chattel. At the same time, in practical terms it is unclear how much the anti-imperialists really could have depended on these US forces for support during their first few weeks in Texas, when hunger and disease severely undermined their effectiveness. As General Sheridan recalled, "The difficulties of [the] entrance at the mouth of the Rio Grande made [the] line of supply very dangerous and precarious," and at times ships bearing desperately needed food and other essentials simply "could not cross the bar at the mouth of the river for nine or ten days" at a stretch. Accordingly, Sheridan ordered the construction of a railroad line from Brazos Santiago to Brownsville. Until the railroad was completed, however, food remained scarce and many soldiers had to make do with half rations. "I am hungry enough to eat almost any thing," wrote one soldier in the 41st USCT, a Pennsylvania-based regiment that was stationed about sixty miles further inland than the 118th.[23]

Lacking fruits and vegetables that were rich in vitamin C, many of the men in the XXV Corps suffered terribly from scurvy, which some had first contracted weeks or even months earlier. "Within one week of their arrival at Brazos Santiago," writes Glatthaar, "the situation was critical. A post hospital with beds for only eighty had five hundred patients, and these were the worst cases." That summer the army's medical inspector in Texas calculated that "60 percent of the Twenty-fifth Army Corps had scurvy," and some men's gums became so swollen that "they completely hid patients' molars, bicuspids, and canine teeth." Thankfully, after several weeks fresh vegetables and fruits finally began to arrive in large quantities, sharply diminishing the number of men who were ill. In the interim, however, several men in Sandy Holt's Company A were hospitalized for the disease, including John D. Murray, who initially showed symptoms on the trip from Virginia to Texas. Once the regiment began its march to Brownsville, Murray became completely incapacitated and had to be returned to Brazos Santiago, where he was hospitalized for two months. Other Company A victims were Henry Barrett, who lost several of his teeth and also developed a "blistering rash," and Silas Letcher, who spent two months in the hospital at Brownsville being treated for scurvy as well as rheumatism.[24]

Other men in the company wrestled with other ailments. For his part, Sandy Holt suffered from a gastrointestinal condition that began on the march to Brownsville, persisted for many months to come, and was eventually diagnosed as dysentery. Although the disease did not kill Sandy, in August it killed Henry Robinson. Indeed, relatively speaking Sandy Holt got off easy. From late June on his comrade John Christian was hospitalized repeatedly for fever, pneumonia, and gonorrhea as well as scurvy and dysentery, and Company A's Alexander Robinson spent most of his time in Texas hospitalized at Brownsville because the leg wound he had received at Dutch Gap became infected, acted up during the arduous march from Brazos Santiago, and eventually "got so bad" that "it gathered, broke, and discharged matter." As he later recalled, "I was not able to do anything much for three years after that." Even the 118th's commander, Colonel Moon, struggled with his health. Soon after wading through the Rio Grande's overflowing waters up to his waist, Moon began to suffer from a "malarial fever," and in August he was finally granted a leave of absence. The colonel resumed command of the regiment in December but he never completely recovered from the illness he contracted in Texas.[25]

Clearly many of the soldiers in the 118th spent large chunks of their time in Texas sick, some of them utterly debilitated. Those who were able to work, however, kept busy, chopping wood for fuel, completing a variety of infrastructure projects, and performing guard duty at various locations. The *Army and Navy Journal* reported in late July that groups of black soldiers had been sent to garrison different points along the Rio Grande to maintain peace and "check the depredations of guerrillas." Men from Company A guarded the post hospital in Brownsville, the headquarters of General Frederick Steele, commander of all US forces stationed along the Rio Grande, and the headquarters of the 1st Division's 1st and 2nd Brigades. Others were detached to work in the quartermaster's department in nearby Clarksville or performed other special duties, sometimes even when they were sick. Despite suffering from scurvy, "bone fever," and piles, for example, Sam Webb worked as a mounted orderly, as did William Williams.[26]

A visit from General Sheridan in late June 1865 surely buoyed the spirits of the hardworking, physically depleted soldiers. On June 20, reported the *Army and Navy Journal,* Sheridan left his headquarters in New Orleans on a "tour of several weeks" through "Galveston, Brazos Santiago, Brownsville, and other points of importance." Sheridan himself recalled that his goal was not so much to cheer the men under his command as "to impress the [Mexican] Imperialists, as much as possible," that the Federals were prepared, if necessary, to commence "hostilities." Indeed, pugnacious Sheridan worried that Secretary of State William H. Seward's diplomatic maneuvers might diminish the potential benefits of the army's threatening presence in the region. Perhaps for this reason, while he was in Brownsville Sheridan decided to flex some military muscle internationally by "demand[ing] the return of certain munitions of war that had been turned over by ex-Confederates to the Imperial General," Tomás Mejía, who was in command at Matamoros. "These demands," Sheridan insisted proudly, "backed up as they were" on the other side of the river by the presence of a large proportion of the XXV Corps, including the 118th, "created much agitation and demoralization among the Imperial troops." On July 10 six pieces of heavy artillery that former Confederates had allegedly sold to the Imperial forces for $17,000 were returned to Brownsville and "parked on the parade-ground near the site of Fort Brown" on the south side of town.[27]

Thanks to a combination of diplomatic efforts and the presence of the

XXV Corps soldiers nearby, the *Army and Navy Journal* was able to report by the end of August 1865 that "the military excitement once stirred up at the Southwest" was ebbing. In a letter to his family Company A's Captain Bullis insisted, not entirely convincingly, that he and the soldiers of the 118th were largely idle and content, "lazily doing nothing." In mid-September the *Army and Navy Journal* similarly commented that along the Rio Grande, "all goes merry as a marriage bell." Still, the paper warned that while the men of the XXV Corps might be happy at the moment to "hob-nob" peacefully with the people they had gone to Texas to monitor and restrain, they would be "none the slower to open fire" and "charge with the bayonet" should conditions change.[28]

Certainly that remained true for Sheridan, who much preferred a vigorous display of armed support for Mexico's republican government to sitting quietly by awaiting the outcome of Seward's diplomatic efforts. "It required the patience of Job," Sheridan later wrote, "to abide the slow and poky methods of our State Department, and, in truth, it was often very difficult to restrain officers and men from crossing the Rio Grande with hostile purpose." For the time being, however, the *Army and Navy Journal* reported, "All is quiet on the Rio Grande." In mid-October the paper also observed that the number of cases of scurvy among the US soldiers in Texas was declining.[29]

Around this time, Sandy Holt and his comrades participated in a review of the XXV Corps's 1st Division by General Frederick Steele. According to the *Army and Navy Journal,* "The division was formed on the prairie, which, cleared of its chaparral, made a good piece of ground for the occasion. In one line of three brigades the body was drawn up, and it looked efficient and steady. . . . There [were] about 3,300 on the ground. . . . The line broke into columns and marched past. As each company went by one could see that the men were clean enough, and that the guides were intelligent." Not long after this review, General Grant ordered several of the USCT regiments in Texas to muster out, beginning with those based in northern states. Grant's decision to release these regiments first reflected his concern about the hostility black soldiers from the South and border states, so many of them former slaves, were bound to face from angry former Confederates once—indeed, *if*—they returned to their antebellum homes.[30]

A reorganization of the XXV Corps in Texas followed, and the 118th USCT now joined the 38th and 46th regiments in the 1st Division's 2nd Brigade. "The corps will now be about 10,000 strong," the *Army and Navy Journal* reported in late October, "of whom two-thirds are fit for duty."

Cooler weather brought further improvement in the men's health, though "great complaints" were still being heard regarding the quality of their rations. Fortunately, the soldiers had still not been required to engage in combat, despite a violent confrontation between the Mexican Liberal and Imperialist forces at Matamoros in late October. "Our neighbors on the opposite shore have lately passed through an ordeal of fire and smoke," Captain Bullis wrote home. Over the next several weeks, even as the conflict on the other side of the border continued, several more black regiments mustered out, now including ones from Southern states. On December 23 the *Army and Navy Journal* reported that twenty more USCT regiments were going home and that the XXV Corps was being consolidated into a single division. "The general health of the troops is good."[31]

As 1865 gave way to 1866, just two cavalry and thirteen infantry regiments of the USCT remained on duty in Texas, including the 118th, for which one more dramatic adventure lay in store before Sandy Holt and his comrades could put their Civil War military service behind them. As it turns out, this adventure cast the 118th's final days under a mysterious cloud. In early January unsubstantiated stories began circulating in the press that an unknown number of soldiers from the regiment had raided, occupied, and plundered the tiny town of Bagdad, Mexico, risking full-scale war with the US's southern neighbor and France. Over the next few weeks the event and the 118th's involvement drew a good deal of attention on both sides of the US-Mexican border.[32]

The basic, blurry outlines of the story are these: in the middle of the night of January 5, 1866, several dozen and perhaps as many as two hundred armed Americans crossed the Rio Grande into Bagdad, for reasons that are not clear. They may have been soldiers or filibusters or a mix of the two. At least one newspaper later reported that the invaders were filibusters who were *also* soldiers, specifically soldiers of the 118th, led by their own lieutenant colonel, Isaac Davis. According to this account, having entered the town, the soldiers captured a Mexican Imperialist garrison and then proceeded "to plunder the place and kill people," creating a "scene" of "indescribable" brutality and chaos. The following day, January 6, another large group of armed men appeared in Bagdad from the US side of the river, some possibly aiming to join in the melee created by the first wave of invaders, others to suppress it. Confusion reigned for several days, in the course of which President Johnson, on January 9, officially disbanded the XXV Corps. Finally, order was restored, the invaders retreated, and war was averted. As Captain Bullis's biographer later commented, "This particular violation of Mexican territory," although troubling to say the least, "happened to cause no international repercussion."[33]

Because the names of the individual soldiers who participated in the so-called Capture of Bagdad never came to light, it is impossible to know if Sandy Holt was among them, though he must have been aware of the events in question. He must also have been aware of the efforts that had been under way since late December to recruit black soldiers like himself and his comrades for some sort of "expedition" into Mexico. "A recruiting office has been opened on the main street," the *Philadelphia Evening Telegraph* had reported from Brownsville on December 23, and it was "doing a lively business" among the soldiers, many of whom were understandably attracted by the high wages being offered by the organizer of the efforts, a former lieutenant colonel of the 1st Tennessee Heavy Artillery, Robert Clay Crawford. Crawford promised anyone who joined the expedition a reward equal to four times what they earned for a month in the Federal service, and he pledged immediate discharge from their US army regiments to those who signed on. "I do not know what authority Colonel Reed," a mysterious figure whose name was associated in some papers with actually leading the expedition, "has for all this," the *Philadelphia Evening Telegraph* correspondent admitted, "but I do know that he has not as yet been interfered with by the authorities here," so "he must have something," or someone, besides Crawford, "to back him up."[34]

The exact relationship between Crawford's recruiting campaign among the remaining USCT soldiers in Brownsville and the Capture of Bagdad remains murky, though the two were unquestionably intertwined. On January 26, the *Washington Evening Star* reported that when Crawford was later captured by US forces in New Orleans and imprisoned on General Sheridan's orders, "many souvenirs of the Bagdad affair" had been "found among his papers." For its part, on January 27 the *Army and Navy Journal* warned against believing *any* of the news that came out of Mexico, most of which, the paper insisted, "seems to have been 'canned for transportation,' and usually, also, arrives badly mined from the voyage." That same issue, which also announced that the 118th would soon be mustering out, speculated on what might have provoked USCT soldiers to get involved in the Bagdad affair to begin with, if indeed they had, given that neither patriotism nor high republican ideals nor a desire for glory nor affection for the Mexican people—whom the paper termed "greasers"—could possibly explain such behavior. The only explanation, the paper concluded, was that the men had grabbed at an opportunity to make some real money, an incentive the paper piously characterized as "worthy of only the gravest censure." A simple glance at the array of injustices these men had endured all of their lives, many of which persisted during their USCT service, exposes the paternalism of such assertions. Moreover, it is easy to believe that an opportunity for both excitement and financial reward would have had considerable appeal to former slaves like Sandy Holt and his comrades as the war and their military service wound down and their futures remained so unclear.[35]

Anticipated and Unanticipated Costs of War

Meanwhile, back in Washington, DC, as the war came to an end and federal occupation and Reconstruction began, the persistence, patience, unflinching courage, and undeniable accomplishments of the USCT only strengthened Judge Advocate General Joseph Holt's dedication to the goals of emancipation and the advancement of black Americans' civil, human, and political rights generally. In December 1864, along with countless others across the North, Holt had been thrilled to learn of the thousands of USCT soldiers who contributed to the collapse of John Bell Hood's army at the battle of Nashville. In January 1865, he had applauded Congress's passage of the Thirteenth Amendment to the US Constitution, which Lincoln then signed and sent out to the states for ratification. On March 3 he welcomed Congress's establishment of the Freedmen's Bureau which, like his own Bureau of Military Justice, fell under the authority of the War Department. The department's main headquarters were located in the Winder Building on 17th Street, not far from the White House, and Judge Advocate General Holt and Freedman's Bureau Commissioner Oliver Otis Howard almost certainly had regular personal contact there. In the months and years ahead, Holt did what he could to support Howard's work with his own.

On April 8, 1865, less than a week after Richmond fell and Sandy Holt and the 118th USCT joined other black soldiers in leading the Union forces into the devastated city, Holt traveled from Washington to South Carolina on the steamer *Arago* with members of the press and a number of other military and civilian dignitaries to participate in the festivities surrounding the restoration of the US flag to its rightful position flying over Fort Sumter. On that occasion, the traveling party included Supreme Court Justice Noah Haynes Swayne, Senator Henry Wilson of Massachusetts, the Reverend Henry Ward Beecher, the great British abolitionist George Thompson—whom Holt had heard speak in Washington earlier in the war—and General Robert Anderson, the hero of Fort Sumter and, like Holt, a Kentuckian. En route to Charleston, Joseph Holt and the others visited Hilton Head, where they observed a colony of approximately three thousand freedpeople at the heart of what came to be known as the "Port Royal experiment." Abandoned by their owners early in the war, these former slaves had defied gloomy predictions that they would sink into indolence in the absence of the overseer's lash. Instead, with US army assistance they had planted crops and established a working town, Mitchelville, complete with "a church, schoolhouse, and other such accessories." "Nothing in the history of Mitchelville," a writer for the *Liberator* commented, "lends endorsement to the oft-repeated assertion, that the freedman neither can nor will support himself, much less perform the higher functions of citizenship and fullest freedom." To the contrary, the settlement proved that with a little help "the freed slave can govern as well as support himself." Attending the Mitchelville church as a group, Holt and the other dignitaries were impressed as they listened to the former slaves sing spirituals and then heard a series of antislavery speeches, including one by William Lloyd Garrison that left them all feeling nothing but "the fullest sympathy with the slave." There the travelers also learned the joyful news of Robert E. Lee's surrender.[36]

Then, on the evening of April 14, Joseph Holt gave a powerful speech in Charleston in which he unequivocally condemned both slavery and the Confederacy. Still unaware of the events then transpiring at Ford's Theater, he denounced the "accursed" Confederate rebellion's "inherent barbarisms and atrocities, as well as its ultimate aims," namely, to preserve race-based human bondage at the cost of the nation's life. To this he compared the tireless efforts of those who had, over four bitter years of war, "seized the clanking fetter of the slave, and the bloody lash of his driver" and had "flung them scornfully into the face of the rebellion." Holt warned that the "fruits of this prolonged and sanguinary conflict" would come to nothing if, when peace finally came, "there remain[ed] a single root of that cancer of slavery which has been eating into the national vitals." He urged vigilance in the effort "not only to strike the last fetter from the limbs of the last slave, but also to see that guarantees are created against the reestablishment of slavery through some cunningly devised system of tutelage, which, enforced by state law, would entail upon this oppressed race the same ignorance, and poverty, and social, and political disfranchisement to which they have heretofore been subjected."[37]

In his Charleston speech, given just three years after he emancipated the last of his own slaves, Joseph Holt also called publicly for the nation to guarantee the rights of the freedpeople, "on whom the wrongs and sorrows of centuries have been pressing." Without these guarantees, Holt insisted, the United States would never be "redeemed from this cankering curse of slavery" or be able "to look the nations of the earth in the face without a blush." The *Liberator* described Holt's Charleston speech as "particularly strong and emphatic" on the idea "that the fullest justice should be meted out to the colored population of the South . . . upon whose loyalty and valor the chief reliance must be placed in holding the South hereafter to the performance of her constitutional duties," including the USCT forces, like the 118th, now serving on occupation duty. The "deepest significance" of the event in Charleston and the most distinctive of the "signs of the times," the paper added, lay "in the speeches of such men as . . . Joseph Holt, claiming citizenship for the black race as the only security and safety for liberty in the future." "What a noble monument to Mr. Lincoln," wrote a Philadelphia correspondent to Holt about a week later, "if we insist upon the rights of the oppressed, thus causing incense to arise perpetually from the altar on which he was sacrificed." Brokenhearted over the death of the wartime president he had served with such vigor and devotion, Holt emphatically agreed.[38]

By the time Joseph Holt returned to Washington from Charleston, Andrew Johnson was president. The period that followed was marked by continuing turmoil as the federal government and its armed forces strove to finish the war, capture John Wilkes Booth, arrest and imprison Booth's co-conspirators, prepare for their trial, locate and arrest Jefferson Davis and those who had abandoned Richmond with him, determine what sort of punishments the Confederate military and civilian leadership should endure, and get the work of the newly established Freedmen's Bureau effectively under way to support the emancipated slaves. Although his Unionist aunt Mary Ann Stephens had been a steady correspondent during the war, it was during this challenging and chaotic period that Holt—whom Secretary of War Stanton had assigned to oversee the assassination investigation and any subsequent trial of Booth's conspirators—received what was apparently his first letter since the war began from any of the pro-Confederate members of his Holt's Bottom family. The letter came from his eighty-two-year-old mother Eleanor.

In the spring of 1865 Eleanor Stephens Holt still lived on the family homestead with Joseph's brother Thomas, Thomas's wife Rosina, their nineteen-year-old son Washington Dorsey Holt, and a number of black men and women the Holts—like so many white slaveholding Kentuckians—still considered their property, including Sandy Holt's old friend Dick. Thomas and Rosina's older son John R. Holt, who had declared himself ready to kill his uncle Joseph should their paths cross during the war, returned home a few weeks later following his release from prison at Point Lookout in Maryland. In her heartfelt letter it is clear that Eleanor was actually responding to one Joseph had sent recently, enclosing money for Dick and the other black men and women who remained on the family property and were now poised to confront the opportunities and hazards that the end of the war and the early days of emancipation presented. Somewhat grudgingly, Eleanor informed her son that Dick and the others had received the money with gratitude. She then quickly turned to the issues that interested her more: her joy that the "savage, barbarous war" was almost over, and her distress that President Lincoln was dead. Despite her pro-Confederate sympathies, the elderly Eleanor believed that Lincoln had been a "kind hearted man," even if he had been "ruled" by men who were "bad" and "ambitious." Like many other white Southerners in the spring of 1865, Eleanor felt sure that Lincoln, in victory, would have adopted a kind and generous approach to the South and she feared—unnecessarily, it turns out—that Andrew Johnson would not be so forgiving.[39]

Perhaps predictably, in her letter to Joseph, Eleanor focused most of her attention on trying to convey the insurmountable misery the Confederate defeat had brought to the family, not least to Holt's brother Robert, now fifty and still living in Mississippi with his wife Ann, and their nine children. Robert, Eleanor reported, was "entirely broken down in spirits," having "lost" almost everything he owned during the war, including thirty-nine slaves: nineteen women or girls and twenty men or boys, ranging in age from thirty-five years down to four months. All Robert had left, Eleanor wrote sadly, was his home, his family, "and some cotton in Atlanta," and she urged Joseph to use his influence in Washington to prevent the last of Robert's possessions being confiscated. She also begged Joseph to write to Robert, who was, she reported, "much discouraged at the prospect of his children growing up in ignorance, for he has nothing with which to give them even a common education." In closing, she expressed her desire to see Joseph as soon as he could possibly come "home." For Eleanor Holt, the future welfare of the family's former bondspeople, let alone the freedpeople generally, held little interest in comparison with the question of how to relieve the suffering the war and emancipation had inflicted on her white blood relations. She dearly hoped that her eldest son, with all his

Washington-based influence, would now join her in the effort to bind the family's wounds.[40]

Eleanor's plea on Robert's behalf—the words of an anxious mother—was sincere and earnest. Still, for Joseph Holt, the vast and widespread human and other costs of the war that were apparent from his vantage point in Washington were far more pressing, not least the profound suffering that awaited the recently emancipated slaves if the federal government did not stand by them. Indeed, it is easy to imagine Holt solemnly shaking his head when he read his elderly mother's plea that he now help white family members in Kentucky who had actively and enthusiastically both defended slavery and tried to destroy the Union. Clearly the philosophical wound that had opened in recent years between himself and most members of his white Kentucky family and community would take time to heal. For now, his greater concern lay in how much work remained before the Federal victory was secure and the former slaves, including his *own* former slaves, like Sandy Holt, could meaningfully claim their freedom and citizenship—their full personhood—in Kentucky and elsewhere. Additionally, despite his mother's warm invitation that he come "home," Joseph Holt was well aware of the very real physical dangers that still awaited him in Kentucky, given his status as a high-profile and influential opponent of both slavery and perpetual white supremacy. For now, he chose to stay away.

Freedom Won, Freedom Contested

On February 6, 1866, Sandy Holt and his surviving comrades from the 118th USCT began the complex process of mustering out at White's Ranch, Texas, near Brazos Santiago, where they had been gathering since January 22. Army regulations stipulated that regiments must "muster out of service at the same location that they mustered in," which for the 118th required a journey of thirteen hundred miles back to Louisville to receive their final pay and discharge papers, hand in their equipment, and be released from the service. They left three more Company A comrades behind in Texas: Jacob Grundy, Bob Taylor, and the second of two men named George Wilson had died there of disease. Now twenty-six of the original hundred enrollees in Company A were dead, including seven (roughly one-quarter) of the twenty-nine fugitive slaves who originally came with Sandy Holt from Holt's Bottom and the surrounding area in the late summer of 1864. The wartime casualty rate for Company A (26 percent) was slightly higher than the rate for the USCT as a whole (22 percent). As was true for the

USCT generally, by far the majority of the men in Company A who died in the service were felled by disease.[41]

More than sixty-three thousand USCT soldiers remained on duty when the 118th headed home to Kentucky, along with their almost twenty-four hundred white officers. The USCT's final muster-out took place just under two years later, in December 1867, when the 124th and 125th regiments—both organized and stationed in Kentucky—were deactivated. Addressing the quality of service the black soldiers had provided during the war, the *Army and Navy Journal* offered neither wild enthusiasm nor undue criticism, concluding that their overall performance had, in fact, been much like that of whites. "The colored soldiers were not," the paper observed, "the chief heroes of the war. On the other hand, they proved much better soldiers than their enemies prophesied." What the writer of this article found most noteworthy was that the black soldiers "achieved no distinction whatever *as* colored troops," and displayed "no special vice or virtue, no special adaptability or character or style in fighting." Rather, they provided "upon the whole, creditable service." Their regiments were comprised of "good and trustworthy material," he concluded, "on which we shall be glad to rely in the future."[42]

For some of the units departing Texas in early 1866, including optimist Henry Hoyle's Pennsylvania-based 43rd USCT, the journey back to their place of origin was treacherous. "En route from Brownsville," Joseph Glatthaar explains, the ship on which a portion of Hoyle's regiment embarked "sprang a leak in heavy seas," which produced a string of interrelated crises. "The pumps failed to remove water rapidly enough, and the flood extinguished a fire in the engine. Troops had to throw horses and goods overboard, and for nearly two days they bailed water to stay afloat." In an ironic stroke of good/bad luck, the ship finally "ran aground on a sandbar" not far from New Orleans and the soldiers were able to complete their journey home to Philadelphia by train.[43]

Sandy Holt and his comrades in the 118th encountered no such disasters on their way back to turbulent Kentucky, but they faced significant challenges nevertheless. Among other problems, the weather at White's Ranch that February was severe and food supplies were scant. Company A's Corporal Samuel Scott of Cloverport developed what became a chronic heart disorder as a result of "exposure to bad weather and improper diet" during his final days in Texas. Conditions did not improve, either: the frigid temperatures at White's Ranch followed the regiment as the soldiers sailed to New Orleans before heading up the Mississippi River to Louisville.

Captain Bullis later remembered that "the weather was very cold," and Sergeant Owen Barrett recalled that he suffered from frostbite on both his feet during the passage from Texas to New Orleans. Sandy Holt's experience was even more debilitating: he endured frozen feet *and* legs on the journey, from which—like the wrist he injured at Dutch Gap—he never completely recovered.[44]

Popular response to the regiment's arrival in Louisville hardly compensated for the men's suffering en route. "Some Northern black regiments," writes Glatthaar, "were fortunate enough to have a dress parade with crowds out to cheer them" when they returned to the places where they had formed, but "most Southern black regiments enjoyed no such celebration." Instead of being fêted upon reaching Louisville, the men of the 118th were simply discharged and sent off to make whatever futures they could in the midst of Kentucky's chaos. "In some instances," Marion Lucas writes, Kentucky's recently discharged USCT veterans faced violence even before they reached their destinations, such as one soldier who, like the men of the 118th, mustered out in Louisville in 1866. This particular soldier was almost immediately attacked by a "gang of 'rowdies'" who "stole his money, clothes, and weapon" and then shot him in the hand as he was attempting "to run for his life."[45]

As might be expected, tracing the postwar lives of USCT veterans like Sandy Holt—most of whom remained poor and illiterate in the years to come—is a significant, sometimes insurmountable challenge, at best only slightly easier than tracing their lives before the war. The paper trails they left behind are spotty, to say the least. Still, pension records and other sources can reveal—in piecemeal fashion—valuable and illuminating details of their postwar activities, experiences, and movements. In contrast with the rich sources available for literate whites like Joseph Holt (and his kin), they offer only limited evidence of individual men's thoughts and feelings as they grappled with the opportunities and hazards post–Civil War America presented. Read collectively, however, they suggest important themes in the men's lives. Certainly this is true for Sandy Holt and his comrades from Holt's Bottom and the surrounding area.[46]

One thing is clear: few if any of the men who enlisted with Sandy Holt in Company A developed a lasting affinity for military life. Historian Donald R. Shaffer writes that only 1 to 2 percent of USCT veterans joined the black regiments Congress established when it reorganized the "peacetime army" in July 1866. Similarly, only one Company A veteran ever went back into the armed services, and even he did not do so right away.

Described later in his life as a "straightforward" man of "fair intelligence" whose "standing for truth is good," Robert Dent was in his early thirties when he enrolled in Company F of the 9th Cavalry in 1875. Now using the last name of his biological father, Coleman, instead of that of his former owner, M. N. Dent, Robert served a standard five-year term of enlistment with the 9th, in the course of which he spent time at Fort Clark in Texas and at Fort Bayard in New Mexico. After mustering out in 1880, Robert Coleman remained in Silver City, New Mexico, not far from Fort Bayard, for about eight years. "We had lots of soldiers there in Silver City," recalled another former 9th Cavalry trooper. "Every branch of the service was represented." Robert Coleman never did return to Kentucky to live, settling instead in El Paso, Texas, where he married and had at least one child. He died in Texas in 1911.[47]

The rest of Sandy's Company A comrades from the Holt's Bottom area lived out their lives as civilians, though few did so permanently in places where they had so recently been slaves. Some spent time back in Breckinridge County when they first returned to Kentucky, and a few remained for good. But fully two-thirds of them moved away within a relatively short span of time, often to other states where they undoubtedly hoped to establish more peaceful, more clearly "free" lives than many white Kentuckians seemed prepared to offer them locally, especially in the early days after the war ended. According to Shaffer, by 1890 "an unusually high percentage" of USCT veterans—almost 27 percent—"could be found living in the Northern states," though "only about seven percent of the general black population in the United States lived there." Sandy Holt's comrades from the Holt's Bottom area were no exception. "Freedmen who lived in counties bordering the Ohio River" like Breckinridge, writes Marion Lucas, "frequently found it better to move across the river than face constant harassment." Consciousness of their own wartime contributions and sacrifices, and their as yet unfulfilled expectation of the full rights of citizenship that their military service and Union victory had seemed to promise, surely amplified black veterans' frustration in the face of whites' active discrimination and violence.[48]

Among the men from the Holt's Bottom area who enlisted with Sandy Holt and then relocated elsewhere after being discharged were his longtime friends James "Lucius" Bates and Ambrose Cooper, both of whom eventually moved to Indiana after first returning to nearby Cloverport and taking up work as general laborers. Cooper was the first to leave, crossing the Ohio River to Tell City, only about fifteen miles away, in 1868.

Subsequently, Cooper moved to Cannelton, still in Indiana but somewhat closer to Cloverport, where he probably still had some strong personal connections. In Cannelton, Cooper worked as a servant for a lawyer named Charles H. Mason and his wife Rachel. By 1880, however, he had moved again, this time twenty-five miles west to Rockport, Indiana, where he met up again with Lucius Bates and a number of other USCT veterans, including more from the 118th. Bates had moved to Rockport the previous year and was working as a general laborer.[49]

Instead of following his brother Robert to Texas, Roland Dent, too, ended up in Indiana after first returning to Cloverport. The Dent brothers shared the same mother, Louisa Johnson, and their former owner, M. N. Dent, was apparently Roland's father. M. N. Dent had a hotel in Cloverport where Roland Dent often worked before the war, though he also hired out as a tobacco factory worker and as a field hand "in the country." After the war, Roland Dent did odd jobs for a couple of years in and around Cloverport, perhaps once again working for his former owner. But he did not stay. Instead, by his own description he "jobbed around" in places ranging from Owensboro and Louisville to Vicksburg, Mississippi, and Madison, Louisiana. As it happens, Roland Dent had something of a reputation during the war as a "troublesome" soldier who frequently got punished for his disobedience; perhaps a similar attitude contributed to his initial difficulty holding down a job after the war. Once he landed in Cannelton, Indiana, around 1870, however, Roland Dent settled down, eventually opening an ice, wood, and coal business and shop with a man named W. T. Bolling, with whom he worked for many years. Roland Dent's longtime friendship with Lucius Bates and Ambrose Cooper—"we were play boys together" during slavery times, he later recalled—likely factored into his decision to settle in Indiana, where he died in 1915.[50]

Just where Sandy Holt's comrade John Christian of Cloverport lived immediately after the war is unclear, but by the late 1870s he, too, had moved across the river to Indiana, where he died in 1878 at the Huff Township home of Dr. Willard Gage, presumably his employer. Still another Company A enlistee from near Holt's Bottom, Sam Webb, moved to Owensboro for a couple of years before relocating to Evansville, Indiana, about thirty miles away. Webb worked as a farm laborer and died unmarried and without children in 1897. Like Webb, David Dowell initially moved to Owensboro after the war, living for a while with his boyhood friends and Company A comrades from Stephensport, Samuel Helm and George Brashears. By the early 1870s, however, David Dowell had moved to Evansville, too. Perhaps even southern Indiana did not feel "free" enough to him, though: some years later Dowell moved again, this time seven hundred miles further north to St. Paul, Minnesota, where he changed his last name to Brown and took a job in a barbershop. He died in 1885.[51]

A number of Sandy Holt's Company A comrades who chose *not* to return permanently to the same area where they had been enslaved nevertheless made their postwar lives in Kentucky, perhaps because of long-standing personal ties in the state, or perhaps because they simply could not gather the financial means and emotional energy to get further away. These men tended to settle in and around the bustling town of Owensboro, which they knew from having enlisted there and which offered a somewhat wider range of employment options than the much more rural area around Holt's Bottom from which they came. Both of the Company A veterans known as John Steves, who had belonged to Joseph and Thomas Holt's cousin James G. Stephens before the war and had known Sandy for many years, moved to Owensboro. For his part, the man identified on his enlistment papers as John Steves (II) lived barely long enough after the war to know what being a freedman meant: he died in 1869 or 1870 of unknown causes. Though he was born several years earlier, John Steves (I)—Sandy Holt's good friend, who subsequently went by the name John Berkley—lived much longer. Immediately after his discharge, this John Steves returned to Holt's Bottom to reunite with his wife from slavery times, Sarah. Subsequently John and Sarah Steves and their children moved to a place near Owensboro and eventually into the town itself, where John continued to do farm work and other labor and Sarah worked as a cook. This John Steves died in 1898.[52]

Company A Corporal Samuel Scott, too, initially returned to the Holt's Bottom area, but by the late 1880s he was living in Owensboro with his wife Mary and their children and working as a laborer; he died in 1904 or 1905. In contrast, brothers Samuel Helm and George Brashears settled in Owensboro directly following their discharges. Little is known about George Brashears's postwar life except that the former Company A sergeant lived for many years there as a "near neighbor" of his comrade and fellow sergeant Owen Barrett. For his part, Samuel Helm's postwar path was a particularly sad one. For several years he worked in and around Owensboro as a common laborer, tobacco factory worker, and steamboat hand, earning a reputation as a generally likeable "character" who was familiar to many of the "older negroes" in the area, especially "the old soldiers." But Samuel Helm also came to be known as unreliable, at least in part because he drank heavily and regularly got into scrapes with the law. These traits diminished his ability to hold down a job and—combined with the violent spells his alcoholism triggered—put great stress on his relationships, especially his postwar marriage. Then, early in 1884, Samuel simply disappeared: a hat presumed to be his was recovered from the site of a recent flood, but his body was never found.[53]

Those of Sandy Holt's comrades who settled in Owensboro were part of a wave of Kentucky freedpeople who did so after the war, for better or worse. "Scarcely a town or city" in Kentucky, writes Marion Lucas, "failed to experience rapid growth" in the postwar period, and "hundreds of freedmen crowded into Owensboro," where they often lived in terrible housing that was "surrounded by stagnant water" in pockets of the town where "disease raged." This massive influx of freedpeople no doubt contributed to the federal government's decision in the spring of 1866 to establish a branch of the Freedmen's Bureau there, and bureau agent A. W. Lawwill soon began to organize a local Freedmen's Sanitary Commission as well. Later that year Lawwill instructed the former slaves in his district that freedom "guarantees to you the right to make and hold property, to educate yourself and children, the right to enjoy the fruits of your own labor, the right to receive justice before the courts of law, the right to serve God in accordance with the dictates of your own conscience and in fact the right to govern all that you call your own in accordance with the laws of the land." Lawwill may have sounded paternalistic; he certainly sounded optimistic.[54]

Yet for all his encouragement, the actual reports that the well-meaning Agent Lawwill provided to his Freedmen's Bureau superiors regarding the former slaves' progress and security in the Owensboro area were mixed. In October 1866 he informed General Ely in Louisville that the crops in the district were doing extremely well, thanks to the freedpeople's hard labor, and that a new "well ventilated and lighted" schoolhouse for local black children situated "in the suburbs of the city" was preparing to open its doors to "at least 150 scholars." In subsequent reports Lawwill reiterated that the crops and the schools in the area were thriving, but he expressed serious concern about what might happen if local whites ever gained control of the schools, given their demonstrated antipathy to black advancement. "I think they wish to educate the colored people in accordance with their idea of the African race," Lawwill wrote in October 1867. This meant teaching the former slaves "to be obedient to their masters," to "reverence the divine institution of slavery," to "humble themselves before their masters and make good menials," to "look upon their late masters as the most chivalrous people the world ever saw," and to hate the Yankees, who had "bestow[ed] on them the curse of Freedom and robbed them of the exhilarating pleasure of being tied up and whipped and insulted."[55]

As was true elsewhere in Kentucky, Lawwill regularly reported that Owensboro's whites—especially former Confederates—continued to express "a deep seated and bitter feeling" against the freedpeople that not uncommonly manifested as violence, including against local USCT veterans. In October 1866 Lawwill described four brutal murders that whites had committed in Owensboro in just the past several months. The dead included William Conyers, a fifteen-year-old boy whom local white men had lynched for allegedly attempting to rape a white woman; a freedwoman who was shot to death for unidentified reasons; a boy whom a group of young white men killed simply for having left the home of his former master; and Andrew Fuqua, a veteran of the 118th's Company B, whom Sandy Holt almost certainly knew, who was shot and killed for no apparent reason in a local grocery store. Four months later, Lawwill reported that local whites had posted notices all over Owensboro threatening to burn down the houses of any other whites who rented property to black tenants.[56]

The situation in Kentucky improved over time, but so slowly that it must have been virtually imperceptible as a lived experience. In June 1867, Agent Lawwill despondently described the freedpeople of Owensboro and the surrounding area as "doing as well as could be expected, considering they have none of the rights of Citizens, only to live (and that uncertain) and pay taxes." The 1866 Civil Rights Bill, he observed unhappily, "is looked upon here as a mere cypher by the class of men who are always seeking difficulties with the Freedmen." That August, Lawwill wrote that blacks in the area were in "a thorough state of terror, almost afraid to leave their homes," and two weeks later he commented that Kentucky's former Confederates still fervently hoped "that their course during the rebellion will yet be justified and that all laws will be crippled or amended or so construed that they will not be punished for cruelties or wrongs practiced against the Freedmen." Local whites, Lawwill declared, "openly proclaim that the future destiny of the county shall be shaped to suit their convenience," and one man even "told me that, in the year 1867 the 'niggers' would be enslaved again." Sandy Holt's former comrades who made their postwar lives in or near Owensboro may have had high hopes for a better future after the war, but it is difficult to conclude from Agent Lawwill's reports and the other available information pertaining to the men's own experiences that their lives in fact became much better, at least in the short run.[57]

One way life *did* get markedly better for many freedpeople after the war, however, lay in the opportunity to create legally recognized marriages and families or to legalize ones that already existed in practice. Sandy Holt's longtime friend and USCT comrade John Steves eagerly took advantage of this opportunity after he returned to Holt's Bottom. As will be recalled, he and his wife Sarah had jumped the broom years before the war, and they already had a child, Henry. One of the first things John and Sarah decided to do when he returned in early 1866 was to legalize their slave marriage and, in turn, their claim as Henry's rightful parents.[58]

The legal marriage of John and Sarah Steves was a manifestation of some of the most dramatic changes and most hopeful promises that were embedded in their new status as free people, even if not all those changes or promises could be claimed right away. Also hopeful, and even somewhat surprising, was the fact that John and Sarah's postwar wedding—a joyful occasion—took place in the heart of the Holt's Bottom community where bitterness over the Confederate defeat would continue to rage for years to come. Indeed, it took place at Joseph Holt's family homestead under the watchful eye of his brother Thomas, who had been one of the area's most fervent Confederates and whose son John R. Holt had served in two different Confederate regiments. That day, at least, Thomas was kind, gracious, and supportive, inadvertently demonstrating to historians of the future the complicated personal dynamics that functioned among the perpetrators and victims of the slave institution. For Sarah Steves, the day and the event produced only happy memories. "Before several people assembled" at the Holt family homestead, she recalled fondly many years later, she and John Steves "publicly declared our intention to live together as husband and wife in pursuance of our slave marriage." The ceremony itself, she added wistfully, "was solemnized under a peach tree in the yard." Gathered around the peach tree on that day in spring 1866 were blacks and whites from the area around Holt's Bottom whose lives had been intertwined since before the national crisis, and would remain so in many cases for many years to come. They included—among others—Sandy Holt; Thomas Holt, his wife Rosina, and their son Washington Dorsey Holt; and John Steves's former owner, Thomas and Joseph's cousin James G. Stephens. How unfortunate that a photographer was not on hand to capture the scene! How sad, too, that Joseph Holt did not—could not—come from Washington, DC, to attend. As was true of such occasions across the state and the nation, however, in the spring of 1866, John and Sarah Steves's wedding was a hopeful event, to be sure. Still, true reconciliation over the war and emancipation in Kentucky's Breckinridge County remained far in the future.[59]

More than 70 percent of Sandy Holt's closest comrades from the 118th claimed the postwar opportunity to marry and establish their families legally in the eyes of the state. But if their emotional lives were potentially rich and more secure, their financial situations usually were not. Like most veterans of the USCT, Sandy Holt and his comrades "remained enmeshed in rural poverty" after the Civil War. It is hardly surprising, therefore, that the theoretically transformative implications of dramatic developments like the July 1868 ratification of the Fourteenth Amendment to the US Constitution, granting black men citizenship, and the February 1870 ratification of the Fifteenth Amendment, granting black men the right to vote, seem to have had very little if any immediate practical impact on their daily lives or political behavior. These veterans' day-to-day concerns were much more fundamental, focused largely on survival. Indeed, wherever they ended up settling, Kentucky's black veterans worked hard simply to make ends meet and manage their many health problems. Of course, the frequently harsh conditions associated with their military service began taking a debilitating toll on the men well before the war ended. After they returned to Kentucky, their suffering increased, in turn diminishing their capacity for labor and leading virtually all of them at some point to turn to the federal government's Pension Bureau for help. In the wake of the startlingly high casualties at the battle of Shiloh, in July 1862 Congress had passed an "epoch making" law granting pensions to Federal soldiers and sailors who could demonstrate that they had become disabled "by reason of wounds received or disease contracted while in the service of the United States and in the line of duty." Subsequent legislation during and after the war steadily increased the pension rates and expanded eligibility to include USCT veterans as well as widows, orphans under the age of sixteen, and unmarried dependent mothers of men killed in battle or by disease in connection with their Federal service. Sandy Holt and just about every man in Company A or his surviving dependents eventually applied for a federal pension. The only exceptions were those who had died in the service, and in some cases their dependents and survivors filed, too.[60]

The legal *availability* of pensions for eligible veterans should not be confused with their actual *accessibility*. According to historian Donald Shaffer, their high rates of illiteracy and poverty, their tendency to adopt new names after the war, and the racist predispositions of the overwhelmingly white Pension Bureau agents meant that black veterans routinely had a significantly harder time than whites producing all the documents and proofs necessary for a successful application. Nevertheless, for some men who had served in Company A, the application process went pretty smoothly. Lucius Bates, for example, first applied for a pension in the mid-1880s, citing rheumatism and injuries to his chest and back resulting specifically from the grueling work he and others had performed on the Dutch Gap project in Virginia. Though compensation for some of his injuries was initially denied, Bates's basic application was approved reasonably quickly, and as his health declined further, Bates's pension rate rose. It bears noting that excessive alcohol consumption as a response to physical pain and perhaps also the challenges of postwar "free" life may well have contributed to Bates's problems, as it had for Samuel Helm. "Drunkenness is increasing at a fearful rate among the Freedmen," wrote Agent Lawwill to John Ely in June 1867. In a 1913 affidavit Bates's wife Eliza, who took in washing and worked as a housekeeper to help support the family, reported that her husband typically spent a large portion of his pension "in drink," and she requested that half his pension be paid to her directly so she could care for herself and their children. Bates's condition continued to worsen: although he lived until he was about eighty, he was "stricken with partial paralysis which affected one side and his bowels and urinary organs," after which he remained bedridden and unable to care for himself. After his death in 1924, Eliza Bates, who lived another dozen years, was grateful to receive a widow's pension.[61]

Beginning in the mid-1880s Ambrose Cooper, too, applied for a veteran's pension on the basis of his persistent suffering from rheumatism and disease of the eyes, rectum, and testicles, all of which were attributed to his having contracted mumps while in the service. In contrast to Bates's case, for Cooper the approval process was painfully slow. Like many other black veterans who encountered obstacles in their quest for a federal pension, therefore, he reached out to his former army comrades for help. Among the several who obliged by filing one or more depositions on his behalf was Bates, his boyhood friend, who described Cooper's severe health problems and his overall disability in detail. Sadly, Cooper, like Bates, was a heavy drinker; one Pension Bureau examiner described him as a "mindless drunk," which inevitably delayed approval of his application. Alcoholism was certainly not Cooper's only ailment, however. A doctor who treated him for years after the war testified that he had regularly prescribed medicines for Cooper's painful "hemorrhoids and chronic conjunctivitis," which the doctor attributed to his military service and which rendered the former slave 25 percent "incapacitated for the performance of manual labor." Eventually, Cooper's pension was approved.[62]

Moreover, like other veterans, in his final years Cooper also spent some time as a patient at a national military home, in his case in Marion, Indiana. "One fact I should mention," Agent Lawwill had written to John Ely in April 1867: "the county has made no arrangement for the old & destitute freedmen," and in his view, "the Govt must take care of this class of unfortunates or there will be great suffering amongst them." Some months later, Lawwill expanded on the theme, warning that "the old and destitute portion of the Freedmen" in his district would surely "suffer the coming winter unless the Bureau extends to them some help. All of them have devoted the prime of their lives to an unrecompensed labor, broke themselves down in the heavy drudgery of the newly cleared ground in this vicinity, and now find themselves old, in want, and the men whose interest they have devoted their past lives [to], turn the cold shoulder on them, telling them to go to the 'Lincoln Bureau and let them take care of you . . . they freed you!!'" It was in recognition of precisely this problem for veterans generally, including the veterans of the USCT, that the federal government in 1866 established the National Homes for Disabled Volunteer Soldiers (NHDVS), a "network of asylums scattered mostly across the North," designed "to provide a refuge for disabled soldiers who were unable to earn a living after the war and had no family willing or able to care for them." The facility in Marion where Ambrose Cooper spent time was one of these "asylums." According to Shaffer, black veterans were far less likely than whites to end up in the national homes: USCT veterans, he writes, "accounted for about 9 percent of Union soldiers and sailors during the Civil War, yet they constituted only around 1 percent of the residents of NHDVS homes between 1876 and 1905." This was at least in part because their life expectancies were so much shorter than those of white veterans. But discrimination also surely played a role, despite the fact that their Army of the James champion, former general Benjamin F. Butler, for over a decade, headed the board of managers. Cooper was fortunate to have the chance to reside in one of the homes. He died in 1916; his widow then received a reduced pension until her own death in 1934.[63]

Among the veterans of Company A most determined to receive a pension was Roland Dent, who began applying in 1892, by which time he was afflicted by a combination of heart disease, disease of the rectum, rheumatism, a hernia, dyspepsia, and impaired vision as a result of smallpox as well as painful shell wounds in the left knee, right arm, and ankle. In his correspondence with the Pension Bureau, Dent repeatedly described the specific events at Dutch Gap in which he and several of his comrades were injured, providing reminders of the grueling conditions the men of the 118th had routinely endured in the course of their military service, even though they were not engaged in battlefield combat. "I was standing up in a boat on a seat in the act of handing a keg of powder to one of the boys," he recalled.

> Had the keg in my arms, just in front of me, when I felt a piece of the shell striking me on the inner part of my right knee. It seemed like 3 or 4 pieces of the shell struck me. . . . I remembered nothing more until I found myself in camp, and then I found a gash on the inner part of my right ankle and also found a gash on my right forearm near the elbow. I was taken to the hospital . . . about 8 or 9 miles from our camp. . . . I did not [return] to my Regt. until . . . just before Richmond was evacuated.[64]

As Shaffer has observed, Pension Bureau examiners, most of whom were white and manifested the racial sensibilities of their era, frequently doubted the veracity of their black applicants. This was certainly true in the case of the examiner who studied Roland Dent's file in the summer of 1895. "He impressed me rather unfavorably," the examiner wrote, "and his reputation for truth is but fair. He is a tall and young looking man"—Dent would have been about fifty—"and judging from his appearance is in fair health, yet he claims that he has not been able to work for nearly three years." As they typically did for one another, former comrades from Company A offered support. Ellis Ayers, for example, declared in a deposition that he "knew Roland Dent very well" when they were in the army, that Dent had been "hurt in the back or side . . . and in the knee or hip" at Dutch Gap, and that his leg had "swelled up when he came from [the hospital] and would swell upon a march." Lucius Bates's brother Elijah provided a deposition, too, but his was somewhat less helpful. Elijah Bates vaguely recalled "a wheel barrow blowing up" after being struck by a rebel shell "while Roland Dent was wheeling it," but he was not entirely sure Roland had been injured by the blast. A second special examiner from the Pension Bureau in October 1895 continued to doubt Roland's story, despite interviewing a number of people in both Indiana and Kentucky who "recalled his lameness without any suggestions from me."[65]

More depositions flowed in to the Pension Bureau from Dent's former comrades in the spring of 1896. Some earnestly supported his claims while others were lukewarm, perhaps reflecting some comrades' lingering resentment of his famously "fractious" behavior as a soldier. Sandy Holt's good friend John Steves, who had known Roland for years—"He and I left Cloverport at [the] same time when we enlisted," Steves recalled—noted that Dent had not been a particularly "good soldier" and was "often punished" on account of being "unruly." Although Steves agreed that Dent had "got hurt some way at Dutch Gap," he could not quite remember how. Alexander Robinson, who had known Dent even longer, recalled him being hospitalized in Virginia, but for measles. "Very near the whole company had measles then," Robinson testified, but he did not recollect Dent getting injured. Not surprisingly, the Pension Bureau's special examiner still found Dent's case dubious.[66]

That summer Dent reapplied, insisting again that he had been perfectly healthy when he enlisted at Owensboro in the summer of 1864 and that his extremely poor health and lameness now, in 1896, were entirely the result of his military service. Aware that some of his former comrades had criticized his performance as a soldier, Dent grumbled that "none of them had any good blood for me." Instead, he now turned to his sister for additional support. In February 1897 Susan Johnson, a laundress in Cloverport who was about five years old when her two brothers ran off to join the army, testified that Roland had returned from the war quite ill with diarrhea and suffering from a "little sore" on his ankle "about as big as [the] end of your thumb" from an injury sustained at Dutch Gap. Dent's mother Louisa Johnson testified, too, as did several more Company A comrades in the years to come. Finally, in 1902, his application was approved. By then he was living out his final years in the National Soldiers' Home in Elizabeth City, Virginia.[67]

As is true for USCT veterans generally, a good deal of intense physical and mental suffering is manifest in the pension records of Roland Dent, Ambrose Cooper, Lucius Bates, and their Company A comrades. Also clearly on display in these files are the men's concerted and often profoundly frustrating efforts to persuade the Pension Bureau to honor their claims and, by association, their wartime sacrifices and contributions. Reading these pension records with the knowledge of the abundant other challenges postwar life and "freedom" presented to Kentucky's black veterans, one cannot help but wonder why *any* of them chose to remain in the Bluegrass State after the war. Why did they not *all* move to places that at least *seemed* more peaceful and more promising for the future, rather than enduring, along with all of their war-related health and financial problems, the severe racial and social turbulence that characterized the state for years after the war? Having already made a break from slavery, why would any black Kentucky veteran of the USCT voluntarily face what was in many ways the ordeal of "freedom" in the very place where, and among the very people to whom, he had been in bondage beforehand?

Of course, as has already been seen, the majority of the men from the area around Holt's Bottom who enlisted in Company A with Sandy Holt did in fact seek their futures and the promises of freedom elsewhere after the war, though some returned temporarily before eventually moving to Owensboro or out of state altogether. Still, about a third of the men from the Holt's Bottom area who had survived their military service in Company A returned there permanently. They included John D. Murray, who before the war had belonged to a wealthy Cloverport merchant and farmer named David R. Murray and his wife Anna. In his mid-thirties when the war ended, John Murray simply came back to Cloverport and resumed working as a farm laborer, probably at least part of the time for David Murray. He continued to suffer from the "bone scurvy" he had contracted on the way from Virginia to Texas, which cost him several teeth, and when he was in his early fifties, he began to receive a pension, thanks in part to the several supporting depositions from Company A comrades. What became of John Murray in the final years of his life is unknown.[68]

Lucius Bates's brother Elijah, in his late twenties when he mustered out of the 118th, also returned permanently to Cloverport where both had been slaves. There Elijah Bates married, fathered ten children, and worked as a farm laborer for at least the next forty years. As in John Murray's case, it is likely that at least one of Elijah's postwar employers was his former owner. Alexander Robinson, who had belonged to Cloverport's William J. Robinson and his wife Virginia before the war, came back, too, although he spent a few months in Owensboro first, working as a tobacco stemmer. Described by his old friend John Steves as "sprightly," and by another comrade as "a lively young fellow," Alexander Robinson worked as a farmer, general laborer, and hostler. In 1869 he married Alice Dean, also a former slave from the area who now worked as a washerwoman. They had three children.[69]

Alexander Robinson began applying for a pension in 1885, focusing on the serious leg injury he had suffered at Dutch Gap, which had never healed properly. In Robinson's case the initial application process was swift, but his subsequent requests for increases were less successful. Throughout the 1890s Robinson filed claims indicating that his leg was in constant pain, that it "swells, [and] gives out in walking," that he also suffered from a loss of vision in his left eye as a result of being struck by a percussion cap, that he had rheumatism in both his shoulders, and that he had chronic diarrhea. Several comrades supplied depositions and his rate was finally increased to $12 per month. Then, in 1902, Robinson died mysteriously, not from his various ailments but from "an injury or blow inflicted on his head from an unknown cause." Alice Robinson received a widow's pension until she died in 1938.[70]

Rough Road to Reconciliation

As for Sandy Holt, he, too, returned permanently to the Holt's Bottom area, where he had spent almost a quarter of a century before the war in bondage, first to Joseph and then to Thomas Holt. Sandy Holt settled in Addison, about a mile and a half northeast of the Holt family homestead, and resumed working as a farm laborer, now for several local landowners, probably including Thomas. "I was until recently very much afraid all the negroes would go off and leave me [to] die [in] a helpless condition," Eleanor Holt had written Joseph in a letter around the time the 118th began its journey back to Kentucky from Texas, "but Tommie has hired all the negroes that belonged to us and things go on much in their usual way." Like his Company A comrades, Sandy Holt left historians limited resources for understanding why he chose to spend the balance of his postwar life in this particular corner of Kentucky. In his case, one suspects that age was a significant factor: Sandy was in his early forties when he left the army, and despite the turmoil Kentucky was experiencing when he returned—and would experience for many years to come—he perhaps rightly anticipated that he would face even greater difficulty than some of his younger comrades should he try to make a new life and market his skills in a place that was unfamiliar. Strong personal connections, too, likely influenced Sandy's decision to return. As already noted, his first wife, Matilda, had died before he enlisted, and the two had no children. But after the war Sandy got a second chance to become a family man. On Christmas Eve 1868, he married a mixed-race former slave named Sarah Moreland, and soon Sarah and Sandy welcomed their first child, Cynthia.[71]

Over the next fifteen years, Sandy and Sarah produced four more living children—Alice (or Allie), Loudon, Josie, and Georgia—while he continued to work as a farm hand and laborer and she kept house and performed a variety of wage-earning tasks that she could handle at home while tending to the children, such as doing other (white) people's laundry. Unfortunately, as was true for so many of his comrades, the physical effects of Sandy Holt's wartime military service on behalf of the Union and black freedom, including the frostbite he had suffered on his legs and feet on the journey home from Texas, took a brutal toll. Around the time his daughter Georgia was born in 1885, Sandy Holt began applying for an invalid pension. Positive results were slow in coming, however, and in the years ahead, as his health deteriorated, Sandy reapplied several times, adding claims of rheumatism, heart trouble, and his permanently disabled wrist from constructing the defensive works at Dutch Gap. All of these problems, Sandy explained in deposition after deposition, sharply diminished his capacity to "earn a support by manual labor." Good friends from the area as well as fellow Company A veterans provided abundant testimony on his behalf, and whatever delayed the Pension Bureau's approval of Sandy's application, it clearly had nothing to do with his universally acknowledged upstanding reputation. Whereas several of his comrades were cited, rightly or wrongly, for alcoholism, other "vicious habits," or even outright deceit, Sandy's good character was never in question.[72]

By the early 1890s, Sandy's physical condition had become dire. In addition, the community of familiar people to which he had returned after the war had suffered decades of strain and loss. Many of the men from the area who had enlisted with him were dead or would die soon, and among those who were still living, most had moved away. Also gone for good were a number of the men and women, white and black, Sandy Holt had known best before the war, including his good friend Wesley Stephens. Wesley, it will be recalled, had belonged to Joseph and Thomas Holt's aunt, Mary Ann Stephens, until he left to serve in the 107th USCT. Both he and Sandy had been stationed on the Richmond-Petersburg front beginning in the fall of 1864, and one imagines them deriving considerable pleasure and comfort from any opportunities they had to encounter each other there before Wesley died in February 1865. Additional losses for Sandy included other former Holt family slaves, such as Dick, with whom he had traveled frequently between Holt's Bottom and Joseph Holt's Louisville home in the years before the war. Dick appears in Holt family letters up to 1870, and not very favorably. According to Eleanor Holt, Dick had "been drunk ever since he has been free," and it is likely that his alcoholism killed him. Indeed, Eleanor Holt herself, the matriarch of the Holt family whom Sandy had known since he arrived in Kentucky as a teenager, was gone, too, having died in 1871 at nearly ninety years of age. Also gone was Sandy's last "owner," Joseph Holt's brother Thomas, who was only sixty-four when he died in 1876. Both Thomas and Eleanor were buried in a small graveyard on the family property along with Thomas and Rosina's infant son, also named Joseph, who had died back in 1843. In 1881, Thomas's widow Rosina was buried there as well. The location of Dick's remains and those of any other former family slaves is unknown.[73]

When Thomas Holt died in 1876 one might have expected ownership and responsibility for the family homestead to pass to the older of his and Rosina's two living sons, John R. Holt, the proud Southern nationalist and former Confederate soldier who returned to the area following his release from Federal prison at Maryland's Point Lookout. For reasons that are unclear, however, John Holt did not return to the family farm. Instead, he became a doctor, married, and opened a practice in Cloverport. "He is an exceedingly skillful and successful physician and surgeon," the *Breckinridge News* boasted in 1881, "and probably the best read member of his profession in all this region of the country." There is some irony in the fact that at one time or another, Dr. John Holt's patients included at least two of Sandy Holt's Company A comrades, whom John Holt had almost certainly known as slaves before the war: Alexander Robinson and, before he moved to Indiana, Roland Dent.[74]

In his own way, John R. Holt struggled emotionally more than some area whites after the war to adjust to the Confederate defeat and the racial and social turbulence that characterized postwar Kentucky. Evidence also suggests that a mysterious physical condition—perhaps the one that had resulted in his abrupt temporary discharge back in June 1861—may have caused him considerable pain and even "convulsive attacks" long after the war was over. John Holt's postwar life was further complicated by a morphine addiction that undermined his ability to sustain his medical practice and almost certainly prompted his attempt, at age forty-one in the summer of 1881, to commit suicide by shooting himself. He recovered, but less than two years later, in January 1883, the local paper reported that he had been confined to an asylum on account of his addiction. He died in January 1888. John R. Holt and his wife Elise, who died in 1896, had no children and, inexplicably, neither was laid to rest in the family plot at Holt's Bottom.[75]

It was therefore Thomas and Rosina Holt's younger son Washington Dorsey Holt, an accomplished lawyer like his uncle Joseph in Washington, who assumed responsibility for the family farm and homestead at Holt's Bottom after Thomas Holt died and John R. Holt settled in Cloverport. Washington Dorsey Holt married Vanda Vineyard in 1870, and their two daughters, Mary and Rose, were born in 1872 and 1874, respectively. This family managed the Holt homestead for many years. Moreover, aided by the healing passage of time and some earnest and heartfelt attempts to reach out in reconciliation, it will be seen that they also finally managed to bring back into the fold the one surviving family member whose passionate support for both the Union and black freedom had put him at odds for years with almost every other white person he knew or was related to there: Joseph Holt.

Over the course of his long postwar life, Joseph Holt never relinquished his rage toward those who had actively sought to destroy the Union. Consequently, he was unable to make peace with his brother Thomas before Thomas died, or—despite his mother's pleas—with his even more recalcitrant, unrepentant brother Robert in Mississippi, who died in 1867. Indeed, for the duration of his life Joseph Holt refused to take a single step back from his commitment to emancipation and the Union victory's long-term promises for black Americans. Although the details of Holt's life during these years have been discussed elsewhere, it bears repeating here that as long as he was judge advocate general—until 1875—this former slaveholder continued, whenever the opportunity arose, to use his office and his influence to support the principle that black Americans—like Sandy Holt and the other slaves he had once owned—were entitled, first and foremost, to the same human, civil, and political rights as white Americans, and to assail "the injustice and inhumanity of the treatment" whites accorded to blacks on a daily basis.[76]

For the rest of his life Joseph Holt pursued this principle professionally; he also asserted it in his correspondence with friends. More directly, he expressed it in his relations with individual blacks, particularly those whom he knew best, because they worked for and even lived with him for many years. Alfred and Jane Lowry, who had come to Washington with Joseph and his wife Margaret back in 1857 and later married, remained in Holt's employ as coachman and cook at his New Jersey Avenue home until Holt retired from the War Department. Later, they lived not too far away in a home he had given them. Subsequently, Holt hired George Johnson, a Maryland native, to serve as his driver, body servant, and overall caretaker. On at least one occasion when Johnson spoke publicly, he emphasized Holt's "kindness to his servants" generally and described being particularly touched by Holt's enthusiastic support for the interracial marriage of another of his black employees, Jim Richardson, and his white housekeeper Annie. According to Johnson, Holt not only endorsed their marriage but also bought the Richardsons a home near his own, as he had done earlier for Alfred and Jane, "fixed it up in good shape," and gave it to the newlyweds to live in. Johnson further recalled how Holt had once lost his temper when a white friend whom he had asked Johnson to assist had begun taking advantage of the black man's patient and generous nature. "I got a little bit tired of being a borrowed servant," Johnson admitted, "and suspected that I was being worked a good deal more than my actual employer [Holt] would have done." Indeed, in a manner reminiscent of his earlier dispute with his friend Mary Cash over her ill treatment of Ellen and Jane, Joseph Holt did more than lose his temper at the person who was exploiting George Johnson. "He was angry," Johnson recalled, "and spoke out good and strong." Subsequently Holt ceased permanently to welcome that former "friend" into his home.[77]

Jane Lowry's sister Ellen, whom Holt had helped emancipate from his former brother-and sister-in-law, the Merricks, stayed on as a cook for Holt into the 1890s, and by 1870 her daughter Frances was living and working there, too. Indeed, evidence indicates that late in his life, Joseph Holt prepared a will that "provided small legacies of a few hundred dollars" for Ellen and Frances. Frances eventually married a black man named Charles Strother, who worked for Holt as a coachman and body servant after George Johnson eventually moved on. As he had done for others, Holt set Frances and Charles Strother up in a house of their own. They eventually became the trusted caretakers of his "fine old mansion" on New Jersey Avenue.[78]

Meanwhile, thanks to Washington Dorsey Holt and his wife Vanda, and despite what might have at one time appeared to be unbridgeable political differences, Joseph Holt did eventually come to terms with his remaining family at Holt's Bottom and, at least to some extent, with the surrounding community of his birth, despite their enduring political differences. In April 1879, when he finally visited the area for the first time since the war, the *Breckinridge News* cheerfully and proudly published word of his arrival. In October 1880, the paper reported favorably on the former judge advocate general's plan to escort his late brother Thomas's wife Rosina to Europe in the fall for her health. In 1882, when he visited to dedicate the chapel he had built on the old family homestead in his late mother's honor, the same paper described Joseph Holt respectfully as a "lawyer and statesman" as well as a "profound scholar and Christian gentleman" of "worldwide fame." By the beginning of the 1880s, the chaos and acrimony of the early postwar years in Kentucky had begun to abate, though the individual suffering of those the war had emancipated had not, as the Company A veterans' stories show. For his part, Joseph Holt felt able, once again, to express love for the place he was born and for at least some of the people who still lived there. "Mrs. Washington Holt was like a daughter to the judge," recalled George Johnson, though Holt had once said that "not a dollar of his should ever go to any of his people who had abused him for his loyalty." The connection he forged with Washington Dorsey Holt's small family was genuinely close, however, and mutually supportive. As Johnson explained it, in the postwar years Washington Holt defended his uncle, "stood by him," and "always spoke of him affectionately," and Joseph Holt responded in kind.[79]

Indeed, George Johnson continued, "the judge's affection for Washington Holt and his wife was more than a show in words. He built, just for her, a splendid house on the old homestead in Kentucky," which he insisted on landscaping magnificently. "One time he and I went out to John Saul's nursery," Johnson reminisced, "and bought a large quantity of trees of all sorts—apples, pears, plums, peaches and apricots and a great many kinds of shade and ornamental trees for the lawn. These we shipped to Kentucky, and the judge himself went on and made a visit and saw to setting them out." Evidence strongly suggests that Holt even named his nephew executor of his will, though there was some dispute about the will later. Joseph Holt died in Washington, DC, in August 1894, but not before he arranged to have his body returned to the family's Breckinridge County homestead, where he was buried in the family plot near the remains of his mother, his brother Thomas, his sister-in-law Rosina, and other members of the family. Upon his death in 1906, Washington Dorsey Holt was buried there, too, as was Joseph Holt's granddaughter Rose in 1932. Vanda and her daughter Mary, however, both moved to California in the late 1890s. Vanda died there in 1940, and Mary in 1952.[80]

Unfinished Story

For two years after Joseph Holt's death in the summer of 1894, his former slave and USCT veteran Sandy Holt—whom, sadly, Joseph probably never saw again after the war began—continued to suffer from a host of physical problems associated with his military service. His dense, thick pension file makes this clear. By February 1895, now in his early seventies and still living in Addison near Holt's Bottom, Sandy Holt claimed that he was completely "unable to earn a support by reason of disease of back, hips, legs, and feet, also of left wrist." Almost a year later, in January 1896, he took the unusual step of traveling forty miles to Rockport, Indiana, where several of his Company A comrades still lived, for a more thorough physical examination. Perhaps because they dealt on a regular basis with the profound postwar health concerns of USCT veterans, or perhaps simply because they examined him more carefully, this board of physicians declared Sandy Holt 50 percent disabled. Still, the Pension Bureau needed additional convincing. As a result, that May, he reached out to several *whites* in the area whom he had known for decades, including James G. Stephens, who had once owned his first wife, Matilda, and his friend John Steves. Stephens, who had known Sandy Holt for half a century and had employed him periodically since the war, seems to have been more than happy to oblige. His deposition indicated that Sandy was much debilitated on account of his many war-related ailments and was therefore "unable to do much labor."[81]

E. H. Miller, too, supplied a deposition for Sandy Holt in the spring of 1896. Miller, a white man who had grown up in Stephensport with Sandy's Company A comrade David Dowell, testified that over the last thirty years since returning to the area Sandy Holt had complained regularly and persuasively of his many physical problems, all of which could easily be traced to his military service. Also providing support for Sandy's latest pension application was William E. Minor, the white man who owned the land in Addison where Sandy Holt and his family lived and for whom his daughter Georgia, who was then only eleven, had recently been working as a servant. Sandy Holt, Minor explained, "is a very old man," "industrious," but also "severely disabled; viz., weak back, injured hips, weak legs, trouble in feet, and an enlargement on his left wrist, which almost destroys its use." According to Minor, Sandy Holt was no longer able "to do daily labor, except at times to use a hoe" and was completely incapable of using a plow or managing draft animals like horses or oxen. Without some form of assistance or "charity," Minor concluded, this "honest" man "of strictly good habits" would need to be hospitalized or placed in an "alms house." Perhaps these local whites were hoping to avoid responsibility for Sandy Holt's upkeep themselves as he declined. But their affidavits seem sincere, concerned, and genuinely affectionate.[82]

The Pension Bureau finally determined that Sandy Holt's many war-related health problems did indeed amount to a "ratable disability," and on November 19, 1896, the bureau granted him a pension of $8 per month. Unfortunately, by the time the Pension Bureau's approval came through, Sandy had been dead for about three weeks, having passed away at home on October 29, just over two years after the death of the man who had brought him to Kentucky as a slave back in the 1830s. Unlike Joseph Holt, who left a sizeable estate, Sandy Holt, like so many of his USCT comrades, died indigent, and the family he left behind continued to struggle for years to come. His widow Sarah, who had "no property, real or personal, mixed or otherwise, and no income except her daily labor and no one legally bound to support her," immediately began applying for a widow's pension, which the Pension Bureau approved about a year later. When Sarah subsequently applied for the back payments on the pension that her late husband had not lived long enough to receive, James G. Stephens and other local whites stepped up again to testify on her behalf. In October 1897, Sarah's additional pension was approved.[83]

Sarah Holt lived for almost thirty years after Sandy Holt died, remaining in the Holt's Bottom area until her death in December 1924 of "old age and general debility." Sarah died at the home of her daughter Georgia—a laundress and domestic servant—and her son-in-law Crawford Dehaven—who worked in a railroad car repair shop and later in a local rock quarry. Because Georgia Holt Dehaven, too, had extremely limited financial resources, and because her mother had died without any insurance, money, real estate, or personal property, she applied to the Pension Bureau for reimbursement for Sarah's funeral expenses from her father's pension: a total of just over $175, including $150 for the casket, $10 for the hearse, $5 for flowers, and about $11 for other incidentals. In May 1925 the Pension Bureau agreed to cover just the cost of the incidentals, less than Sandy Holt had earned in a month as a USCT soldier. That this black Civil War veteran's survivors in the Holt's Bottom area remained mired in poverty, and the Pension Bureau proved so ungenerous, reflects the long, hard road that lay ahead even at the end of the nineteenth century for the families and descendants of the USCT soldiers.[84]

The postwar road Sandy Holt and his family walked was profoundly different from the one Joseph Holt and his white family and birth-community members traveled down, though that road, too, had many painful twists and turns. At the same time, one should not dismiss the moments when these roads intersected, along with the fragile signs of hope those intersections sometimes offered: John and Sarah Steves's wedding, for example, and the occasions when community whites—once ardent Confederates—provided meaningful support to their former slaves, such as in their depositions on behalf of local black veterans in which they spoke fondly and appreciatively of those who had once been their human property. Of course, one must not exaggerate the importance of such individualized examples for the evolution of racial and social justice in the region. Still, they offered glimmers of possibility for the future. And it was arguably in such reimagined interpersonal connections that the best hope lay for true reconciliation and lasting positive change.[85]

Notes

Abbreviations

JAG Office, Letters Sent	RG 153, Records of the Office of the Judge Advocate General (Army), 1692–1981, Letters Sent, National Archives and Records Administration, Washington, DC. (See bibliography for dates covered by specific volumes).
M1904	RG 105, Records of the Bureau of Refugees, Freedmen, and Abandoned Lands: Records of the Field Offices for the State of Kentucky, 1865–1872, National Archives and Records Administration, Washington, DC (microfilm).
Military Service Records	RG 94, Records of the Adjutant General's Office, 1780s–1917, Compiled Military Service Records for Volunteers in Company A, 118th United States Colored Infantry Regiment, National Archives and Records Administration, Washington, DC.
OR	*The War of the Rebellion: A Compilation of the Official Records of the Union and Confederate Armies,* 130 vols. (Washington, DC: Government Printing Office, 1880–1901).
Pension Files	RG 15, Records of the Veterans Administration, Pension Records for Enlisted Men and Officers in the 118th United States Colored Infantry Regiment, National Archives and Records Administration, Washington, DC. (See bibliography for specific pension file numbers.)

Preface

1. Kentucky did not ratify the Thirteenth Amendment to the US Constitution until 1976, more than a century after the necessary two-thirds of the states had done so.

2. Leonard, *Yankee Women;* Leonard, *Lincoln's Avengers;* Leonard, *Lincoln's Forgotten Ally;* Leonard, "One Kentuckian's Hard Choice."

Part One

1. Joseph Holt's maternal grandfather, Richard Stephens, had first laid claim in the 1780s to land in the area of Breckinridge County that came to be known as Holt's Bottom, located on the Ohio River about ten miles northeast of Cloverport. Over the years Richard Stephens and his kin steadily expanded their holdings, which eventually encompassed over one hundred thousand acres. The Holts and Stephenses also owned dozens of slaves. According to the US Census, Richard Stephens owned thirty slaves in 1830. Holt's uncle Daniel J. Stephens owned seven; his uncle Robert Stephens owned thirteen; and his parents owned six. (1830 US Census.)

Holt's first wife, Mary Harrison Holt, grew up in a slaveholding family and had no apparent qualms about the institution. At the time she married Holt, her father, Dr. Burr Harrison of Bardstown, Kentucky, owned about twenty men, women, and children. (This number is an estimate based on the 1820 US Census, which indicates that Harrison owned eighteen slaves then, and the 1850 US Census, which indicates that he owned twenty-three.) Mary Harrison Holt died in 1846. Four years later, Holt married Margaret Wickliffe, whose eminent father, Charles A. Wickliffe of Bardstown, Kentucky, claimed at least twenty-six slaves in 1850. If the Charles A. Wickliffe who owned a dozen slaves in neighboring Washington County in 1850 is the same person—which seems highly likely—the total was thirty-eight (1850 US Census Slave Schedules.) Holt's Kentucky law mentors, Robert Wickliffe of Lexington and Benjamin Hardin of Elizabethtown, both owned many slaves and advocated for the institution in their law practices. According to the 1840 US Census, Robert Wickliffe owned thirty-three slaves and Benjamin Hardin owned more than forty.

2. Martin, *The Anti-slavery Movement in Kentucky,* 54–55; Leonard, *Lincoln's Forgotten Ally,* 66–67; Robert Stephens to Joseph Holt, October 6, 1845, container 11, Joseph Holt Papers, Library of Congress.

3. "Speech of Joseph Holt to the Democratic Association of Frederick, Maryland," July 26, 1856, reel 3, Joseph Holt Papers, Huntington.

4. "Speech of Joseph Holt to the Democratic Association of Frederick, Maryland," July 26, 1856, reel 3, Joseph Holt Papers, Huntington.

5. Lucas, *A History of Blacks in Kentucky,* 23; Clark-Lewis, *First Freed,* xvii–xviii.

6. Clark-Lewis, *First Freed,* xvii, 3, 44, 71–72; Whyte, *The Uncivil War,* 27; Ingle, "The Negro in the District of Columbia," 22.

7. Notably, Joseph Holt did not *emancipate* the black men and women he owned, perhaps in part, at least, because of the disruptive implications of the existing Kentucky law that required freed slaves to leave the state.

8. Joseph Holt to Margaret Wickliffe Holt, April 17, 1857, container 17, Joseph Holt Papers, Library of Congress.

9. Joseph Holt to Margaret Wickliffe Holt, April 1, 1857, April 17, 1857, container 17, Joseph Holt Papers, Library of Congress. Jane's son stayed behind in Bardstown and quickly disappears from the historical record. See Joseph Holt to Margaret Wickliffe Holt, November 26, 1858, container 19, Joseph Holt Papers, Library of Congress.

Although Jane Clark appears elsewhere as Jane Cox (see, for example, Jane Cox to Joseph Holt, July [date unknown], 1864, container 44, Joseph Holt Papers, Library of Congress) and also as Jane Lowry, careful cross-referencing of the evidence in the various documents in which "Jane" appears indicates that Jane Cox, Jane Clark, and Jane Lowry are the same person. Other black men and women who worked in the Holt household included Thomas, about whom nothing is known beyond his name and the fact that Joseph Holt deemed him competent; and Leonard, whom Holt described in November 1858 as "anxious, laborious, & most cleanly in his person & work" and as having given him "in every thing complete satisfaction." In July 1859, Holt also mentioned a much less satisfactory hired servant, James, whom he was then on the verge of firing. "I think the dismissal of James," he wrote to Margaret, "which will occur in a few days, will be a popular movement in the family," by which he meant the entire household, white and black. "I am quite sure," Holt noted, "that our servants believe he took your diamond pin, & he gave them mortal offense on yesterday by refusing to dine with them & the friends they had invited. He assigned no reason but that such was his imperial pleasure" (Joseph Holt to Margaret Wickliffe Holt, November 13, 1858, container 19; July 27, 1859, container 21; January 27, 1860, container 23, Joseph Holt Papers, Library of Congress).

10. Joseph Holt, Manumission of Jane, October 16, 1860, folio 319, Washington, DC, Slave Emancipation Records, 1851–1863; James Speed to Joseph Holt, December 12, 1861, container 31, Joseph Holt Papers, Library of Congress; undated newspaper clipping from the *Washington Post,* "Who Had Holt's Will," Joseph Holt Rose Scrapbook. Many thanks to Joseph Holt Rose for sharing this rich family resource with me.

11. Draft of speech (or possibly speeches) from spring and early summer 1860, container 22, Joseph Holt Papers, Library of Congress.

12. 1860 US Census Slave Schedules; Robert S. Holt to Joseph Holt, November 9, 1860, container 25, Joseph Holt Papers, Library of Congress; Joseph Holt to John Cadwalader, November 30, 1860, Cadwalader Collection Series VI (Judge John Cadwalader), box 268, Historical Society of Pennsylvania, Philadelphia. Many thanks to historian Jonathan White for bringing this document to my attention.

13. Robert S. Holt to Joseph Holt, February 11, 1861, container 27, Joseph Holt Papers, Library of Congress; see Leonard, *Lincoln's Forgotten Ally* for details on Holt's activities during this period, including his involvement with the initial attempt in early January 1861 to resupply Fort Sumter.

14. Harlan, *Some Memories of a Long Life,* 47–48. See also John Marshall Harlan to Joseph Holt, March 11, 1861, container 28, Joseph Holt Papers, Library of Congress. According to biographer Loren P. Beth, This letter represents "Harlan's first recorded

thought on the subject [of Kentucky Unionism] after Lincoln's election and the secession crisis." See *John Marshall Harlan,* 42.

15. Clark-Lewis, *First Freed,* 12, 73–74. In May, Major General Benjamin F. Butler, in command of the Federal forces at Fortress Monroe, Virginia, made his famous decision not to return three fugitive slaves who had sought safety there. With this decision Butler helped establish a principle that became federal law that summer in the First Confiscation Act: namely, that slaves of rebel masters who would otherwise be useful to the Confederacy could be confiscated just like any other type of property the enemy might deploy against the government. The flood of "contraband" into Washington and other locations where the Union army was stationed began.

16. Open letter from Joseph Holt to Joshua F. Speed, May 31, 1861, container 29, Joseph Holt Papers, Library of Congress.

17. *New York Times,* July 18, 1861; Speech of Joseph Holt to the Troops Gathered at Camp Jo Holt, July 31, 1861, reel 2, Joseph Holt Papers, Huntington; Speech of Joseph Holt to the New York Chamber of Commerce, September 3, 1861, reel 3, Joseph Holt Papers, Huntington.

It is interesting to note that Holt took the opportunity of his letter to Joshua Speed to level an attack not just on slavery but on the international slave trade, which he predicted the seceded states would soon reinstitute. "Kentucky, in her soul," he declared, "abhors the African slave-trade, and turns away with unspeakable horror and loathing from the red altars of King Dahomey." And he asked, "Is Kentucky prepared to see the hand upon the dial plate of her civilization rudely thrust back a century, and to stand before the world the confessed champion of the African slave-trader? Is she, with her unsullied fame, ready to become a pander to the rapacity of the African slave-trader, who burdens the very winds of the sea with the moans of the wretched captives whose limbs he has loaded with chains, and whose hearts he has broken? I do not, I cannot, believe it." (See the open letter from Joseph Holt to Joshua F. Speed, May 31, 1861, container 29, Joseph Holt Papers, Library of Congress.)

18. Clark-Lewis, *First Freed,* 12–14, 59–60, 74–75, 116, 118. The law also "included a provision"—$100,000—"for sending freedpeople out of the country" (59–60). The highest price paid for a single slave was $2,000; the largest single claim was for sixty-eight slaves (60). Whyte, *The Uncivil War,* 32.

19. In the emancipation papers Holt referred to Alfred as "Alfred Allen," but I am convinced that this is the same man who appeared in the 1860 census as Alfred Semmes, Holt's "hostler," and later as "Alfred Lowry." As will be seen, it was common for former slaves to use a variety of last names in their lives, a reflection of the disruptions to actual kinship ties that slavery produced. See Joseph Holt, Petition for Compensation, May 24, 1862, Washington, DC, Slave Emancipation Records, 1851–1863. Whether they stayed in Washington or moved away, the first freed exploited whatever educational opportunities they could identify and afford for their children and themselves. Clark-Lewis, *First Freed,* xii, 74–78. See also Ingle, "The Negro in the District of Columbia," 26–27. See also "Emancipation in the District of Columbia," 65; the record

for Alfred Allen, Civil War Draft Registration Records, 1863–1865; undated newspaper clipping from the *Washington Post,* "Who Had Holt's Will," in the Joseph Holt Rose Scrapbook; and the 1874 District of Columbia City Directory, which shows Alfred Lowry living at 236 New Jersey Avenue—Joseph Holt's address—as a coachman.

20. 1860 US Census Slave Schedules; 1860 US Census; Petition of Joseph Holt on Behalf of Caroline Robinson, September 30, 1862, Washington, DC, Slave Emancipation Records, 1851–1863. The 1860 US Census entry for William Merrick listed two black "domestics" in the home: Caroline Robinson, age thirty-five, and Ellen Cox, age seventeen, both born in Kentucky. As has already been noted, Jane, too, at one time used the surname name Cox, and evidence suggests that she, Ellen, and Annie (who remained in Kentucky with William) were all sisters.

21. Ingle, "The Negro in the District of Columbia," 39; *Liberator,* October 11, 1861, and November 8, 1861 (see also *Liberator,* September 27, 1861); "Speech of Hon. C. A. Wickliffe, of Kentucky, on the Bills to Confiscate the Property and Free from Servitude the Slaves of Rebels, and Other Matters," May 26, 1862.

22. *Liberator,* August 22, 1862; Joseph Holt, Report on the Subject of the Operation of the Confiscation Act on the Property of Mrs. Anne P. Thom &c., September 10, 1862, JAG Office, Letters Sent, vol. 1. See also Joseph Holt to Edwin M. Stanton, September 10, 1862, October 6, 1862, and November 7, 1862; and Joseph Holt to L. C. Turner, September 19, 1862, JAG Office, Letters Sent, vol. 1.

23. Hugh Campbell to Joseph Holt, September 26, 1862, container 34, Joseph Holt Papers, Library of Congress.

24. Open letter from Joseph Holt to Hiram Barney, *New York Times,* October 25, 1862; Hugh Campbell to Joseph Holt, November 15, 1862, container 35, Joseph Holt Papers, Library of Congress.

25. *Christian Recorder,* December 6, 1862; *Liberator,* December 19, 1862.

26. *Weekly Western Sun* (Vincennes, IN), December 20, 1862; Petition of Joseph Holt to the Manumission Commission, October 13, 1862, Washington, DC, Slave Emancipation Records, 1851–1863.

27. Jesse W. Kincheloe to Joseph Holt, November 26, 1862, container 35; E. T. Bainbridge to Joseph Holt, December 23, 1862, container 36, Joseph Holt Papers, Library of Congress.

28. "Speech of C. A. Wickliffe in the House of Representatives," February 2, 1863.

29. "Speech of C. A. Wickliffe in the House of Representatives," January 29, 1863. In early February 1863, Wickliffe gave another speech in the House of Representatives in which he directly attacked Lincoln's final Emancipation Proclamation as "an alarming assertion of power" that violated the rights of the states and constitutional protections on property and undermined the orderly "social relations" that slavery supposedly ensured. Wickliffe scoffed, too, at the idea that the slavery had caused the war in the first place. "Slavery was not the cause of the present war," he declared. "This is nothing more, nor less, than the hypocritical assertion of the abolitionists, to induce the President to assume a power as commander-in-chief which does not belong to him as such, nor to

him and the Congress combined." "Speech of C. A. Wickliffe in the House of Representatives," February 2, 1863.

30. Joseph Holt to Edwin M. Stanton, March 13, 1863, JAG Office, Letters Sent, vol. 2. Holt hoped that Oberholtzer would be discharged, and in August, it seems, he was.

31. Joseph Holt to Edwin M. Stanton, March 14, 1863, March 30, 1863, April 2, 1863, May 1, 1863, May 21, 1863, JAG Office, Letters Sent, vol. 2. See also Joseph Holt to Edwin M. Stanton, November 11, 1863, JAG Office, Letters Sent, vol. 5; June 1864 letter from P. H. Burghardt to the widow of a soldier in his regiment named Smith Davis, from Cold Harbor, Virginia, in the Case Files of Approved Pension Applications of Widows and Other Dependents of Civil War Veterans, ca. 1861–ca. 1910; telegram from Isaac J. Wistar to Abraham Lincoln, March 12, 1863, and letter from Isaac J. Wistar to Abraham Lincoln, March 15, 1863, Abraham Lincoln Papers.

32. Joseph Holt to Edwin M. Stanton, June 10, 1863, JAG Office, Letters Sent, vol. 2.

33. Clark-Lewis, *First Freed,* 80; Charles A. Dana to Edwin M. Stanton, June [date illegible], 1863, container 12 (microfilm reel 5), Edwin M. Stanton Papers.

34. Wilson, *The Black Phalanx,* 318. See also Joseph Holt to Abraham Lincoln, August 19, 1863, JAG Office, Letters Sent, vol. 3.

35. Francis Lieber to Joseph Holt, June 11, 1863, container 39, Joseph Holt Papers, Library of Congress; Joseph Holt to Francis Lieber, July 15, 1863, Francis Lieber Papers.

36. *New York Times,* September 7, 1863; Joseph Holt to Edwin M. Stanton, August 20, 1863, container 39, Joseph Holt Papers, Library of Congress.

37. Lieber, who lived in New York City and taught at Columbia University, personally experienced the riots. On July 17 he wrote to Holt, "The cruelty against the poor negroes" that he had witnessed in the riots, "clubbing them to death like rats, surpasses . . . the first French Revolution." See Francis Lieber to Joseph Holt, July 17, 1863, container 39, Joseph Holt Papers, Library of Congress. See also Schneider and Schneider, *Slavery in America,* 420, for the quote from Lincoln.

38. Joseph Holt to Abraham Lincoln, July 13, 1863, JAG Office, Letters Sent, vol. 4; General Order No. 265, August 3, 1863, and other relevant papers in Military Service Record of Robert Sutton. See also Joseph Holt to Abraham Lincoln, July 14, 1863, regarding the related case of Private Richard Green, JAG Office, Letters Sent, vol. 4.

39. Joseph Holt to Abraham Lincoln, January 26, 1864, JAG Office, Letters Sent, vol. 4. See also an article about the case in the *Army and Navy Journal,* May 14, 1864.

40. Joseph Holt to Abraham Lincoln, March 5, 1864, JAG Office, Letters Sent, vol. 8. See also Joseph Holt to Abraham Lincoln, April 19, 1864, JAG Office, Letters Sent, vol. 7.

41. Joseph Holt to Abraham Lincoln, May 17, 1864, JAG Office, Letters Sent, vol. 9. See also the Military Service Records of William Striblen, Sterling Bradley, and Charles Davis. For Holt's handling of the cases of Fountain Brown, John J. Glover, and West Bogan, see Joseph Holt to Abraham Lincoln, May 24, 1864, and June 6, 1864, container 43, Joseph Holt Papers, Library of Congress; and Leonard, *Lincoln's Forgotten Ally,* 176ff.

42. *Liberator,* April 15, 1864; E. D. Townsend to Joseph Holt, July 12, 1864, in *OR,* ser. 3, vol. 4, 488.

43. Leonard, *Lincoln's Forgotten Ally,* 139.

44. 1860 US Census; Military Service Record of John R. Holt; Leonard, *Lincoln's Forgotten Ally,* 191. As I wrote in *Lincoln's Forgotten Ally,* "According to Will Sterett, Holt's old friend and his late sister Elizabeth's husband, this was actually John's second imprisonment, his first having occurred about a year earlier, on which occasion Thomas had spent $2,000 to get him released on the promise of his good conduct. Thomas had then brought John back to Stephensport, but John had refused to remain home for long: after three months he rejoined the Confederate forces, leaving Thomas without the money or his son."

45. Jane Cox to Joseph Holt, July 24, 1864, and July [date unknown], 1864, container 44, Joseph Holt Papers, Library of Congress.

46. *OR,* ser. 2, vol. 7, 940. In the correspondence from the JAG Office Holt's name begins appearing again on August 5. See JAG Office, Letters Sent, vol. 9. For a more detailed discussion of Holt's investigation and report from his journey west, see Leonard, *Lincoln's Forgotten Ally,* 184–86. See also his full report, *OR,* ser. 2, vol. 7, 930–53.

47. *OR,* ser. 2, vol. 7, 940, 949. See also *Nashville Daily Union,* June 26, 1864, for an article that describes this act of sabotage.

48. John R. Grissom to James B. Fry, June 1, 1865, "The Negro in the Military Service," roll 4, chapter 6.

49. Joseph Holt to Edwin M. Stanton, July 28, 1864, in *OR,* ser. 1, vol. 39, pt. 2, 208. Among those involved in the killing was the well-known Confederate guerrilla Champ Ferguson. See William H. Gardner to J. S. Butler, October 26, 1864, in *OR,* ser. 1, vol. 39, pt. 1, 554–55; James S. Brisbin to Lorenzo Thomas, October 20, 1864, in *OR,* ser. 1, vol. 39, pt. 1, 556–57.

50. See Leonard, *Lincoln's Forgotten Ally,* 184. In November, Lincoln offered Holt the opportunity to become attorney general, replacing Edward Bates, who had recently retired. Holt graciously turned Lincoln down, saying that for the time being, at least, he felt his abilities were better used in the office of judge advocate general (188–89).

51. Joseph Holt to Edwin M. Stanton, October 13, 1864, and January 20, 1865, JAG Office, Letters Sent, vol. 11; Military Service Records of James Castle, Edwin R. Fox, and Henry Edwards.

52. Joseph Holt to Edwin M. Stanton, October 22, 1864, JAG Office, Letters Sent, vol. 10; Military Service Record of Adam Laws. See also Joseph Holt to Abraham Lincoln, March 17, 1865, JAG Office, Letters Sent, vol. 11; Military Service Record of Charles Baltimore; Joseph Holt to Abraham Lincoln, December 19, 1864, JAG Office, Letters Sent, vol. 6; Military Service Record of John Johnson; Joseph Holt to Edwin M. Stanton, October 17, 1864, JAG Office, Letters Sent, vol. 11.

53. Joseph Holt to Abraham Lincoln, November 17, 1864, JAG Office, Letters Sent, vol. 12; Military Service Record of Robert Richardson.

54. Joseph Holt to Edwin M. Stanton, November 12, 1864, JAG Office, Let-

ters Sent, vol. 11; Joseph Holt to Abraham Lincoln, November 17, 1864, JAG Office, Letters Sent, vol. 12; Military Service Record of Robert Richardson. As already noted, Joseph Holt's position also afforded him opportunities to speak out on behalf of black civilians, and when he could, he did. In November 1864, for example, Holt followed up on the case of Fountain Brown of Arkansas, a white man who had been convicted of "re-enslaving persons freed by the Emancipation Proclamation." Some unnamed "military authorities," however, were seeking a pardon for Brown on the premise that he had been "ignorant of the injunctions of the proclamation" when he attempted to sell several of his former slaves to another white man. Calling Brown's actions a "case of atrocious criminality," Holt pointed out that the evidence "distinctly proved" that the convicted man had "told his slaves before this sale that they were freed by that decree," and had "confessed that he knew he was doing wrong and violating the law." Rather than consider a pardon for Brown, Holt "earnestly recommended that the full measure of his penalty be enforced with energy and without abatement." See Joseph Holt to Edwin M. Stanton, November 22, 1864, JAG Office, Letters Sent, vol. 6.

55. Simpson et al., *Advice After Appomattox,* 104–5n13.

56. Joseph Holt to Abraham Lincoln, November 22, 1864, JAG Office, Letters Sent, vol. 11. On at least two other occasions, Holt spoke up vigorously against white officers' ill treatment of black women who provided support (including sexual) services for the USCT regiments. See Joseph Holt to Edwin M. Stanton, December 3, 1863, JAG Office, Letters Sent, vol. 5, in which Holt condemned a white lieutenant's "grossly unbecoming conduct with colored prostitutes in his quarters"; and Joseph Holt to Abraham Lincoln, April 2, 1864, JAG Office, Letters Sent, vol. 8, in which he expressed his disgust over certain "disgraceful proceedings" and "disorderly, indecent, and disgraceful conduct" toward their black regiment's six "colored" laundresses.

57. For a full discussion of this story, see Leonard, *Lincoln's Forgotten Ally,* 195–96. See also Jane Cox to Joseph Holt, October 4, 1864, container 45, Joseph Holt Papers, Library of Congress.

Part Two

1. Washington, *Eagles on Their Buttons,* x; 1860 US Census Slave Schedules.

2. McDougle, "The Development of Slavery," 214; Lucas, *A History of Blacks in Kentucky,* xi, xv, 2.

3. Lucas, *A History of Blacks in Kentucky,* xiv; McDougle, "The Legal Status of Slavery," 242, 248; Littell and Swigert, *Digest of the Statute Law of Kentucky,* 1149–59.

4. Lucas, *A History of Blacks in Kentucky,* 29, 30, 33; McDougle, "The Legal Status of Slavery," 261.

5. *Slave Narratives,* 69; Lucas, *A History of Blacks in Kentucky,* 290; McDougle, "The Legal Status of Slavery," 240–41, 276–77; Hudson, "In Pursuit of Freedom," 290–92, 314.

6. Lucas, *A History of Blacks in Kentucky,* 140; *Slave Narratives,* 3, 6, 18, 23, 34, 67; Harrison, *Kentucky's Road to Statehood,* 163; Leonard, *From Slavery to Affluence,* 35; McDougle, "The Legal Status of Slavery," 241.

7. Lucas, *A History of Blacks in Kentucky,* 2–4.

8. Lucas, *A History of Blacks in Kentucky,* 3; *Slave Narratives,* 70.

9. Lucas, *A History of Blacks in Kentucky,* 2–3; *Slave Narratives,* 34, 51, 59, 72.

10. McDougle, "Public Opinion Regarding Emancipation and Colonization," 312; Lucas, *A History of Blacks in Kentucky,* 2, 42–43; McDougle, "The Development of Slavery," 221; *Slave Narratives,* 29, 45–47.

11. Howard, *Black Liberation in Kentucky,* 12; Lucas, *A History of Blacks in Kentucky,* 147, 149; William T. Sherman to John B. Turchin, October 15, 1861, in *OR,* ser. 1, vol. 4, 307.

12. Alexander M. McCook to William T. Sherman, November 5, 1861; William T. Sherman to Alexander M. McCook, November 8, 1861, in "The Negro in the Military Service," roll 1, chapter 4.

13. Ulysses S. Grant to Eleazer A. Paine, January 19, 1862; Quincy A. Gilmore to Gordon Granger, December 11, 1862, in "The Negro in the Military Service," roll 1, chapter 4.

14. G. Robinson to Abraham Lincoln, November 19, 1862; H. G. Wright to Henry Halleck, November 23, 1862; M. Mundy to Abraham Lincoln, November 27, 1862, in "The Negro in the Military Service," roll 1, chapter 4; Joseph Holt to Edwin M. Stanton, April 9, 1863, JAG Office, Letters Sent, vol. 2. Holt also recommended as a general rule that "any military officer"—including Boyle—"detected in prostituting his police power over his camp to give aid, however remote, to such practices as these, should be at once dishonorably dismissed [from] the service." Some months later Boyle wrote directly to Provost Marshal General James B. Fry urging Fry to oppose the enlistment of Kentucky's black men, slave or free, into the US army. See Jeremiah T. Boyle to James B. Fry, June 25, 1863, Abraham Lincoln Papers.

15. Joseph Holt to Edwin M. Stanton, April 23, 1863, JAG Office, Letters Sent, vol. 2.

16. Washington, *Eagles on Their Buttons,* 39; Glatthaar, *Forged in Battle,* 65; description of an address by Charles A. Wickliffe to the House of Representatives on July 5, 1862, in "The Negro in the Military Service," roll 1, chapter 4. See also the descriptions given in "The Negro in the Military Service" of speeches by Wickliffe and others on May 28, June 9, and July 3, 1862. Kentuckians continued to speak out against arming the state's blacks in 1863. See documents dated January 28, 1863, and March 2, 1863, in "The Negro in the Military Service," roll 2, chapter 5.

17. Lucas, *A History of Blacks in Kentucky,* 151; Howard, *Black Liberation in Kentucky,* 52. According to Dudley Cornish, "A group of leading Kentuckians petitioned the secretary of war in December of 1863. . . . They wanted recruiting camps for colored troops at Clarksville and Fort Donelson, Tennessee, removed 'to points farther South of

the Kentucky Border—say Columbia and Jackson.' If that suggestion would not suit the War Department, then they asked that 'officers of camps in Tennessee be forbidden to receive Kentucky negroes within their lines.'" *The Sable Arm,* 249.

18. Lucas, *A History of Blacks in Kentucky,* 152; Lorenzo Thomas to Edwin M. Stanton, February 1, 1864, in "The Negro in the Military Service," roll 3, chapter 6.

19. Lucas, *A History of Blacks in Kentucky,* 153; Howard, *Black Liberation in Kentucky,* 57; General Orders No. 34, Headquarters of the District of Kentucky, April 18, 1864, in "The Negro in the Military Service," roll 3, chapter 6. See also Lorenzo Thomas to E. D. Townsend, July 26, 1864, in the last-cited work.

20. Glatthaar, *Forged in Battle,* 73; Lucas, *A History of Blacks in Kentucky,* 154–55. See also General Orders No. 20, issued by Lorenzo Thomas for Edwin M. Stanton on June 13, 1864, in "The Negro in the Military Service," roll 3, chapter 6.

21. Lucas, *A History of Blacks in Kentucky,* 153; Cornish, *The Sable Arm,* 249; Glatthaar, *Forged in Battle,* 68; W. H. Sidell to James B. Fry, March 14, 1864; Stephen G. Burbridge to Lorenzo Thomas, April 5, 1864, in "The Negro in the Military Service," roll 3, chapter 6. See also Rhyne, "'A Blood Stained Sin.'"

22. John R. Grissom to W. H. Sidell, March 16, 1864, in "The Negro in the Military Service," roll 3, chapter 6; Lucas, *A History of Blacks in Kentucky,* 153. See also various documents pertaining to Wolford in "The Negro in the Military Service," roll 3, Chapter 6.

Lucas writes: "Many Kentuckians simply enlisted their slaves at the local recruiting office with little or no payment of money to the bondsmen, while others promised slave substitutes cash they never received. In some instances, however, owners paid slaves premium prices for taking their places in the military." And he adds, "Since Federal policy loosely defined 'runaways' and 'refugees' as eligible for induction, making it difficult for them to escape military service, black Kentuckians sometimes concluded that they had no choice but to become substitutes. Some bondsmen signed up with agents of wealthy Northerners who swarmed into Kentucky promising large bounties. These slaves frequently found that trusted 'substitute brokers' were in reality 'bounty scalpers' who took most of the money, leaving them with a pittance" (152). See also Paradis, *Strike the Blow for Freedom,* 34. According to Glatthaar, "Bounties varied from state to state, even locality to locality, throughout the course of the war. Usually the federal government provided some money, as did the state and local community, and in the end, the bounty could be substantial. But they could also be paltry" (*Forged in Battle,* 65).

23. Report from the Provost Marshal's Headquarters, 4th Congressional District of Kentucky, May 31, 1864, in "The Negro in the Military Service," roll 3, chapter 6; Lucas, *A History of Blacks in Kentucky,* 156. A similar story appears in Part One of this book, perhaps a reference to the same event.

24. See Leonard, *Men of Color to Arms!;* Washington, *Eagles on Their Buttons,* xi; Glatthaar, *Forged in Battle,* 73, 174; Lucas, *A History of Blacks in Kentucky,* 152, 154, 166; Joseph Holt to Edwin M. Stanton, July 31, 1864, in *OR,* ser. 1, vol. 39, pt. 2, 213–14.

25. "Departure of Negro Soldiers," reprinted from the *Owensboro Monitor* in the *Maysville (KY) Weekly Bulletin,* June 23, 1864.

26. *Maysville (KY) Weekly Bulletin,* June 30, 1864, July 28, 1864, August 4, 1864, and August 11, 1864.

27. Encyclopedia Virginia, http://www.encyclopediavirginia.org/culpeper_county_during_the_civil_war. The population of Culpeper County in 1820 was 20,944; in 1830 it was 24,027. See the enlistment card in the Military Service Record of Sandy Holt. Sandy's height was precisely average for a USCT recruit; Washington, *Eagles on Their Buttons,* 15; Paradis, *Strike the Blow for Freedom,* 35; Thomas Holt to Joseph Holt, June 4, 1840, container 8, Joseph Holt Papers, Library of Congress.

28. Leonard, *Lincoln's Forgotten Ally,* 49–52; Thomas Holt to Joseph Holt, July 4, 1837, container 6; Robert Holt to Joseph Holt, April 6, 1840, container 7; and April 12, 1840, container 8, Joseph Holt Papers, Library of Congress. Many years later, Sandy recalled being brought to Kentucky as a youth. See Sandy Holt's disability affidavit, dated February 28, 1885, in the Sandy Holt Pension File.

29. 1840 US Census. The Holts' Louisville home was located at 574 Walnut Street (now Muhammad Ali Boulevard), between 5th and 6th Streets, not far from Holt's Jefferson Street office and an area of the city that was largely inhabited by relatively well-to-do free blacks and domestic slaves who did not live in or directly behind their owners' homes. Lucas, *A History of Blacks in Kentucky,* 110.

30. Kentucky Marriage Records, 1852–1914, entry for James G. Stephens. Sarah Stephens died of cancer in 1859 (see also 1860 US Census and US Federal Census Mortality Schedules, 1850–1885); Affidavits of James G. Stephens and Mary Brook Stephens in the Sandy Holt Pension File; Thomas Holt to Joseph Holt, November 13, 1853, container 16, Joseph Holt Papers, Library of Congress. By 1860, James G. Stephens owned ten slaves. 1860 US Census Slave Schedules.

31. Thomas Holt to Joseph Holt, June 4, 1840, container 8; May 16, 1843, container 10; April 20, 1845; March 27, 1853, container 15, Joseph Holt Papers, Library of Congress. For whatever reason, among the slaves that Joseph Holt owned in this period, Dick seems to have had particularly warmhearted feelings for him: "Your Dick came to the door & wished his love sent to you," wrote Aunt Mary Ann Stephens to her nephew on one occasion. Mary Ann Stephens to Joseph Holt, May 15, 1848, container 13, Joseph Holt Papers, Library of Congress. One female slave whose name was frequently associated with Dick's in the early years was Celia, a skilled young seamstress and "lady's maid" whom Joseph Holt's wife Mary found delightful (Mary Harrison Holt to Joseph Holt, September 24, 1839, container 98, folder 1, Joseph Holt Papers, Library of Congress). Mary and Joseph traveled frequently, however, and when they did they left Celia at Holt's Bottom under Thomas's "care." There Celia became, at least in Thomas's eyes, feisty, "trifling," "troublesome," and "saucy." Indeed, the stern Thomas soon began to recommend that she be sold, and after 1846, Celia disappears from the historical record. Thomas Holt to Joseph Holt, May 16, 1843, and April 2, 1844, container 10, Joseph Holt Papers, Library of Congress.

Other slave men and women Sandy worked with on a daily basis in the prewar years and who were important members of his community included Joshua who, along with his wife Ellen, Joseph Holt had also purchased in Mississippi when he bought Sandy. Once Joseph Holt returned to Kentucky in 1842, Sandy, Joshua, and Ellen all divided their labor between Holt's Bottom and Louisville. Indeed, it was in Louisville in the winter of 1843–1844 that both Ellen and Joshua fell gravely ill with cholera; Joshua survived, but Ellen did not, which contributed, no doubt, to Joshua's lifelong struggle with alcohol. George Robards to Joseph Holt, February 17, 1844, and Rosina Holt to Joseph Holt, April 2, 1844, container 10; Thomas Holt to Joseph Holt, April 5, 1846, container 12; and January 29, 1853, container 15, Joseph Holt Papers, Library of Congress. Joshua did remarry in 1845, this time to a slave named Letty. See George Robards to Joseph Holt, January 27, 1845, container 11; Eleanor Stephens Holt to Joseph Holt, February 2, 1866, container 23, Joseph Holt Papers, Library of Congress.

Joseph Holt's Petition for the Emancipation of Alfred Allen [aka Alfred Lowry/Simmes/Semmes], July 2, 1862, Washington, DC, Slave Owner Petitions, 1862–1863, contains the information about Joseph and Thomas trading Dick for Alfred.

32. Mary Ann Stephens to Joseph Holt, December 10, 1863, container 41, Joseph Holt Papers, Library of Congress. See also the 1860 US Census Slave Schedule; depositions of Sandy Holt, James G. Stephens, and Rosina Board Holt, July 13, 1877; and of Thomas Holt, July 20, 1873, and June 24, 1874, Wesley Stephens Pension File; "Register of the Births of the Negroes of T[homas] Holt," reel 3, Joseph Holt Papers, Huntington; Mary Ann Stephens to Joseph Holt, December 10, 1863, container 41, Joseph Holt Papers, Library of Congress; Military Service Record of John Steves (I); and the deposition of Sarah Steeves, May 1, 1911, John Steves (I) Pension File.

33. Thomas Holt to Joseph Holt, November 13, 1853, container 16; and "Slave Policy," issued by the Kentucky Mutual Life Insurance Company, container 98, folder 4, Joseph Holt Papers, Library of Congress. According to the *Dictionary of Afro-American Slavery,* less than 3 percent of all slaves were covered by insurance during the 1850s, at least in part because of the high cost. See Miller and Smith, eds., *Dictionary of Afro-American Slavery,* 403. See also Savitt, "Slave Insurance in Virginia and North Carolina"; and Ryder, "'Permanent Property.'"

34. Handwritten statement dated May 29, 1896, and handwritten affidavit dated May 29, 1896, Sandy Holt Pension File.

35. Deposition of Henry Barrett, October 22, 1904, Henry Barrett Pension File. Barrett gave his owner's name as Miss Virginia Barrett of Henderson. See the Military Service Record of Henry Barrett.

The formation of the 118th USCT was authorized by the adjutant general of the army (Special Orders No. 132) on July 22. See Special Orders No. 132, July 22, 1864, in "The Negro in the Military Service of the United States," roll 3, chapter 6. Writes Cornish, "General Order 143 . . . directed that colored regiments be 'numbered ad seriatim, in the order in which they are raised.'" Only a few black regiments raised in the North (including the famed 54th Massachusetts) fell outside this rule (*The Sable Arm,* 239).

As Owensboro recruiting agent John R. Grissom explained later, "I established an invariable rule that all colored volunteers (if slaves) should bear their owners' surname at the date of enlistment. The reason for this was that in this state," Kentucky, "slaves have no lawful patronymic and among themselves they have as many as four different names. And as it always happens in states where men are held to service by sale and purchase they change owners and at the same time their names. In view of these facts I have followed the above rule that the history and identity of the enlisted and mustered man might be more readily ascertained both by the Government and the claimant." John R. Grissom to James B. Fry, June 1, 1865, in "The Negro in the Military Service," roll 4, chapter 6.

As their individual Military Service Records reveal, the men from the Holt's Bottom area who enlisted in Company A at the same time as Sandy Holt were Elijah and James "Lucius" Bates, Edward Boyd, George Brashears, John Christian, Ambrose Cooper, Robert and Roland Dent, David Dowell—"He told me," Dowell's widow later recalled, "that he run away from" his owners "and enlisted in the army" (Deposition of Isabella Watkins, June 12, 1902, David Dowell Pension File)—George McGavock, James Mouldin, John D. Murray, George Sawyer, and John Steves, identified officially in the military records as "John Steves (II)." ("Steves"—sometime spelled "Steeves"—was a distortion: John Steves (II) belonged to the same Holt relative who owned Sandy's Matilda: James G. Stephens.) Others from the area who followed soon after were Samuel Helm, Henry, Jerry, Lawrence, and Sandy Moorman, Henry, Alexander, Essex, and Harry Robinson, Samuel Scott, Sam Webb, and two more of James G. Stephens's slaves, George and John Steves (the latter, identified officially as "John Steves (I)," was the slave known as John who was Sandy's friend and was married to Thomas Holt's slave Sarah). Area slaves who enlisted in Company H were Anthony, Elijah, Edward, Jake, George, and Joseph Dean.

A note: Determining exact numbers when it comes to slavery and the enslaved is always extremely difficult. That said, an examination of the Federal Slave Schedules indicates that in 1860 there were (counting conservatively) approximately sixty male slaves in the Stephensport/Cloverport area specifically who were between the ages of thirteen and forty-one, putting them—if they lived—between the ages of seventeen and forty-five in the summer of 1864.

36. Howard, *Black Liberation in Kentucky,* 66; Deposition of Owen G. K. Barrett, July 26, 1902, David Dowell Pension File. According to the 1860 US Census Slave Schedules, Grissom's father owned five slaves in 1860, and he probably still owned them in the summer of 1864.

37. John L. Bullis and John C. Moon Military Service Records; Fogel and Engerman, *Time on the Cross,* 125; Affidavits of James G. Stephens and Mary Brook Stephens, Sandy Holt Pension File; Glatthaar, *Forged in Battle,* 70.

38. Deposition of Alexander Robinson, February 18, 1897, Alexander Robinson Pension File; Glatthaar, *Forged in Battle,* 76, 77.

39. Surgeon's Certificate, June 3, 1891, Isaac Bugg Pension File; C. W. Foster to Edwin M. Stanton, June 7, 1864, in "The Negro in the Military Service," roll 3, chapter 6. Among those physicians assigned to examine Kentucky's black recruits was Joseph

Holt's good friend T. S. Bell in Louisville. In June 1864 Bell wrote, "I am now examining from 40 to 60 negro recruits daily, and not one of them is rejected. Every one of them can be put to some good use." See T. S. Bell to Joseph Holt, June 28, 1864, container 44, Joseph Holt Papers, Library of Congress.

40. Military Service Record of Sandy Holt. Dr. John W. Compton is listed in the 1860 US Federal Census as living in Owensboro, but he is not on the 1860 Slave Schedules as a slave owner.

41. Franklin and Schweninger, *Runaway Slaves,* 156, 160; Howard, *Black Liberation in Kentucky,* 192n34. Some owners' pursuit of their slave runaways extended beyond the end of the war. The service record of Company A's James Atchison of Owensboro includes his former owner's claim for compensation, dated January 14, 1867. Austin Atchison insisted that he himself was a loyal citizen of the United States at the time that James enlisted, and was therefore entitled to fair compensation for his loss. There is no indication in the record that this claim was honored. See the Military Service Record of James Atchison. See also the Military Service Record of Marion Davis, who was one of the very first fugitive slaves to enlist in the 118th (in late July 1864), and whose owner, Arthur N. Davis of Greenville, Kentucky, sought compensation, as did Isaac Morton of Hartford, for the loss of Sylvester Morton (Military Service Record of Sylvester Morton).

42. Thomas Bramlette to Abraham Lincoln, September 3, 1864; and Lorenzo Thomas to Edwin M. Stanton, September 20, 1864, in "The Negro in the Military Service," roll 3, chapter 6.

43. Lucas, *A History of Blacks in Kentucky,* 175–76.

44. Lucas, *A History of Blacks in Kentucky,* 156; Military Service Record of Robert Eaves.

45. *OR,* ser. 1, vol. 39, pt. 1, 492; *Daily National Republican* (article reprinted from the *Louisville Journal*), September 3, 1864.

46. *Daily National Republican* (article reprinted from the *Louisville Journal*), September 3, 1864; Military Service Record of David Heston.

47. Downs, *Sick from Freedom,* 22, 98; Washington, *Eagles on Their Buttons,* 30. "During the Civil War," writes Arthur Allen, "smallpox was of relatively little import to either side in comparison to the pervasive gastrointestinal disorders, the respiratory invasions of packed sleeping tents, the malarial mosquitoes, and gangrene-infested operating wards." See Allen, *Vaccine,* 131–32.

48. Washington, *Eagles on Their Buttons,* 30. Writes Glatthaar: "From the very beginning, the War Department had great difficulty procuring competent physicians for the USCT. Throughout the North there were a limited number of properly trained physicians who were physically able to handle both the strain of army life and its professional demands. Black commands had to compete with white volunteer units, which had organized earlier and therefore had first crack at qualified physicians. In addition, like the rest of [white] Northern society, not everyone wanted to serve in the USCT." *Forged in Battle,* 187–88, 194–95.

49. Russell D. Adams to E. P. Morang, April 11, 1865, Military Service Record of

Russell D. Adams. See also the Military Service Records of Alexander M. Winn, Joel T. Tevis, Ellis Ayer, Robert Dent, and John Christian.

50. Military Service Records of Dick Rapier, Jack Younger, Jefferson Gibson, and Henry Houston.

51. Military Service Record of James Bell; *Maysville (KY) Weekly Bulletin,* September 15, 1864. Jacob Grundy also died in the service, in October 1865, of chronic diarrhea. See the Military Service Record of Jacob Grundy.

52. Cornish, *The Sable Arm,* 239; Lorenzo Thomas to Edwin M. Stanton, October 8, 1864, in "The Negro in the Military Service," roll 3, chapter 6.

53. Lorenzo Thomas to Benjamin F. Butler, October 17, 1864, in "The Negro in the Military Service," roll 3, chapter 6; Military Service Record of George Martin; Wallace, "General John Lapham Bullis (I)," 457–58; Military Service Record of Henry Moorman.

Ambrose Cooper's pension record includes a document ("Proof of Disability" affidavit, dated February 10, 1900) in which Walter Whitinghill, also of Company A, commented that the regiment marched from Louisville all the way to Virginia. This contradicts other evidence and also seems highly unlikely. I believe Whitinghill meant they marched from Baltimore to City Point. See the Ambrose Cooper Pension File.

54. See Cornish, *The Sable Arm,* 118; *OR,* ser. 1, vol. 42, pt. 3, 336. In July 1864, Lorenzo Thomas wrote to Secretary of War Stanton regarding the difficulties he was experiencing finding officers for the black regiments being organized in Kentucky. Lorenzo Thomas to Edwin M. Stanton, July 3, 1864, in "The Negro in the Military Service," roll 3, chapter 6. See also Lorenzo Thomas to Stephen G. Burbridge, July 24, 1864, in the same source, in which Thomas wrote: "In the organization" of the black regiments in Kentucky to date, "I have taken all the officers reported to me from the Boards at Washington, Cincinnati, St. Louis, Davenport, and Lexington, and a few from Nashville. I have no personal acquaintance with these officers, but have taken them as they have been sent to me, and although you may not know them, I think you can depend on them—especially those from the Army of the Potomac—as I know they have to pass through a most rigid examination, occupying sometimes, from one to three days."

55. See Captain D. D. Wheeler, October 25, 1864, circular, in *OR,* ser. 1, vol. 42, pt. 3, 354; see also "Organization of Troops in the Department of Virginia and North Carolina . . . October 31, 1864," in *OR,* ser. 1, vol. 42, pt. 3, 467; *OR,* ser. 1, vol. 42, pt. 3, 1126. Subsequently, the 118th, 22nd, 36th, and 38th regiments under Alonzo Draper became the first brigade of the first division (commanded by August V. Kautz) of the XXV Corps. See *OR,* ser. 1, vol. 46, pt. 1, 579; see also *OR,* ser. 1, vol. 46, pt. 1, 139ff.; D. D. Wheeler, October 28, 1864, circular, in *OR,* ser. 1, vol. 42, pt. 3, 422.

See the Military Service Record of Henry Moorman. Henry's "effects" amounted to his uniform, a rubber blanket, a pair of shoes, a haversack, a knapsack, and a canteen.

Sawyer is buried at Fort Harrison in Virginia. See http://lestweforget.hamptonu.edu/page.cfm?uuid=9FEC4857-9679-946D-5BDE698C2B8421A8. Record and Pension Office Document, June 17, 1895, Harry Robinson Pension File.

56. Military Service Record of John C. Moon. For his part, Bullis later became famous for his leadership of a group of black Seminole scouts during the Indian Wars. See Leonard, *Men of Color to Arms!* 117, 119.

57. Glatthaar, *Forged in Battle,* 167. See also Cornish, *The Sable Arm,* 266; Longacre, "Black Troops in the Army of the James," 1. "The Army of the James," notes Longacre, "used its 'sable arm' in the most responsible positions, to spearhead assaults and to secure footholds in enemy territory; provided it with the best rations and materiel; maintained regiments of black cavalry and sought to recruit black cannoneers despite War Department disapproval; and even traded white regiments to another army in exchange for an equal number of blacks. Moreover, the army constantly sought to bolster the morale of its USCTs, from designing medals honoring their bravery in combat to providing sustenance to their dependence through its Office of Negro Affairs." See also Becker, "The Dutch Gap Canal."

The USCT regiments that participated in the May 4–June 19, 1864, operations against Petersburg and Richmond—before the army settled in for the siege—were (with the location where they were organized in parentheses) the 1st (DC), 4th (Maryland), 5th (Ohio), 6th (Pennsylvania), 10th (Virginia), 19th (Maryland), 22nd (Pennsylvania), 23rd (Virginia), 27th (Ohio), 30th (Maryland), 31st (New York), 37th (North Carolina), 39th (Maryland), and 43rd (Pennsylvania) USCT infantry regiments; the 1st (Virginia) and 2nd (Virginia) USCT cavalry regiments; and Battery B of the 2nd Regiment USCT Light Artillery (Virginia). The USCT regiments that departed at the end of the year were the 1st (December 7, 1864), 4th (December 7), 5th (December 6), 6th (December 17), 27th (December 7), 30th (December 7), 37th (December 7), 39th (December 7), 107th (December 7), 1st Cavalry (August 1864), 2nd Cavalry (February 1865), and Battery B (July 7, 1864). The USCT regiments that arrived starting in late summer 1864 were the 7th (August 1864), 8th (August 1864), 9th (August 1864), 28th (July 1864), 29th (June 19, 1864), 36th (July 1864), 38th (late June 1864), 41st (October 1864), 45th (September 1864), 107th (November 1864), 109th (October 1864), 114th (January 1865), 115th (December 1864), 116th (September 1864), 117th (October 1864), 118th (October 1864), 122nd (February 1865), and 127th (September 1864). Regiments that stayed throughout the 118th's time there were the 7th (to May 1865), 8th (to May 1865), 9th (to June 1865), 10th (to June 1865), 19th (to June 1865), 22nd (to May 1865), 23rd (to June 1865), 28th (to June 1865), 29th (to May 1865), 31st (to May 1865), 36th (to May 1865), 38th (to May 1865), 41st (to May 1865), 43rd (to May 1865), 45th (to May 1865), 109th (to May 1865), 114th (to May 1865), 115th (to May 1865), 116th (to May 1865), 117th (to June 1865), 118th (to June 1865), 122nd (to June 1865), and 127th (to June 1865).

58. Glatthaar, *Forged in Battle,* 150–51; *OR,* ser. 1, vol. 46, pt. 1, 139; Leonard, *Men of Color to Arms!* 12–13. Thirteen other USCT soldiers also earned medals for their performance at Chaffin's Farm (Cornish, *The Sable Arm,* 266).

59. McPherson, *Ordeal by Fire,* 481; *OR,* ser. 1, vol. 46, pt. 1, 139ff.; Greene, *The Final Battles of the Petersburg Campaign,* 12.

60. See Paradis, *Strike the Blow for Freedom,* 15, for a description of a "typical" day for a black regiment at Petersburg in the fall of 1864; R. B. Marcy to Lorenzo Thomas, November 30, 1864, in "The Negro in the Military Service," roll 3, chapter 6; Peter S. Michie to J. G. Barnard, October 25, 1864, in *OR,* ser. 1, vol. 42, pt. 1, 664–65; Greene, *The Final Battles of the Petersburg Campaign,* 8.

61. Washington, *Eagles on Their Buttons,* 41, 45; Military Service Record of Wesley Stephens; War Department document dated March 2, 1888, Sandy Holt Pension File; Deposition of James L. Bates, August 22, 1896; and F. M. Hackleman to Commissioner of Pensions, April 27, 1896, Ambrose Cooper Pension File.

62. Military Service Records of George Wilson, John Peyton (Peyton's service record indicates that he died of "jaundice," which is a symptom of liver failure), Thornton Stout, Sandy Moorman, Charley Turner, Joseph Roberts, Charles H. Tickenor, George Steves, and Edward Boyd. George Steves's effects included a cap, a greatcoat, a pair of trousers, a pair of shoes, two pairs of socks, two blankets, and a knapsack. See also Deposition of Roland Dent and Samuel Scott, June 22, 1869; medical testimony of Dr. Jesse W. Holmes, November 1, 1868; joint affidavit of Samuel Scott and James L. Bates, June 22, 1869; and Claim for a Mother's Pension, July 12, 1869, Edward Boyd Pension File.

Among the men of the 5th USCT, writes Washington, "the average strength for the companies" during their service in the area declined "from 77 to 58," with typhoid fever and sunstroke serving as "the primary causes." *Eagles on Their Buttons,* 45.

63. Department of the Interior document, February 26, 1901, in Sidney Smith Pension File; Military Service Records of George Rowan, Benjamin F. Baker, and Isaac Bugg. See also Isaac Gibson Bugg Declaration for Original Invalid Pension, 1890; War Department document dated May 13, 1891; Affidavit of James Taylor, March 28, 1891; Surgeon's Certificate, June 3, 1891, Isaac Bugg Pension File.

64. Military Service Records of Richard Thompson and Jacob Miles.

65. Military Service Records of Elijah Bates, Caleb Nelson, Jack Griffith, Walter Whitinghill, Jim Johnson, Sam Webb, Joshua Howard, Alfred Stiles, Rolly Reed, Robert White, Lewis Beverly, Jerry Moorman, and Sidney Smith.

66. See "Annual Report of the Secretary of War for 1865," 946ff.; *OR* (Navy), ser. 1, vol. 10, 345.

67. Longacre, *A Regiment of Slaves,* 110–11; Faust, *Historical Times Illustrated Encyclopedia,* 231. According to Longacre, Dutch Gap was named "in memory of a European immigrant who, some years before, had tried unsuccessfully to connect the two prongs of the hairpin by means of a canal" (*A Regiments of Slaves,* 110). See also "The Dutch Gap Canal," *New York Herald,* January 5, 1865; Becker, "The Dutch Gap Canal," *Frank Leslie's Popular Monthly,* June 1894; "Dutch Gap Canal," *Overland Monthly and Out West Magazine,* January 1870; "Annual Report of the Secretary of War for 1865," 948; *Army and Navy Journal,* January 7, 1865.

68. "Dutch Gap Canal," *Overland Monthly and Out West Magazine,* January 1870. Adds the article's author, "To live in putrid holes; to be exposed daily to a hostile fire,

with no chance to retaliate; to suffer a soldier's dangers, while deprived of his spirit as a combatant; to wield a spade only under fire—all this is depressing and demoralizing, and to the impressible and depressible negro race, it was doing much to deprive him of his soldierly ardor." See also Deposition of Alexander Robinson, October 25, 1888, and various other related documents in Alexander Robinson Pension File.

69. Peter S. Michie to J. G. Barnard, September 10, 1864, in *OR,* ser. 1, vol. 42, pt. 1, 657–58. See also Peter S. Michie to J. G. Barnard, September 18, 1864, in *OR,* ser. 1, vol. 42, pt. 1, 659; and Peter S. Michie to J. G. Barnard, October 10, 1864, in *OR,* ser. 1, vol. 42, pt. 1, 660–61, 663; Longacre, *A Regiment of Slaves,* 111; "Dutch Gap Canal," *Overland Monthly and Out West Magazine,* January 1870;*Army and Navy Journal,* December 10, 1864, December 17, 1864; *New York Times,* October 22, 1864, October 24, 1864; Longacre, "Black Troops in the Army of the James," 4.

70. Paradis, *Strike the Blow for Freedom,* 61; Longacre, *A Regiment of Slaves,* 111; "Dutch Gap Canal," *Overland Monthly and Out West Magazine,* January 1870; Military Service Records of Sandy Holt, Frank Bell, David Howard, George Brashears, and Edward Boyd; Joint Affidavit of Roland Dent and Samuel Scott, June 22, 1869; the medical testimony of Dr. Jesse W. Holmes, November 1, 1868; and the Claim for a Mother's Pension, July 12, 1869, Edward Boyd Pension File; Affidavit of Walter Whitinghill, April 19, 1898, Walter Whitinghill Pension File; Claimant's Affidavit, February 2, 1893; Surgeon's Certificate, January 22, 1896; Claimant's Affidavit, June 24, 1893, Sandy Holt Pension File; and relevant documents in James L. Bates Pension File and George Brashears Pension File.

71. Greene, *The Final Battles of the Petersburg Campaign,* 30; Godfrey Weitzel, Orders dated February 20, 1865, "In the Field," from the database "American Broadsides and Ephemera, Series I," no. 12160. Dudley Cornish describes the XXV Corps, "an entire army corps made up of Negro regiments, thirty-two in all," as "unique in American military history" (*The Sable Arm,* 266).

72. *Army and Navy Journal,* January 7, 1865, January 21, 1865; Military Service Record of William Williams; William A. Parker to David D. Porter, January 1, 1865, in *OR* (Navy), ser. 1, vol. 11, 400. See also H. H. Pierce to H. L. Abbott, January 1, 1865, in *OR,* ser. 1, vol. 46, pt. 2, 7; William R. King to J. G. Barnard, January 10, 1865, in *OR,* ser. I, vol. 46, pt. 1, 376–77; Faust, *Historical Times Illustrated Encyclopedia,* 232.

73. "The Dutch Gap Canal," *New York Herald,* January 5, 1865.

74. *Christian Recorder,* January 28, 1865; Farewell message of Benjamin Butler, January 8, 1865, in "The Negro in the Military Service," roll 4, chapter 6. Writes Edward Longacre, Butler "crusaded for equalization of pay between the races" and "publicly vowed that 'every enlisted colored man shall have the same uniform, clothing, arms, equipment, camp equipage, rations, medical and hospital treatment, as are furnished to the United States soldiers of a like arm of the service.'" Butler also "established a system by which blacks' grievances could be recorded and injustices against them rectified." He was "careful to secure the best officers . . . for his Colored Troops," and he also strove to

educate them and provide them with religious instruction and guidance. "Black Troops in the Army of the James," 1–3.

75. A September 27, 1910, letter from an unnamed agent in the Pension Bureau to the chief of the Special Examination Division, Roland Dent Pension File, mentions the company's involvement at Fort Brady. See also Henry L. Abbot to Richard Delafield, March 2, 1865, in *OR,* ser. 1, vol. 46, pt. 1, 165; Long, *The Civil War Day by Day,* 628; John Gibbon to John Rawlins, January 23, 1865, in *OR,* ser. 1, vol. 46, pt. 2, 210; communications between John W. Turner and C. A. Heckman, January 24, 1865, in *OR,* ser. I, vol. 46, pt. 2, 245–46; Henry H. Pierce to C. A. Truesdell, January 26, 1865, in *OR,* ser. 1, vol. 46, pt. 1, 176–77; *Army and Navy Journal,* January 28, 1865; *OR,* ser. 1I, vol. 46, pt. 1, 378–79.

76. http://www.angelfire.com/wv/wasec5/formations.html; R. B. Marcy to Lorenzo Thomas, November 30, 1864, in "The Negro in the Military Service of the United States," roll 3, chapter 6. Glatthaar notes, "Throughout their service black soldiers complained bitterly over the lack of opportunities for advancement into the officers' ranks" (*Forged in Battle,* 178).

77. Military Service Records of Anderson Green, Samuel Scott, David Howard, Walter Whitinghill, George McClarty, George Brashears, Owen Barrett, Jack Griffith, Robert White, Alexander Ayer, John Smith, Henry McClarty, Horace Morton, Henry Barrett, Frank Bell, Sylvester Morton, Albert Delanor, and Silas Letcher.

78. Military Service Records of James Atchison, John Craig, and Sandy Holt.

79. In the years before the war, John Moon was a schoolteacher in Wilmington, Ohio, about forty miles north of his boyhood home and fifty miles northeast of Cincinnati (1860 US Census). John Moon joined the army in June 1862 on a three months' enlistment as a captain in the 85th Ohio's Company F. That September he reenlisted, perhaps inspired to do so by the gruesome news coming from Antietam. This time Moon mustered in for three years as captain of Company B of the 88th Ohio Infantry, with which he served until July 1864, when he accepted the commission as lieutenant colonel of the newly forming 118th USCT. (See various documents in John C. Moon Pension File and the Military Service Record of John C. Moon.) During the spring and summer of 1865, Moon also commanded the XXV Corps's 1st Brigade, 1st Division.

Five years older than Moon, Royall began his Civil War service as second lieutenant of Company G of the 54th Ohio, with which he served at the battle of Shiloh, where he was wounded. Royall left the service temporarily, but he returned in April 1864 as a captain in the 27th USCT, which had recently been organized in Ohio and was deployed to the Richmond-Petersburg area in May. Royall's transfer from the 27th to the 118th coincided with the 27th's December departure from Petersburg. Contributing to the decision to promote Royall to lieutenant colonel, no doubt, was a glowing November 1864 letter to General Butler from General Thomas Kilby Smith, who had organized the 54th Ohio. Smith described Royall as "a gallant soldier, a profound scholar, and a most accomplished gentleman" (Military Service Record of Albert Royall). Clearly Weitzel did not agree.

80. See relevant documents in the Military Service Records of Edmund DeBuck and Martin V. B. Wagoner. See also US Civil War Soldier Records and Profiles, 1861–1865; Military Service Records of Willard M. Farr (who resigned in June 1865), George H. Willis, Russell D. Adams, Joel T. Tevis, Alexander M. Winn, and Asa E. Everest. See also Glatthaar, *Forged in Battle,* 187–88; 1850 and 1860 US Census.

81. 1860 US Census; US Find a Grave Index, 1600s–Current; Wallace, "General John Lapham Bullis (I)," 453–61; John Bullis Pension File; 1850 and 1860 US Census and 1913 *Harvard Alumni Directory;* Military Service Records of Robert N. Verplanck and Joseph A. Robinson. According to Glatthaar, "For many white men with ambition, service as an officer in the USCT became a dead end, due to the extremely limited opportunities in which to shine in either battle or drill" (*Forged in Battle,* 184).

82. General Orders No. 10, March 12, 1865, in "The Negro in the Military Service," roll 4, Chapter 6.

Part Three

1. Military Service Record of Henry Hoyle; *Christian Recorder,* September 23, 1865.

2. Marshall, *Creating a Confederate Kentucky,* 34; Lucas, A *History of Blacks in Kentucky,* 178.

3. Lucas, *A History of Blacks in Kentucky,* 178, 182; Marshall, *Creating a Confederate Kentucky,* 37; *Slave Narratives,* 19, 26, 28, 29, 108.

4. Lucas, *A History of Blacks in Kentucky,* 178–79, 182.

5. Lucas, *A History of Blacks in Kentucky,* 185.

6. M1904, roll 127, introduction; Howard, *Black Liberation in Kentucky,* 112; Lucas, *A History of Blacks in Kentucky,* 186–87. Howard notes that the standard bounty for a Kentucky USCT soldier was $300. Their service records indicate that virtually all of the men in Company A were due $100 of the allotted bounty money when they mustered out. The records of the Owensboro branch of the bureau, whose jurisdiction—a complicated and shifting matter for the Freedmen's Bureau in Kentucky—included Breckinridge County at least part of the time, contain documents dating from the fall of 1866 to the spring of 1868 associated with the bounty claims for back pay and/or bounty by Company A's Johnson Griffiths, William Conyers, James Taylor, Caleb Nelson, James Mouldin, Henry Greenwill, George Brashear, Sam Webb, David Dowell, James Atchinson, George Steves (deceased), James L. Bates, Robert Dent, and Alexander Robinson. See A. W. Lawwill to William Fowler, March 30, 1867, April 3, 1867, April 4, 1867, April 10, 1867, April 13, 1867, and April 15, 1867, M1904, roll 126; and A. W. Lawwill to William Fowler, September 14, 1866; William Fowler to A. W. Lawwill, May 4, 1867, and May 6, 1867; A. W. Lawwill to John Ely, May 9, 1867; A. W. Lawwill to William Fowler, May 23, 1867; A. W. Lawwill to Oliver O. Howard, December 17, 1868; Ben Runkle to A. W. Lawwill, December 26, 1867; and A. W. Lawwill to Oliver O. Howard, April 14, 1868, M1904, roll 127.

7. *Army and Navy Journal,* September 30, 1865, and October 7, 1865. See also

the issues from October 21, 1865, October 28, 1865, and December 23, 1865, for material on the situation in Kentucky.

8. *Army and Navy Journal,* November 4, 1865. Lucas indicates that martial law actually ended in Kentucky in mid-October. *A History of Blacks in Kentucky,* 179.

9. *Army and Navy Journal,* December 23, 1865; Lucas, *A History of Blacks in Kentucky,* 185; Howard, *Black Liberation in Kentucky,* 147–48; John R. Grissom to James B. Fry, June 1, 1865; James L. Fidler to W. H. Sidell, June 15, 1865; and W. H. Sidell to James B. Fry, undated, in "The Negro in the Military Service," roll 4.

10. Marshall, *Creating a Confederate Kentucky,* 56, 61; Astor, *Rebels on the Border,* 3; *Army and Navy Journal,* February 24, 1866. Lucas indicates that the worst years were from 1865 to 1870. See *A History of Blacks in Kentucky,* 187, 190, 312, 313.

11. Howard, *Black Liberation in Kentucky,* 97–98, 100–101, 106; *Slave Narratives,* 62; "Memorial of a Committee Appointed at a Meeting of Colored Citizens of Frankfort, Ky., and Vicinity." The phrase "as amended" here refers to all three Reconstruction amendments: the Thirteenth, Fourteenth, and Fifteenth.

According to Howard, in the postwar period "Kentucky was the only state outside the Confederacy" where the KKK's activities were "significant" *Black Liberation in Kentucky,* 178). See also Marshall, *Creating a Confederate Kentucky,* 58, 60.

12. *Army and Navy Journal,* January 6, 1866; Lucas, *A History of Blacks in Kentucky,* 187, 292; M1904, roll 127, introduction; Howard, *Black Liberation in Kentucky,* 122; Marshall, *Creating a Confederate Kentucky,* 38–39. The *Army and Navy Journal* of March 31, 1866, announced the resignation of John Palmer.

13. M1904, roll 127, introduction; Lucas, *A History of Blacks in Kentucky,* 186; A. W. Lawwill to John Ely, October 31, 1866, M1904, roll 126; Marshall, *Creating a Confederate Kentucky,* 62; Howard, *Black Liberation in Kentucky,* 161–63; John Ely to members of the Ely School Board, May 6, 1867, M1904, roll 127.

14. Howard, *Black Liberation in Kentucky,* 166–67; "Memorial of a Committee Appointed at a Meeting of Colored Citizens of Frankfort, Ky., and Vicinity," 2; A. W. Lawwill to A. Benson Brown, June 24, 1868, M1904, roll 127.

15. Manarin, *Richmond Occupied,* 12; *OR,* ser. 1, vol. 46, pt. 1, 139.

16. *OR,* ser. 1, vol. 46, pt. 3, 816; Military Service Record of Jerry Moorman. The card reads: "Shot accidentally by a guard at Head Quarters Ambulance Corps near City Point Va. April 19th, 1865."

17. Glatthaar, *Forged in Battle,* 218; *Army and Navy Journal,* June 10, 1865; Military Service Record of Jacob Green.

18. Philip H. Sheridan to John A. Rawlins, June 13, 1865, in *OR,* ser. 1, vol. 48, pt. 2, 865; Wallace, "General John Lapham Bullis (I)," 458; Extract from the Returns of the XXV Army Corps, June 1865, in "The Negro in the Military Service," roll 4; *OR,* ser. 1, vol. 46, pt. 1, 139–40. See also E. R. S. Canby to Frederick Steele, June 1, 1865, in *OR,* ser. 1, vol. 48, pt. 2, 716–17. See R. H. Jackson to D. D. Wheeler, July 31, 1865, in *OR,* ser. 1, vol. 48, pt. 2, 1140–41, for a detailed description of the transfer of the XXV Corps's 2nd Division to Texas, which must have been similar to the 1st Division's.

An extract from the returns of the 1st Brigade, 1st Division, XXV Corps for May 1865 reads, "The Brigade," which included the 118th USCT, "remained quiet in camp of instruction during the month with the exception of the last two days. May 30th it embarked on transports bound for Texas." See "The Negro in the Military Service," roll 4.

19. *Army and Navy Journal,* June 17, 1865, and July 8, 1865; Glatthaar, *Forged in Battle,* 291; Military Service Record of Edmund Reese. See also the US Register of Deaths of Volunteers, 1861–1865, 90.

20. Report of Philip H. Sheridan, November 14, 1866, in *OR,* ser. 1, vol. 48, pt. 1, 299; *Christian Recorder,* July 29, 1865; *Army and Navy Journal,* August 5, 1865.

21. E. R. S. Canby to Frederick Steele, June 1, 1865, in *OR,* ser. 1, vol. 48, pt. 2, 716–17; Deposition of Owen Barrett, July 3, 1897, Alexander Robinson Pension File; Glatthaar, *Forged in Battle,* 219. See also Philip H. Sheridan to John A. Rawlins, June 4, 1865, in *OR,* ser. 1, vol. 48, pt. 2, 767; Philip H. Sheridan to Ulysses S. Grant, June 8, 1865, in *OR,* ser. 1, vol. 48, pt. 2, 813–14; Frederick Steele to Philip H. Sheridan, June 10, 1865, in *OR,* ser. 1, vol. 48, pt. 2, 841–42.

According to Confederate general Hamilton P. Bee, the weakly defended Brownsville was a center for Mexican trade until the Civil War began. "The foreign merchants at Matamoros are English and German," Bee wrote in October 1861, and "friendly" to the Confederate cause, whereas the Mexicans were "neutral" and "not to be relied on in case of invasion." In fact, should invasion by the Union army occur, Bee was convinced in 1861 that the Mexicans would side with the North. See *OR,* ser. 1, vol. 4, 118–19.

22. *OR,* ser. 1, vol. 46, pt. 1, 140; Report of Philip H. Sheridan, November 14, 1866, in *OR,* ser. 1, vol. 48, pt. 1, 297; Sheridan, *Personal Memoirs,* 403–4.

23. Report of Philip H. Sheridan, November 14, 1866, in *OR,* ser. 1, vol. 48, pt. 1, 299–300; E. R. S. Canby to Frederick Steele, June 1, 1865, in *OR,* ser. 1, vol. 48, pt. 2, 716–17; Glatthaar, *Forged in Battle,* 220; *Christian Recorder,* July 29, 1865.

24. Glatthaar, *Forged in Battle,* 220; Declaration for Original Invalid Pension, February 6, 1885, and Proof of Disability forms supplied by Alexander Robertson and George Miller, February 28, 1885, John D. Murray Pension File; Depositions of Henry Barrett and Daniel Conway, December 2, 1891, Henry Barrett Pension File; Military Service Record of Silas Letcher; Deposition of William Williams, August 29, 1890, and the Declaration for Invalid Pension, August 28, 1901, Silas Letcher Pension File. Glatthaar notes: "To aid his men, [one] surgeon even traveled south into Mexico to purchase barrels of onions and tomatoes, but Mexican authorities would not permit such a large quantity of vegetables and fruit to pass over the border" (*Forged in Battle,* 220–21).

25. War Department document dated March 2, 1888, Sandy Holt Pension File; Record and Pension Office document, June 17, 1895, Harry Robinson Pension File; Military Service Record of John Christian; Affidavit of George Brashear, March 28, 1891, and Deposition of Alexander Robertson, October 25, 1888, Alexander Robinson Pension File; Military Service Record of John C. Moon; John C. Moon Pension File.

26. Military Service Records of Henry Barrett, Lewis Beverly, David Dowell,

John Smith, Alexander Ayer, Henry Row, Frank Bell, Marion Davis, Samuel Scott, George McClarty, William Williams, Walter Whitinghill, Lawrence Moorman, Sylvester Morton, Anderson Green, and Sam Webb; Declaration for Original Invalid Pension, March 11, 1890, Sam Webb Pension File; *Army and Navy Journal,* July 29, 1865, and August 12, 1865. For a discussion of the casualties from disease in the USCT as a whole, see "Extract from the Final Report of the Provost Marshal General," March 17, 1866, in "The Negro in the Military Service," roll 4.

27. *Army and Navy Journal,* August 5, 1865; Sheridan, *Personal Memoirs,* 404.

28. *Army and Navy Journal,* August 26, 1865, and September 16, 1865; Wallace, "General John Lapham Bullis (I)," 458.

29. Sheridan, *Personal Memoirs,* 405–6; *Army and Navy Journal,* September 30, 1865, and October 14, 1865.

30. *Army and Navy Journal,* October 14, 1865, and October 28, 1865. The USCT regiments whose mustering out the paper announced were the 8th, 22nd, 28th, 29th, 31st, 41st, 43rd, 45th, and 127th.

31. *Army and Navy Journal,* October 28, 1865, November 4, 1865, November 11, 1865, November 18, 1865, December 23, 1865, and December 30, 1865; Wallace, "General John Lapham Bullis (I)," 459–60. The USCT regiments mustered out in late December were the 11th, 12th, 13th, 21st, 30th, 33rd, 39th, 47th, 48th, 55th, 61st, 63rd, 76th, 78th, 92nd, 100th, 104th, 136th, 137th, and 138th. Soon General Weitzel hoped to be headed home to Cincinnati, too. *Army and Navy Journal,* January 6, 1866. In fact, Weitzel's departure was delayed until the end of January by the events that followed. See *Army and Navy Journal,* February 10, 1866.

32. See *Washington Evening Star,* January 26, 1866. See also *Army and Navy Journal,* January 27, 1865. Reporting on the so-called Capture of Bagdad, the *Army and Navy Journal* correspondent described the town as a "very insignificant" place, "a little settlement of the 'one-horse' kind," with a "good sprinkling of 'American merchants' therein," whose "intrinsic beauty, size, and importance have never been sufficient, hitherto, to procure it the slightest notoriety" (*Army and Navy Journal,* January 27, 1866). Indeed, by the 1890s Bagdad had vanished into the sprawling city of Matamoros, from which it originally stood twenty-five miles away. "Bagdad, Texas," in the Handbook of Texas Online, http://www.tshaonline.org/handbook/online/articles/htb04.

The USCT infantry regiments still in Texas were the 7th, 9th, 19th, 36th, 38th, 46th, 62nd, 109th, 114th, 115th, 116th, 117th, and 118th.

33. The *New Orleans Times* seems to have been the first US newspaper to report on the events. On January 7, 1866, the paper announced that "Bagdad was captured on the morning of the 5th, and that "the attacking party consisted of sixty men." The *Times* did not identify the "attacking party" in any way but informed readers that the men had "captured nearly 200 prisoners" in Bagdad, at least half of whom were Mexican "Liberals." See also *Cleveland Daily Leader,* January 19, 1866; *Army and Navy Journal,* January 27, 1866, February 3, 1866, February 10, 1866, and March 3, 1866; *Charleston*

Daily News, February 5, 1866; Wallace, "General John Lapham Bullis (I)," 460; *Philadelphia Daily Evening Telegraph,* January 16, 1866, January 22, 1866, January 30, 1866, and February 17, 1866; *Norfolk Post,* February 22, 1866; *National Republican,* January 22, 1866; *Charleston (SC) Daily Phoenix,* January 23, 1866; *Daily Ohio Statesman,* January 23, 1866; *Wheeling (WV) Daily Intelligencer,* January 23, 1866; *Washington Evening Star,* January 23, 1866.

For more on the Capture of Bagdad, see also U. S. Grant, Endorsement on Report of the Military Commission in Relation to the Capture of Bagdad, Mexico, January 5, 1866, dated March 1, 1866; and General Orders No. 2, January 8, 1866, in "The Negro in the Military Service," roll 4. See also George D. Ruggles to the Commissioner of Pensions, June 17, 1881, in "The Negro in the Military Service," roll 4. And see the Military Service Record of Robert Clay Crawford; Court Martial Orders No. 43, June 14, 1865, Military Service Record of Arthur F. Reed; R. F. Halstead to W. T. Clark, January 29, 1866, Military Service Record of Arthur F. Reed.

34. *Philadelphia Evening Telegraph,* January 16, 1866; *Washington Evening Star,* January 26, 1866. Crawford had been dismissed from the service following a November 1864 court-martial. See Military Service Record of Robert Clay Crawford.

35. *Washington Evening Star,* January 26, 1866; *Army and Navy Journal,* January 27, 1866, February 3, 1866; Wallace, "General John Lapham Bullis (I)," 460.

36. *Liberator,* April 28, 1865, and May 12, 1865.

37. *Liberator,* April 28, 1865; Holt, *Treason and Its Treatment.*

38. Holt, *Treason and Its Treatment; Liberator,* April 28, 1865, and June 9, 1865; *New York Herald,* April 18, 1865; William Welsh to Joseph Holt, April 21, 1865, container 47, Joseph Holt Papers, Library of Congress.

39. Military Service Record of John R. Holt; Leonard, *Lincoln's Forgotten Ally,* 191; Eleanor Stephens Holt to Joseph Holt, April 25, 1865, container 38, Joseph Holt Papers, Library of Congress; 1860 US Census Slave Schedules.

40. Eleanor Stephens Holt to Joseph Holt, April 25, 1865, container 38, Joseph Holt Papers, Library of Congress; 1860 US Census Slave Schedules.

41. War Department document dated June 16, 1885, Sandy Holt Pension File; Glatthaar, *Forged in Battle,* 234. Jacob Grundy died of chronic diarrhea in August, Bob Taylor died of the same disease in September, and the second George Wilson died of "congestive intermittent fever" in November. See the Military Service Records of Grundy, Taylor, and Wilson. The other men from the area who had died were Edward Boyd, Henry, Jerry, and Sandy Moorman, Henry Robinson, George Sawyer, and George Steves.

42. *Army and Navy Journal,* April 7, 1866.

43. Glatthaar, *Forged in Battle,* 233.

44. General Affidavit of Samuel Scott, January 4, 1892, Samuel Scott Pension File; John Bullis to the Bureau of Pensions, November 23, 1893, Anderson Green Pension File; E. W. Morgan to Cesar DePriest, June 10, 1932, Owen G. K. Barrett Pension File; Sandy Holt, Application for an Invalid Pension, 1885, Sandy Holt Pension File.

45. Glatthaar, *Forged in Battle,* 234; Lucas, *A History of Blacks in Kentucky,* 190–91.

46. I have been completely unable, for example, to find reliable records of the postwar lives of three of the men who enlisted with Sandy from the Stephensport/Cloverport area: George McGavock, Lawrence Moorman, and James Mouldin. For Moorman and Mouldin I found nothing. In the case of McGavock, I located a black man by the name of George McGavock in the city directories of Nashville, Tennessee, about 130 miles south of Cloverport, from 1876 through 1924, but efforts to connect this man to the man by the same name who enlisted in the 118th have been unsuccessful. See Nashville, Tennessee, City Directories, 1876–1924, accessed via ancestry.com.

47. Shaffer, *After the Glory,* 39; Leonard, *Men of Color to Arms!;* Letter from [illegible] to J. L. Davenport, December 27, 1910; Letter from [illegible] to the Chief of the Special Examination Division, September 27, 1910; Deposition of John Bullis, December 13, 1910; Deposition of Gabriel Joyner, December 10, 1910; Deposition of Calvin Tipton, December 9, 1910; Deposition of William A. Henderson, December 13, 1910; Maria Coleman to the Pension Bureau, June 2, 1928, all in Robert Dent Pension File. (Robert's Military Service Record describes his complexion as "copper," which suggests that even if his father was not his former owner, he was white.)

Robert Dent began to collect a pension of $12 per month on account of his rheumatism and persistent kidney trouble (he had begun applying for a pension sixteen years earlier). Three years after his benefits began Robert sought an increase, and among those who gave testimony on his behalf was John Bullis, now much better known for his postwar command of the Seminole-Negro Indian Scouts. (Leonard, *Men of Color to Arms!* 117, 119.) A busy man, Bullis nevertheless found time in 1910 to meet with Dent in order to identify him for the Pension Bureau agent. "O yes! I know this man," Bullis exclaimed when he saw Robert, whose face he apparently recognized instantly "as one of my old soldiers" and to whom he reportedly held out his hand and offered a vigorous "Howdy do Robert." Letter from [illegible] to J. L. Davenport, December 27, 1910; and Deposition of John L. Bullis, December 13, 1910, Robert Dent Pension File. After Robert died the following year, his widow Arcadia received a widow's pension, much of which she seems to have spent on a series of patent medicines—less expensive than going to a physician—in the hope of improving her perennially fragile health. Arcadia died in early 1928. Maria Coleman to the Pension Bureau, June 2, 1928, Robert Dent Pension File.

48. Shaffer, *After the Glory,* 46; Lucas, *A History of Blacks in Kentucky,* 195.

49. Military Service Record of James L. Bates; Ambrose Cooper Pension File; 1870 and 1900 US Census. Sometime in the early 1900s Ambrose returned to Kentucky, but not to Cloverport. He died in 1916 in Louisville and was buried in the city's Greenwood Cemetery.

50. Deposition of Roland Dent, August 14, 1895; S. M. Custer to Commissioner of Pensions, October 25, 1895; Deposition of Roland Dent, July 16, 1896; Deposition of W. T. Bolling, February 6, 1894; and Widow's Pension document, April 19, 1928, all in Roland Dent Pension File.

"I remember he was 'bucked' and 'gagged' down in Texas once," recalled Company A's Johnson Griffiths many years later. "I don't know what this punishment was for." Deposition of Johnson Griffiths, May 16, 1896, Roland Dent File. See also Walter Whitinghill's recollection and others in this file.

In her February 1897 deposition for his pension application, Roland Dent's sister recalled that after the war he returned to Cloverport for a few years, got married, had two children, and also "got into some trouble and left and went south." She added: "The trouble he got into here was neglecting his own wife to run after an old white woman." See the deposition of Susan Johnson, February 18, 1897, Roland Dent Pension File.

51. Typescript document that begins, "Be it remembered that . . ." in the John Christian Pension File; Sam Webb to Commissioner of Pensions, February 1, 1891, and related documents in Sam Webb Pension File; D. S. M. Integro to "Sire," June 21, 1902; Deposition of Alexander Robertson, June 20, 1902; Deposition of Silas Letcher, June 9, 1902; Deposition of Isabella Watkins, October 5, 1901; and Affidavit of Charles F. Denny, March 19, 1891, all in David Dowell Pension File.

52. Deposition of Owen G. K. Barrett, September 14, 1889; Deposition of Hannah Duncan, May 2, 1911, in John Steves (I) Pension File; Entry for Sarah Berkley, 1901 City Directory for Owensboro, Kentucky.

53. Samuel Scott Pension File; Military Service Record of Owen G. K. Barrett; Deposition of Henry Munday, April 24, 1907, Samuel Helm Pension File; Affidavit of George Brashears, January 16, 1895, Walter Whitinghill Pension File, identifies the Samuel Helm and George Brashears (who was also known as George Helm) as brothers. Barrett lived in Louisville for about eight years after the war, then moved back to Owensboro, where he remained until after World War I. In 1918 or 1919 he moved to Chicago, where he died in the early 1930s. See various documents in Owen G. K. Barrett Pension File. It is not known when George Brashears died, but he is buried in Owensboro's Elmwood Cemetery. See Headstones Provided for Deceased Union Civil War Veterans, 1879–1903.

54. Lucas, *A History of Blacks in Kentucky,* 195, 198, 199; A. W. Lawwill to Levi F. Burnett, June 6, 1866, and A. W. Lawwill, "To the Freedmen of Owensboro, Kentucky," November 11, 1866, M1904, roll 127. Much of the rest of the speech is highly, if predictably, patronizing, e.g.: "You will remember and always keep before your mind the one important fact that you are now accountable for your own acts and deeds. If you are virtuous, honest, and sober you will experience no trouble, but if you are vicious, dishonest, and intemperate you will find the law a harder master than the one you formerly served."

55. A. W. Lawwill to John Ely, October 31, 1866, M1904, roll 126, vol. 172; A. W. Lawwill to John Ely, April 30, 1867, June 30, 1867, August 31, 1867, September 30, 1867, October 31, 1867, M1904, roll 127.

56. A. W. Lawwill to John Ely, October 4, 1866, October 31, 1866, and February 27, 1867, M1904, roll 126, vol. 172.

57. A. W. Lawwill to John Ely, June 30, 1867, August 11, 1867, August 31, 1867,

and September 30, 1867, M1904, roll 127. See also "Freedmen's Affairs in Kentucky and Tennessee," 3–4.

58. Deposition of Sarah Steves, May 1, 1911, John Steves (I) Pension File.

59. Deposition of Sarah Steves, May 1, 1911, in John Steves (I) Pension File.

60. Shaffer, *After the Glory,* 53, 122; Glasson, *History of Military Pension Legislation,* 73–75, 78, 79, 95, 105, 114, 303–4.

61. Shaffer, *After the Glory,* 123–124, 128, 131; A. W. Lawwill to John Ely, June 14, 1867, M1904, roll 127; 1910 US Census; J. L. Davenport to L. N. Savage, March 28, 1913, James L. Bates Pension File.

62. John A. Crawford to H. Clay Evans, September 11, 1897, Alexander Robinson Pension File; Dr. F. M. Hackleman of Rockport to the Pension Bureau, April 27, 1896, Ambrose Cooper Pension File.

63. A. W. Lawwill to John Ely, April 30, 1867, and October 31, 1867, M1904, roll 127; "Freedmen's Affairs in Kentucky and Tennessee," 2; Shaffer, *After the Glory,* 137; Ambrose Cooper Pension File.

64. Pension document, February 21, 1905; Invalid Pension document, June 24, 1902; and Deposition of Roland Dent, August 14, 1895, Roland Dent Pension File.

65. John Teicher to Commissioner of Pensions, August 15, 1895; Deposition of Ellis Ayers, October 26, 1895; Deposition of Elijah Bates, October 16, 1895; and S. M. Custer to Commissioner of Pensions, October 26, 1895, all in Roland Dent Pension File. Among the veterans of Company A whose pension records I examined, I found abundant examples of men deposing on behalf of their comrades: In 1869, Roland Dent and Samuel Scott filed two joint affidavits on behalf of Clara Oglesby's application for a pension as the mother of Edward Boyd, who had died of pneumonia while in the service (Edward Boyd Pension File). In 1885, Alexander Robinson/Robertson and George Miller filed depositions on behalf of John D. Murray (John D. Murray Pension File). In 1888, Walter Whitinghill and Owen Barrett filed depositions for the supposedly dependent children of Harry Robinson (Harry Robinson Pension File). In 1889, Owen Barrett filed a deposition for John Steves (I) (John Steves (I) Pension File). In 1891, George Brashears filed a deposition for Alexander Robinson (Alexander Robinson Pension File). In the 1890s, Lucius Bates provided a series of depositions in conjunction with Ambrose Cooper's pension application and then, after Ambrose died in 1916, on behalf of his widow (Ambrose Cooper Pension File). In 1894, Silas Letcher and Daniel Conway filed depositions for Sam Webb (Sam Webb Pension File). In 1895, George Brashears filed an affidavit on behalf of Walter Whitinghill's pension application (Walter Whitinghill Pension File). In 1895–1896, Ellis Ayers, Elijah Bates, John Steves (I), Walter Whitinghill, Johnson Griffiths, Owen Barrett, Samuel Scott, and Alexander Robinson filed depositions for Roland Dent (Roland Dent Pension File). In 1896–1898, Daniel Conway, Silas Letcher, Ambrose Cooper/Frey, Samuel Scott, John Steves (I), Owen Barrett, Walter Whitinghill, James L. Bates, and Essex Robinson filed depositions for Alexander Robinson (Alexander Robinson Pension File). In 1896, Owen Barrett filed a deposition for Harry Robinson (Harry Robinson Pension File).

In 1910, even John A. Bullis filed a deposition for Robert Dent (Robert Dent Pension File). And in December 1918, at the age of seventy-six, Elijah Bates filed an affidavit on behalf of Ambrose Cooper's widow in conjunction with her application for a widow's pension (Ambrose Cooper Pension File). Clearly these men aimed to assist one another whenever they could in gaining help from the federal government they had served during the war.

66. Deposition of Silas Letcher, March 27, 1897; Deposition of Johnson Griffiths, May 16, 1896; Deposition of Walter Whitinghill, May 16, 1896; Deposition of Owen G. K. Barrett, May 5, 1896; Deposition of John Steves (I); Deposition of Sam Scott, May 4, 1896; Deposition of Alexander Robinson, March 3, 1896; and John A. Crawford to Commissioner of Pensions, May 16, 1896, all in Roland Dent Pension File.

67. Deposition of Roland Dent, July 16, 1896; Deposition of Susan Johnson, February 18, 1897; Invalid Pension document, June 24, 1902; Documents labeled "Act of February 6, 1907" and "Act of March 3, 1899," all in Roland Dent Pension File. According to the US Burial Registers, Military Posts and National Cemeteries, 1862–1960, p. 646, Roland Dent is buried at Hampton National Cemetery in Virginia.

68. 1860 US Census; John D. Murray Disability Affidavit, April 4, 1885; Declaration for an Original Invalid Pension, February 6, 1885; John D. Murray Disability Affidavit, April 4, 1885; and other related documents, John D. Murray Pension File.

69. Deposition of John Steves (I), August 27, 1897, and Deposition of Daniel Conway, January 25, 1898, Alexander Robinson Pension File; Deposition of Alexander Robinson, February 6, 1896, Harry Robinson Pension File; 1870, 1880, and 1900 US Census; S. M. Custer to William Lochren, October 26, 1895, Roland Dent Pension File. Elijah Bates's pension file seems to be lost: efforts to access it via the National Archives were unsuccessful

70. Invalid Pension document, May 29, 1896; Deposition of Alexander Robinson, October 25, 1888; Affidavit of George Brashear, March 28, 1891; Deposition of Alexander Robinson, February 18, 1897; Document filed for increase of pension, May 11, 1898; Deposition of Daniel Conway, January 25, 1898; Deposition of Silas Letcher, January 29, 1898; John A. Crawford to H. Clay Evans, September 11, 1897; Deposition of Sam Scott, September 9, 1897; Deposition of Owen Barrett, July 3, 1897; Deposition of Walter Whitinghill, July 3, 1897; Deposition of James L. Bates September 11, 1897; Deposition of Ambrose Cooper/Frey, September 11, 1897; Deposition of Essic [Essex] Robertson, December 28, 1896; all in Alexander Robinson Pension File. Some of this testimony was supportive, some of it less so. Deposition of Martha Robertson, December 28, 1896; Widow's Pension document March 24, 1903; and Affidavit of A. A. Simons, January 15, 1903, Alexander Robinson Pension File; Kentucky Death Records, 1852–1953.

Alexander's brothers Harry and Essex Robinson also made their postwar lives in the area around Holt's Bottom. In 1872 Harry married Polly Ann De Jarnett, with whom he had seven or eight children. Beginning in 1891 Harry applied for a pension claiming rheumatism and neuralgia, which he attributed to exposure during his military service. Harry Robinson's initial claim was rejected on the premise that his ailments did not disable him from doing manual labor, but as his health continued to decline he reapplied several times while continuing to work as a cook for one of his former master's grandsons, William Moorman. Finally, in June 1896, by which time he was a semi-invalid "confined to his house & bed for as long as two or three weeks at a time," Harry Robinson began receiving a pension of $12 per month. He died of "cardiac asthma" on April 7, 1908. Polly applied for a widow's pension, which she received until her death in November 1914. See Affidavit of Jesse A. Moorman, September 1, 1892; Statement of Harry Robertson, April 22, 1895; Declaration for Invalid Pension, January 6, 1891; Deposition of Harry Robinson, February 10, 1896; Affidavit of Thomas J. Spencer, May 29, 1897; Invalid Pension Claim, June 20, 1896, Accrued Pension form, August 25, 1910; statement of P. E. Dempster, June 22, 1910; Ben Johnson to Commissioner of Pensions, June 24, 1910; and Bureau of Pensions Notice of Check Cancellation, February 9, 1915, Harry Robinson Pension File.

71. Eleanor Stephens Holt to Joseph Holt, February 2, 1866, container 23, Joseph Holt Papers, Library of Congress; Copy of Sarah and Sandy's marriage license, and copy of Sarah and Sandy's marriage certificate, both dated December 24, 1868, Sandy Holt Pension File; 1870 US Census. When the census taker came to Sandy and Sarah's home in the summer of 1870, he noted that they had a daughter, Cynthia, who was two.

72. Undated "Proof of Birth" by John Bowmer of Cloverport; Sandy Holt Application for Invalid Pension, July 23, 1890; Depositions of A. A. Simons and Wesley Dent; Surgeon's Certificate, July 11, 1894; all in Sandy Holt Pension File. The 1910 Census indicates that Sarah Holt bore ten children, but only four of them survived.

73. Eleanor Stephens Holt to Joseph Holt, May 19, 1870, container 63, Joseph Holt Papers, Library of Congress.

Ironically, in her will Mary Ann Stephens left Wesley to her nephew Joseph. Had Wesley survived the war, of course, he would have been free. Moreover, it seems reasonable to assume that even if the Thirteenth Amendment had never been ratified, a transformed Joseph Holt would have emancipated him. See Mary Ann Martha K. Stephens Will, July 11, 1857, Breckinridge County Archives, Hardinsburg, KY.

When Wesley died, his two children became orphans. In 1872, through a guardian, Columbus V. Wedding, they applied for a pension, which was approved in 1874 for $8 per month. Interestingly, Thomas Holt supplied at least two depositions in support of Wesley and Joanna's children's application, and his wife Rosina and son Washington Dorsey supplied depositions as well. Sandy testified, too, and when Rosina was asked about Sandy's reputation for honesty, she declared that he was a "truthful negro." See Wesley Stephens Pension File.

74. *Breckinridge News*, June 29, 1881; Deposition of Alexander Robinson, October 25, 1888, Alexander Robinson Pension File; Deposition of Susan Johnson, February 18, 1897, Roland Dent Pension File.

75. *Breckinridge News*, June 29, 1881, July 6, 1881, July 13, 1881; and January 24, 1883; *Hartford (KY) Herald*, January 11, 1888.

76. *Breckinridge News,* April 16, 1879; Leonard, *Lincoln's Forgotten Ally;* Joseph Holt to Andrew Johnson, December 27, 1865, in Graf and Haskins, *The Papers of Andrew Johnson,* 9:541–42; Joseph Holt to Ulysses S. Grant, October 2, 1867, in Simon, *The Papers of Ulysses S. Grant,* 18:309–15; Joseph Holt to Andrew Johnson, February 26, 1869, in Graf and Haskins, *The Papers of Andrew Johnson,* 15:478–80. A single piece of evidence indicates that Washington Dorsey Holt may have served in the Confederate army: a card from a provost marshal file that lists his name and the detail "Co A, 10 Ky Cav." But I have been unable to locate any military service record for him.

77. Stephen C. Burbridge to Joseph Holt, July 20, 1865, container 28, reel 10, Edwin M. Stanton Papers. See also W. G. Snethen to Joseph Holt, September 15, 1865, container 49; Jesse Kincheloe to Joseph Holt, October 9, 1865, container 50; Jesse Kincheloe to Joseph Holt, January 17, 1866, container 50; W. G. Snethen to Joseph Holt, April 29, 1867, container 56; A. Alderson to Joseph Holt, July 18, 1869, container 61, Joseph Holt Papers, Library of Congress; 1870 and 1880 US Census; Washington, DC, City Directories, 1874, 1878; Joseph Holt to Mary and Rose Holt, 1883, Holt Family Private Collection; "Baffled by Witness," newspaper clipping dated May 29, 1896, and "Judge Holt's Will" and "Who Had Holt's Will," undated newspaper clippings in the Joseph Holt Rose Scrapbook. The 1879 Washington, DC, City Directory shows James and Annie Richardson living just down the street at 432 New Jersey Avenue SE.

78. Washington, DC, City Directories for 1886, 1887, 1889, 1890, 1891; 1870 US Census; "Who Had Holt's Will" and "No New Clue," undated newspaper clippings, Joseph Holt Rose Scrapbook.

79. *Breckinridge News,* April 16, 1879, October 20, 1880, November 22, 1882, and October 16, 1889; "Judge Holt's Will," "Who Had Holt's Will," and "The Will Mystery," undated newspaper clippings, Joseph Holt Rose Scrapbook; *Breckinridge News,* October 25, 1899.

80. "Judge Holt's Will," "Who Had Holt's Will," and "The Will Mystery," undated newspaper clippings, Joseph Holt Rose Scrapbook; *Breckinridge News,* October 25, 1899.

81. Declaration for Invalid Pension, February 23, 1895; Surgeon's Certificate, January 22, 1896; and Deposition of James G. Stephens, May 29, 1896, Sandy Holt Pension File.

82. Deposition of E. H. Miller, May 29, 1896; William E. Minor Affidavit, May 29, 1896; and Jacob E. Hanks Deposition, May 29, 1896, Sandy Holt Pension File; 1900 US Census for William E. Minor.

83. General Affidavit of Sarah Holt, March 24, 1897, and Declaration for Widow's Pension, November 26, 1896, Sandy Holt Pension File; 1880 US Census for William H. Bowmer.

84. 1880 US Census for William H. Bowmer; 1910, 1920, 1930 US Census; Bill issued to Georgia Dehaven, January 17, 1925, from H. Hamman and Son, "Furniture

Dealer, Funeral Director, and Embalmer," and Application for Reimbursement, January 19, 1925, both in Sandy Holt Pension File.

85. The pension record of Essex Robinson is particularly suggestive on this score. See the various depositions in the record by whites who had known him for many years.

Bibliography

Archival Materials

Joseph Holt Papers. Huntington Library, San Marino, CA.

Joseph Holt Papers. Library of Congress, Washington, DC.

Francis Lieber Papers. Huntington Library, San Marino, CA.

"The Negro in the Military Service of the United States, 1639–1886" (microfilm T823). National Archives and Records Administration, Washington, DC.

RG 15, Records of the Veterans Administration, Pension Records for Enlisted Men and Officers in the 118th United States Colored Infantry Regiment. National Archives and Records Administration, Washington, DC.

Henry Barrett (app. 733813, cert. 588147)
Owen G. K. Barrett (app. 472979, cert. 515572)
James L. Bates (app. 485316, cert. 684882)
Edward Boyd (app. 170148, cert. 131911)
George Brashears (app. 1062319, no cert. #)
Isaac Bugg (app. 941269, cert. 908034)
John L. Bullis (app. 1046422, cert. 827648)
John Christian (app. 970721, no cert. #)
Ambrose Cooper (app. 650104, cert. 477755)
Isaac D. Davis (app. 342542, cert. 243163)
Robert Dent (app. 1004026, cert. 1163737)
Roland Dent (app. 1115262, cert. 1045203)
David Dowell (app. 485419, no cert. #)
Anderson Green (app. 764687, cert. 1030760)
Samuel Helm (app. 526547, cert. 727807)
Sandy Holt (app. 534068, cert. 919884)
Silas Letcher (app. 724903, cert. 502407)
John C. Moon (app. 437144, cert. 333348)
John D. Murray (app. 532446, cert. 334678)

Alexander Robinson (app. 534111, cert. 669774)
Essex ("Easick") Robinson Pension File (app. 239551, cert. 451814)
Harry Robinson (app. 1011213, cert. 974209)
Samuel Scott (app. 935465, cert. 764231)
Sidney Smith (app. 1024508, cert. 1026622)
Wesley Stephens (app. 204445, cert. 178308)
John Steves (I) (app. 707253, cert. 555856)
Sam Webb (app. 762055, cert. 548034)
Walter Whitinghill (app. 1007588, cert. 918004)

RG 105, Records of the Bureau of Refugees, Freedmen, and Abandoned Lands: Records of the Field Offices for the State of Kentucky, 1865–1872 (M1904). National Archives and Records Administration, Washington, DC.

RG 153, Records of the Office of the Judge Advocate General (Army), 1692–1981, Letters Sent. National Archives and Records Administration, Washington, DC.
Volume 1 (1842–1863)
Volume 2 (1863)
Volume 3 (June 18, 1863–September 20, 1863)
Volume 4 (June 16, 1863–February 15, 1864)
Volume 5 (September 17, 1863–December 1863)
Volume 6 (December 23, 1863–January 11, 1865)
Volume 7 (January 4, 1864–May 16, 1864)
Volume 8 (February 13, 1864–July 14, 1864)
Volume 9 (May 3, 1864–October 12, 1864)
Volume 10 (July 11, 1864–December 5, 1864)
Volume 11 (October 13, 1864–April 1, 1865)
Volume 12 (September 30, 1864–unknown)

Joseph Holt Rose Scrapbook and other items. Personal Collection of Joseph Holt Rose, Pasadena, CA.

Edwin M. Stanton Papers. Library of Congress, Washington, DC.

Archival Materials Retrieved via ancestry.com

Headstones Provided for Deceased Union Civil War Veterans, 1879–1903.

Kentucky Death Records, 1852–1953.

Kentucky Marriage Records, 1852–1914.

Abraham Lincoln Papers, Series I: General Correspondence, 1833–1916. Library of Congress.

US Burial Registers, Military Posts and National Cemeteries, 1862–1960.

US Census Records.US City Directories, 1822–1995.

US Civil War Draft Registration Records, 1863–1865.

US Civil War Soldier Records and Profiles, 1861–1865.

US Federal Census Mortality Schedules, 1850–1885.
US Find a Grave Index, 1600s–Current.
US Register of Deaths of Volunteers, 1861–1865.
Washington, DC, Slave Emancipation Records, 1851–1863.
Washington, DC, Slave Owner Petitions, 1862–1863.

Archival Materials Retrieved via Fold3.com

Case Files of Approved Pension Applications of Widows and Other Dependents of Civil War Veterans, ca. 1861–ca. 1910.
Organization Index to Pension Files of Veterans Who Served between 1861 and 1900.
RG 94, Records of the Adjutant General's Office, 1780s–1917, Compiled Military Service Records for Volunteers in Company A, 118th United States Colored Infantry Regiment. National Archives and Records Administration, Washington, DC.

Other Primary Sources

"Annual Report of the Secretary of War for 1865." House of Representatives Exec. Doc. No. 1, pt. 3, vol. 2, 39th Cong., 1st sess., 1866.
Becker, Joseph. "The Dutch Gap Canal." *Frank Leslie's Popular Monthly,* July 1894.
"Dutch Gap Canal." *Overland Monthly and Out West Magazine,* January 1870.
"Emancipation in the District of Columbia." House of Representatives Exec. Doc. No. 42, 28th Cong., 1st sess., February 17, 1864.
"Freedmen's Affairs in Kentucky and Tennessee." House of Representatives Exec. Doc. No. 329, 40th Cong., 2nd sess., July 7, 1868.
Graf, LeRoy P., and Ralph W. Haskins, eds. *The Papers of Andrew Johnson.* 16 vols. Knoxville: University of Tennessee Press, 1967.
Harlan, Malvina Shanklin. *Some Memories of a Long Life, 1854–1911.* New York: Modern Library, 2003.
Higginson, Thomas Wentworth. *Army Life in a Black Regiment.* New York: Penguin Books, 1997.
Holt, Joseph. *Treason and Its Treatment.* New York: New York Young Men's Republican Union, 1865.
Leonard, Daisy Anderson. *From Slavery to Affluence: Memoirs of Robert Anderson, Ex-Slave.* Steamboat Springs, CO: Steamboat Pilot, 1927.
Littell, William, and Jacob Swigert. *Digest of the Statute Law of Kentucky.* Vol. 2. Frankfort: Kendall and Russell, 1822.
"Memorial of a Committee Appointed at a Meeting of Colored Citizens of Frankfort, Ky., and Vicinity." Senate Mis. Doc. No. 49, 42nd Cong., 1st sess., April 11, 1871.
Sheridan, Philip H. *The Personal Memoirs of P. H. Sheridan.* Cambridge, MA: Da Capo, 1992.

Simon, John Y., ed. *The Papers of Ulysses S. Grant.* 32 vols. Carbondale: Southern Illinois University Press, 1967–2012.

Simpson, Brooks D., et al., eds. *Advice After Appomattox: Letters to Andrew Johnson, 1865–1866.* Knoxville: University of Tennessee Press, 1988.

Slave Narratives: A Folk History of Slavery in the United States from Interviews with Former Slaves. Vol.7: *Kentucky Narratives.* Washington, DC, Federal Writers' Project, 1941.

"Speech of C. A. Wickliffe in the House of Representatives," January 29, 1863. Archives of the Kentucky Historical Society, Frankfort.

"Speech of C. A. Wickliffe in the House of Representatives," February 2, 1863. Archives of the Kentucky Historical Society, Frankfort.

"Speech of Hon. C. A. Wickliffe, of Kentucky, on the Bills to Confiscate the Property and Free from Servitude the Slaves of Rebels, and Other Matters," May 26, 1862. Archives of the Kentucky Historical Society, Frankfort.

Taylor, Susie King. *A Black Woman's Civil War Memoirs: Reminiscences of My Life in Camp.* New York: M. Wiener, 1988.

War of the Rebellion: A Compilation of the Official Records of the Union and Confederate Armies. 130 vols. Washington, DC: Government Printing Office, 1880–1901.

Newspapers

Breckinridge News
Charleston Daily News
Charleston Daily Phoenix
Christian Recorder
Cleveland Daily Leader
Daily National Republican
Daily Ohio Statesman
Hartford (KY) Herald
Liberator
Maysville (KY) Weekly Bulletin
Nashville Daily Union
New York Herald
New York Times
Norfolk Post
Owensboro Monitor
Philadelphia Evening Telegraph
United States Army and Navy Journal
Washington Evening Star
Washington Post
Weekly Western Sun (Vincennes, IN)
Wheeling (WV) Daily Intelligencer

Secondary Sources

Allen, Arthur. *Vaccine: The Controversial Story of Medicine's Greatest Lifesaver.* New York: Norton, 2007.

Astor, Aaron. *Rebels on the Border: Civil War, Emancipation, and the Reconstruction of Kentucky and Missouri.* Baton Rouge: Louisiana State University Press, 2012.

Beth, Loren P. *John Marshall Harlan.* Lexington: University Press of Kentucky, 1992.

Bryant, James K. *The 36th Infantry United States Colored Troops in the Civil War: A History and Roster.* New York: McFarland, 2012.

Clark-Lewis, Elizabeth. *First Freed: Washington, D.C., in the Emancipation Era.* Washington, DC: Howard University Press, 2001.

Cornish, Dudley Taylor. *The Sable Arm: Black Troops in the Union Army, 1861–1865.* Lawrence: University Press of Kansas, 1987.

Downs, Jim. *Sick from Freedom: African-American Illness and Suffering during the Civil War and Reconstruction.* New York: Oxford University Press, 2012.

Faust, Patricia L., ed. *Historical Times Illustrated Encyclopedia of the Civil War.* New York: HarperPerennial, 1991.

Fogel, Robert W., and Stanley L. Engerman, *Time on the Cross: The Economics of American Negro Slavery.* New York: Little, Brown, 1974.

Franklin, John Hope, and Loren Schweninger. *Runaway Slaves: Rebels on the Plantation.* New York: Oxford University Press, 1999.

Glasson, William H. *History of Military Pension Legislation in the United States.* New York: Columbia University Press, 1900.

Glatthaar, Joseph T. *Forged in Battle: The Civil War Alliance of Black Soldiers and White Officers.* New York: Meridian, 1991.

Greene, A. Wilson. *The Final Battles of the Petersburg Campaign: Breaking the Backbone of the Rebellion.* Knoxville: University of Tennessee Press, 2008.

Harris, William C. *Lincoln and the Border States: Preserving the Union.* Lawrence: University Press of Kansas, 2011.

Harrison, Lowell H. *The Civil War in Kentucky.* Lexington: University Press of Kentucky, 1975.

———. *Kentucky's Road to Statehood.* Lexington: University Press of Kentucky, 1992.

Howard, Victor B. *Black Liberation in Kentucky: Emancipation and Freedom, 1862–1884.* Lexington: University Press of Kentucky, 1983.

Hudson, J. Blaine. "In Pursuit of Freedom: Slave Law and Emancipation in Louisville and Jefferson County, Kentucky." *Filson History Quarterly* 76 (Summer 2002): 287–325.

Ingle, Edward. "The Negro in the District of Columbia." *Johns Hopkins University Studies in Historical and Political Science,* ser. 11, vols. 3–4 (March–April 1893).

Johnson, Allen. *Jefferson and His Colleagues: A Chronicle of the Virginia Dynasty.* New Haven: Yale University Press, 1921.

Leonard, Elizabeth D. *Lincoln's Avengers: Justice, Revenge, and Reunion After the Civil War.* New York: Norton, 2004.

———. *Lincoln's Forgotten Ally: Judge Advocate General Joseph Holt of Kentucky.* Chapel Hill: University of North Carolina Press, 2011.

———. *Men of Color to Arms! Black Soldiers, the Indian Wars, and the Quest for Equality.* New York: Norton, 2010.

———. "One Kentuckian's Hard Choice: Joseph Holt and Abraham Lincoln." *Register of the Kentucky Historical Society* 106 (Summer–Autumn 2008): 373–407.

———. *Yankee Women: Gender Battles in the Civil War.* New York: Norton, 1994.

Long, E. B. *The Civil War Day by Day.* New York: Da Capo, 1985.

Longacre, Edward G. "Black Troops in the Army of the James, 1863–65. *Military Affairs* 45 (February 1981): 1–8.

———. *A Regiment of Slaves: The 4th United States Colored Infantry, 1863–1866.* Mechanicsburg, PA: Stackpole Books, 2003.

Lucas, Marion B. *A History of Blacks in Kentucky: From Slavery to Segregation, 1760–1891.* Frankfort: Kentucky Historical Society, 2003.

Manarin, Louis H., ed. *Richmond Occupied: Entry of the United States Forces into Richmond, Va., April 3, 1865.* Richmond: Richmond Civil War Centennial Committee, 1965.

Marshall, Anne E. *Creating a Confederate Kentucky: The Lost Cause and Civil War Memory in a Border State.* Chapel Hill: University of North Carolina Press, 2013.

Martin, Asa Earl. *The Anti-slavery Movement in Kentucky Prior to 1850.* Louisville: Filson Club, 1918.

McDougle, Ivan E. "The Development of Slavery." *Journal of Negro History* 3 (July 1918): 214–39.

———. "The Legal Status of Slavery." *Journal of Negro History* 3 (July 1918): 240–80.

———. "Public Opinion Regarding Emancipation and Colonization." *Journal of Negro History* 3 (July 1918): 303–28.

McPherson, James M. *Ordeal by Fire: The Civil War and Reconstruction.* New York: McGraw Hill, 2001.

Miller, Edward A., Jr. *The Black Civil War Soldiers of Illinois: The Story of the Twenty-Ninth U.S. Colored Infantry.* Columbia: University of South Carolina Press, 1998.

Miller, Randall M., and John David Smith, eds. *Dictionary of Afro-American Slavery.* Westport, CT: Praeger, 1997.

Paradis, James M. *Strike the Blow for Freedom: The 6th United States Colored Infantry in the Civil War.* Shippensburg, PA: White Mane, 1998.

Rhyne, J. Michael. "'A Blood Stained Sin': Slavery, Freedom, and Guerrilla Warfare in the Bluegrass Region of Kentucky, 1863–1865. *Register of the Kentucky Historical Society* 112 (Autumn 2014): 553–87.

Ryder, Karen Kotzuk. "'Permanent Property': Slave Life Insurance in the Antebellum Southern United States, 1820–1866." PhD diss., University of Delaware, 2012.

Savitt, Todd L. "Slave Insurance in Virginia and North Carolina." *Journal of Southern History* 43 (November 1977): 583–600.

Schneider, Dorothy, and Carl J. Schneider. *Slavery in America.* New York: Facts on File, 2007.

Shaffer, Donald R. *After the Glory: The Struggles of Black Civil War Veterans.* Lawrence: University Press of Kansas, 2004.

Smith, John David, ed. *Black Soldiers in Blue: African American Troops in the Civil War Era.* Chapel Hill: University of North Carolina Press, 2002.

Taylor, Amy Murrell. *The Divided Family in Civil War America.* Chapel Hill: University of North Carolina Press, 2005.

Wallace, Edward S. "General John Lapham Bullis: Thunderbolt of the Texas Frontier, I." *Southwestern Historical Quarterly* 54 (April 1951): 452–61.

———. "General John Lapham Bullis: Thunderbolt of the Texas Frontier, II." *Southwestern Historical Quarterly* 55 (July 1951): 77–85.

Washington, Versalle F. *Eagles on Their Buttons: A Black Infantry Regiment in the Civil War.* Columbia: University of Missouri Press, 1999.

Whyte, James H. *The Uncivil War: Washington during the Reconstruction, 1865–1878.* Woodbridge, CT: Twayne, 1958.

Williams, George Washington. *A History of the Negro Troops in the War of the Rebellion, 1861–1865.* New York: Fordham University Press, 2012.

Wilson, Joseph T. *The Black Phalanx: African American Soldiers in the War of Independence, the War of 1812, & the Civil War.* New York: Da Capo, 1994.

Index

Military units appear in numerical order at the beginning of the index.

Index